THE RHETORICAL ROAD TO
BROWN V. BOARD OF EDUCATION

Race, Rhetoric, and Media Series
Davis W. Houck, General Editor

The Rhetorical Road
to *Brown v. Board of Education*

*Elizabeth and Waties
Waring's Campaign*

Wanda Little Fenimore

University Press of Mississippi / Jackson

The University Press of Mississippi is the scholarly publishing agency of the Mississippi Institutions of Higher Learning: Alcorn State University, Delta State University, Jackson State University, Mississippi State University, Mississippi University for Women, Mississippi Valley State University, University of Mississippi, and University of Southern Mississippi.

www.upress.state.ms.us

The University Press of Mississippi is a member of the Association of University Presses.

Any discriminatory or derogatory language or hate speech regarding race, ethnicity, religion, sex, gender, class, national origin, age, or disability that has been retained or appears in elided form is in no way an endorsement of the use of such language outside a scholarly context.

An earlier version of chapter 4, "Brickbats and Bouquets," originally appeared in *Rhetoric & Public Affairs* 24, no. 4 (Winter 2021).

Copyright © 2023 by University Press of Mississippi
All rights reserved

First printing 2023
∞

Library of Congress Cataloging-in-Publication Data available

LCCN 2023002319
ISBN 9781496843968 (hardcover)
ISBN 9781496843975 (trade paperback)
ISBN 9781496843982 (epub single)
ISBN 9781496843999 (epub institutional)
ISBN 9781496844002 (pdf single)
ISBN 9781496844019 (pdf institutional)

British Library Cataloging-in-Publication Data available

To Daisy

CONTENTS

Acknowledgments ♦ ix

Introduction ♦ 3

1. Baptism ♦ 17
2. It All Started with a Bus ♦ 33
3. I Hope to Make More Friends ♦ 54
4. Brickbats and Bouquets ♦ 73
5. Only Force Will Work ♦ 94
6. The Year of Decision ♦ 115
7. The Day Dreamed and Prayed Would Arrive Has Come ♦ 135
8. Democracy and Decency Prevail ♦ 156

Conclusion ♦ 172

Notes ♦ 183

Bibliography ♦ 225

Index ♦ 237

ACKNOWLEDGMENTS

Nearly ten years in the making, telling Waties and Elizabeth's story has been a labor of love and hate, just like their lives. Their love for each other sustained them while white supremacists bombarded them with hate. My conviction that their story needed to be told sustained me through the years as I persevered through rejections. I first "met" Elizabeth many years ago through Davis Houck. He was in an archive, not looking for anything related to the Warings, and came across the Charleston YWCA speech manuscript. As he does, he copied it, held on to it, then handed it to me. Thank you for sharing your best finds with people like me. Through the years, I have expressed my frustration that no other speech texts were preserved. Thank you, Davis, for reminding me that an absence can be as significant as a presence. Thank you for bringing me to UPM.

Researchers like me rely upon the kindness of strangers, and archivists are the kindest. Regardless of the archive, I have encountered knowledgeable and competent professionals who are always willing to help. After Davis schooled me in proper etiquette in the archives, I made my first visit to the Avery Research Center in Charleston. Georgette Mayo welcomed this rookie then and again during subsequent visits. The judge bequeathed his papers to the Moorland-Spingarn Research Center at Howard University, so I made many trips to Washington, DC, from Florida, from Virginia, and from South Carolina. A constant throughout the years was Joellen ElBashir and Richard Jenkins's unfailing professionalism. Through email and phone calls, archivists at South Caroliniana, Tamiment, Beinecke, Winthrop, Clemson, and South Carolina State Archives assisted me with timely responses and without complaint. I could not have completed the manuscript during the coronavirus pandemic without their help.

Academic publishing is simultaneously a minefield and roller coaster. Through the years, Carole, Melody, Camille, Ruth, Maegan, and Deb offered hand-holding, virtual hugs, and shoulders to cry on. They cheered me through the successes, then reminded me of them when I was in the pits of self-doubt.

To Ann M. Hyde, Will Gravely, Sean O'Rourke, and those anonymous reviewers who resisted the Reviewer 2 urge: Thank you for affirming that Elizabeth's story needed to be told. This manuscript was only possible because of the generosity of the American Council of Learned Societies' Mellon/Community College Faculty Fellowship. The stipend afforded me time without teaching or service responsibilities to immerse myself into the Warings and their campaign.

THE RHETORICAL ROAD TO
BROWN V. BOARD OF EDUCATION

INTRODUCTION

In 1892, Homer Plessy boarded a train in New Orleans as a planned challenge to the state law that allowed railroad companies to provide "equal, but separate" cars for Black and white passengers.[1] After his arrest, Plessy appealed the guilty verdict rendered by parish criminal court Judge John Howard Ferguson until the case eventually arrived at the Supreme Court. In the majority opinion, Justice Henry Billings Brown wrote that the plaintiff's argument that the "enforced separation of the two races stamps the colored race with a badge of inferiority" was a fallacy. Instead, Justice Brown reasoned that any sense of inferiority was "solely because the colored race chooses to put that construction upon it."[2] The 1896 decision in *Plessy v. Ferguson* provided legal sanction for separate-but-equal and paved the way for state legislatures to mandate separate facilities under the pretense that they were equal.

As a consequence of *Plessy*, race defined life in the South for the better part of the twentieth century. Every human institution was organized overtly around a racial hierarchy.[3] Jim Crow restricted what bodies could enter spaces, who had a voice in the electoral process, and whose children deserved an education. Scholars disagree as to when Jim Crow originated, but by mid-twentieth century it was firmly entrenched. The most visible manifestation of Jim Crow was segregation—the legal separation of Black and white bodies. "White" and "colored" signs littered the South. Buses, streetcars, schools, restaurants, parks, playgrounds, prisons, theaters, and hospitals were designated as "white" or "colored." Oklahoma required separate phone booths for white and Black people. In South Carolina, Black and white workers in cotton textile factories could not work in the same room or use the same entrances, exits, stairways, windows, or toilets.[4] Race dictated every aspect of daily life, from birth to burial. Segregation codified the beliefs of most white southerners about the inferiority of Black people. NAACP attorney Constance Baker Motley wrote that legal segregation was "a state-imposed badge of servitude" upon Black people. She concluded that *Plessy*'s most devastating result "was its reaffirmation of a majority of the population's belief in the inherent inferiority of African-Americans."⁵ Although the Thirteenth Amendment abolished slavery, the habits, customs, and prejudices associated with it persisted in the South. Jim Crow retained slavery in all but name.

In the lone *Plessy* dissent, Justice John Marshall Harlan wrote "Our constitution is color-blind, and neither knows nor tolerates classes among citizens. In respect of civil rights, all citizens are equal before the law."⁶ African American people lived as less than second-class citizens because segregation was sanctioned by *Plessy* and enforced by states. The separate spaces were supposed to be equal, but as Thurgood Marshall wrote in 1951, "It is, of course, common knowledge that no separate facility maintained for Negroes is even remotely the physical equal of that maintained for whites."⁷ Therefore, legal segregation had to be eliminated in order for Black people to exercise their rights under the Constitution. The American Fund for Public Service, known as the Garland Fund, financed studies to determine possible courses of action to reverse *Plessy*. In a report prepared in the early 1930s, Nathan Margold outlined strategies to overturn *Plessy*. Margold recognized that lawsuits in separate jurisdictions were a costly piecemeal approach. However, an attack on the unequal conditions under *Plessy* had the potential to force the Supreme Court to reckon with the constitutional dilemma that segregation presented. As dean of Howard University's School of Law, Charles Hamilton Houston traveled across the South and documented the unequal conditions in Black schools. On June 16, 1935, Houston prepared a ten-page memorandum with suggested edits to compile the evidence into a film, *Examples of Educational Discrimination Among Rural Negroes in South Carolina*, for the National Association for the Advancement of Colored People's (NAACP) annual conference.⁸ Instead of attacking segregation head-on, Houston brought a series of lawsuits demanding that states comply with *Plessy* by providing "equal allocations of financial and other resources for black students in segregated schools."⁹

Margold had recommended forcing the issue in the courts "on the least risky terrain as possible." The cases on the "least risky terrain" were graduate and law schools because, as Richard Kluger reports, white people were most vulnerable in segregated higher education and also "least likely to respond with anger."¹⁰ Oliver Hill, the NAACP attorney for the Prince Edward County school segregation case, said, "We realized we had to overturn Plessy versus Ferguson. . . . That the best thing for us to do would be to challenge segregation at its weakest point, that is the inequality . . . and we had great success in all of our lawsuits under that approach."¹¹ Houston laid the foundation to overturn *Plessy v. Ferguson* with a series of victories in graduate and law school cases. Although the Supreme Court inched closer with each case, it stopped short of an outright reversal of *Plessy*. James M. Nabrit Jr., faculty at Howard University and member of the NAACP Legal Defense and Educational Fund, pointed out, "It should be remembered that in every case where the Court has been given a chance to decide a segregation case on the ground of lack of equality it has so decided and declined to pass upon the question of segregation per se."[12] After the Supreme Court bypassed the question for decades, the figurative and literal roads that Houston traveled culminated in *Brown v. Board of Education* when the Supreme Court ruled in its unanimous decision that "separate educational facilities are inherently unequal."[13]

A number of scholarly works detail the politico-legal dimensions of *Brown* and its role in the civil rights movement. Political scientists and legal scholars have examined the legal arguments as the cases made their way from local federal district courts to the Supreme Court. Historians have studied the local grassroots organizing. However, a significant gap still exists: the rhetorical road to *Brown*. The social and political consequences stemming from *Brown* were as great as those resulting from an act of Congress.[14] Many perceive the 1954 decision as a watershed in civil rights history, focusing too often on the consequences of, but not the impetus for, the decision. Those scholars who have examined the events and people culminating in the *Brown* decision have done so from historical, sociological, and legal perspectives, with scant attention paid to the rhetorical dimension except in terms of the pleadings, oral arguments, and judicial opinions.

The Rhetorical Road to Brown v. Board of Education*: Elizabeth and Waties Waring's Campaign* traces the symbolic battle that provided the locus for change in the landmark Supreme Court decision.[15] This book offers an account of resistance to white supremacy through the lives and words of Elizabeth and Waties Waring. The husband, federal Judge J. Waties Waring, was an eighth-generation Charlestonian whose family had enslaved people of African descent. The wife, Elizabeth Avery Waring, was a twice-divorced northern socialite. The circumstances surrounding their marriage created a scandal in Charleston, South Carolina. The dramatic narrative of their private lives serves as a backdrop to their public address. The Warings launched a rhetorical campaign with a series of speeches delivered from 1949 to 1952. As a consequence of their stance, their lives were filled with verbal assaults, impeachment attempts, harassing phone calls, threatening letters, and attacks on their Meeting Street home.

The timing of the Warings' rhetorical campaign is significant in terms of the Clarendon County school segregation case, *Briggs v. Elliott*. The case began in 1947, and after landing on Judge Waring's docket on three separate occasions, it was consolidated with four other cases and decided in *Brown v. Board of Education*. Aware of Black parents' resistance, Elizabeth and Waties delivered fourteen speeches in 1950 that condemned white supremacy and segregation. In each speech, they called for public pressure on elected representatives to force southern states to end legal segregation. In 1951, after *Briggs* was scheduled for trial in federal district court, Waties and Elizabeth delivered seven more speeches, repeating the themes from the 1950 speeches. The next year, 1952, as *Briggs* made its way to the Supreme Court, Waties delivered more than ten speeches. In approximately three years, the Warings delivered over thirty speeches. The Warings' goal was to influence the outcome of *Briggs v. Elliott* by arousing public opinion to the extent necessary to force the federal government to intervene in the South and end legally mandated school segregation. They crafted a rhetorical campaign to ambush white supremacists. As the Warings poked at the defenses of segregation and its incongruence with "all men are created equal," white supremacists pushed back. This book examines the Warings' public address within the historical context of the Jim Crow South.

Elmer W. Henderson, the plaintiff in a case about segregated dining cars on trains, outlined a three-pronged attack to eliminate segregation: repeal state statutes, declare them unconstitutional, and "build public opinion against the law and the practice of segregation to the extent that both will be abandoned."[16] Because southern state legislatures were not likely to voluntarily repeal Jim Crow statutes, efforts should be focused on the Supreme Court reversing its precedent, *Plessy v. Ferguson*.[17] Continuing the ideas developed by the President's Committee on Civil Rights, the Warings believed that federal intervention was necessary to remedy race relations in the South. However, American voters had not protested loudly enough to create an unfavorable environment for segregation. A shift in public opinion against segregation would enhance the possibility that the judiciary would overturn *Plessy*. The Warings developed their rhetorical campaign so that the Supreme Court would agree, as Thurgood Marshall argued, "that the time is ripe for the 'separate but equal' doctrine to be further delimited."[18]

After World War II, in the midst of political debates and court cases, a symbolic battle ensued—a battle in which the United States grappled with the lag between its public morals and promise of democracy. The Warings entered this battle, sometimes officially through Waties's rulings as a federal judge and sometimes unofficially through networking and speeches. This book integrates the Warings' words and their lived experience. Their activism occurred within a repressive rhetorical culture that constrained and prompted their discourses. The couple's public utterances did not occur in isolation. Just as discourses impacted the Warings, the Warings' speeches circulated and influenced their environment. Michael Leff argued that rhetorical discourses are conditioned by other discourses and by the progression of events.[19] The Warings' speeches circulated among a network of discourses, spawning yet more discourses in response. My underlying premise is that the Warings were dissatisfied with some aspect of their environment, desired change, made efforts to alter the environment, and these efforts resulted in some degree of success or failure. Their efforts to alter their environment were rhetorical.

The state laws and local customs that constituted Jim Crow created the impression of consensus. The rhetorical culture of the Jim Crow South created barriers to speech in order to maintain that consensus. Marouf Hasian Jr., Celeste Michelle Condit, and John Louis Lucaites define rhetorical culture as "the range of linguistic usages available to those who would address a particular audience as a public" such as analogies, euphemisms, characterizations, myths, ideographs, narratives, and public vocabulary. By changing the rhetorical culture that demarcates the "symbolic boundaries within which public advocates find themselves constrained to operate," an interest group may exact a change in power relations.[20] However, symbolic border guards monitor and enforce the boundaries of the rhetorical culture.[21] White supremacists and racial conservatives "mounted a righteous crusade" to maintain the Southern way of life.[22] The crusade included threats of physical violence, economic retaliation, and social ostracism that silenced the voices of white people who questioned segregation. As a result, the public conversation about race relations was one-sided. As early as 1944, Lillian Smith, author of the controversial *Strange Fruit*, called for white people to voice their opposition to segregation:

> We who do not believe in segregation as a way of life, must say so. We must break the conspiracy of silence which had held us in a grip so strong that it has become a taboo. We must say why segregation is unendurable to the human spirit. We must somehow find the courage to say it aloud. For, however, we rationalize our silence, it is fear that is holding our tongues today. A widespread denial of a belief in segregation and all that it implies will shake this way of life to its roots. Each of us in his heart knows this . . . To remain silent while the demagogues, the Negro haters, the racists, the mentally ill, loudly reaffirm their faith in segregation and the spiritual lynching which their way of life inflicts, is to be traitorous to everything that is good and creative and sane in human values.[23]

Smith was correct—people were afraid. They were afraid of losing their jobs, homes, social standing, and families. White supremacists' terrorist tactics were not reserved for "uppity Negroes." White people who criticized the racial status quo were subject to repercussions as Theodore Bilbo warned in 1944, "We people of the South must draw the color line tighter and tighter, and any white man or woman who dares to cross that color line shall be promptly and forever ostracized."[24] Jeanne Theoharis explains that white people supported segregation through their actions and their inaction. For white people who knew the system was deeply wrong, they "felt there was little they could do about it or feared risking their family's safety and security, so they hung back."[25] Just as Jim Crow created physical boundaries between the races, it also created rhetorical boundaries.

Based on the number of speeches that the Warings delivered, when they delivered them, and the consistent themes among them, their public address was a thoughtful and deliberate campaign to turn public opinion against segregation. However, their voices circulated within a rhetorical culture that suppressed open discussion. The illusion of white consensus about segregation existed because Jim Crow barred criticism and opposition. In *The Mind of the South*, W. J. Cash tried to explain the overwhelming pressure to conform to white supremacy: "And one thought it, said it, did it, exactly as it was ordained, or one stood in pressing peril of being cast out for a damned n-word-loving scoundrel in league with the enemy."[26] When they launched their campaign with Elizabeth's explosive speech to the Black Charleston YWCA on January 16, 1950, the Warings believed, as did George Washington Cable, Lillian Smith, and leaders of the Southern Conference Educational Fund, that a constituency existed of white people who opposed segregation but remained silent due to the risk of reprisals. In 1947, Waties wrote, "But there is a silent, thinking minority who are as yet little heard of."[27] Five years later, he concluded that of those who secretly sympathized with him, "no one would dare back him openly."[28] The Warings' rhetorical strategy to break the grip of fear was to disseminate their speeches and circulate the responses. The Warings took purposeful steps to ensure that their oratory reached audiences beyond those physically present. With each speech and media interview, they received letters—positive and negative—that they then circulated to more audiences. The strategic circulation of the responses served two rhetorical purposes. First, the negative responses confirmed that white supremacists were sick, just as Elizabeth and Waties claimed. Second, the positive responses supported the Warings' assertion that other white people agreed with them. Once publicly circulated, the positive letters had the potential to remove the barriers to speech that quashed dissent. The Warings' rhetoric contained a persistent, recurring message that they progressively layered in each speech and media interview for a dual purpose: strike at the core of segregationists' defense and activate public opinion. The issue of race relations in the South could be remedied or at least altered rhetorically.

With my account, I employ a rhetorical lens to deepen our understanding of *Brown v. Board of Education*. Throughout his career, Martin J. Medhurst advocated rhetoric as a pathway into public affairs: "Rhetoric is a mode of analytical thinking that helps the critic ask important questions and explore significant dimensions of public culture—dimensions that our friends in history, political science, and sociology often miss."[29] Other works have examined Judge Waring's career. Tinsley Yarbrough, a political scientist, authored a compelling judicial biography, *A Passion for Justice*, that focused on Waties's rulings. Because his interest was legal history, Yarbrough did not delve into Waties's speeches, even though he accounted for some of them in his book. While Yarbrough mentions Elizabeth, she is included to highlight the drama of the Warings' divorces and marriage.[30] Federal Judge Richard Gergel's *Unexampled Courage* explores the impact of Isaac Woodard's blinding on Waties and President Truman. Gergel adopts a top-down approach that points to Truman's civil rights initiatives in the executive branch and Waties's bold rulings as a federal judge as heralding a new era of racial equality in the United States. Gergel discusses four of Waties's speeches by date, location, and occasion. He speculates that "Waring's outspoken advocacy on the speaker's circuit" was a possible reason for his rift with Judge John J. Parker; yet, Gergel goes no further.[31] Because their interests were legal and political, neither Yarbrough nor Gergel pursued the possibility that Waties *and* Elizabeth designed a multifaceted rhetorical campaign to end school segregation.

The Rhetorical Road employs a case-study approach rather than a theoretical one to examine the Warings' little-known rhetorical campaign. This book is the first step in recovering the rhetorical history of *Brown v. Board of Education*. In "Four Senses of Rhetorical History," David Zarefsky identifies four lines of inquiry where rhetoric and history are interlocked. Zarefsky insists that his mapping of the four senses does not imply boundaries. Instead, the four senses "open possibilities for productive inquiry." The first sense involves the history of rhetoric from classical times to the present. The rhetoric of history, the second sense, studies the practices of historians as a "specialized discourse community." From the third sense, the "historical study of rhetorical events," scholars may proceed by considering rhetoric as "a force in history" or as "an index or mirror of history." The last and fourth sense comprises the "study of historical events from a rhetorical perspective." The subject matter for the rhetorical historian and historian is the same, "human life in all its totality and multiplicity." But as a rhetorician, I approach a subject from a different perspective and ask different questions, namely, "how messages are created and used by people to influence and relate to one another." As Zarefsky indicates, I view history "as a series of rhetorical problems." The Warings viewed race relations as a rhetorical problem that called for public persuasion "to advance a cause or overcome an impasse."[32] The ways that the Warings crafted their speeches imparted their understanding of the obstacles to ending segregation. Martin J. Medhurst argued that the close examination of texts is both intellectually respectable and potentially productive of various forms of critical knowledge.[33] We gain critical knowledge about the multiple aspects of activism, beyond the legal case, that culminated in *Brown*.

My concern is how Elizabeth and Waties crafted their speeches to influence others in a specific context. The context, as Martin Medhurst argued, "includes the audiences that are addressed, whether directly or indirectly, immediately or at some future moment."[34] Because rhetoric "seeks to move audiences in the direction suggested by the speaker," I answered Amos Kiewe and Davis Houck's call for rhetorical critics "to engage a text's interlocutors in order to understand how a message has resonated (or failed to resonate) with them, especially when such evidence is available."[35] Such evidence is available in archives, databases, microfilm, and digital platforms. Those who disagreed with the Warings spewed racist stereotypes, often politely. Those who agreed with the Warings yearned for others to publicly denounce segregation. The responses to the Warings' speeches reveal how white Americans conceived of citizenship, namely as rights conferred upon those who looked like them and therefore, deserved those rights.

Examining *Brown v. Board of Education* from a rhetorical perspective disputes the idea that the Supreme Court decision was inevitable. Robert Hariman writes that the study of public address "offers a narrow yet reliable passage in the lived experience of public culture in particular historical periods."[36] The Warings' speeches evinced opposition to segregation among white people in the years leading up to *Brown*. The response demonstrates how Black and white people navigated the complexities and contingencies of a critical moment in American history. It is only through rhetorical history that we learn about the public conversation about an issue. It is only through audience responses that we learn if, and how, private conversations aligned with the public conversation. Finally, Kathleen Turner argues that "rhetorical history can trace symbolic social constructions."[37] Rhetorical history reveals the contested processes of conceiving and defining "politically sensitive words" like *citizen, democracy,* and *equality*.[38]

Scholars in other disciplines recognize the role of rhetoric in maintaining white supremacy and creating barriers to upend the status quo. In "Toward New Histories of the Civil Rights Era," Charles W. Eagles, professor of history emeritus at the University of Mississippi, outlined several areas of the Black Freedom Struggle that needed further study. He wrote that "the formal ideas and ideologies of the people involved at all levels in the movement as well as their unarticulated assumptions and beliefs warrant serious analysis." While Eagles called this an "intellectual history," ideas, ideologies, beliefs, and assumptions are expressed through language and rhetorical analysis reveals them. Eagles went further to recommend that students of the movement study "how the rhetoric and its meanings varied among contemporaries and how definitions have changed over time."[39] Jeanne Theoharis persuasively argues that the silences and coded language of "polite racism" maintain racial injustice.[40] Growing up in Richmond, Virginia, Edward H. Peeples learned that white supremacy "included an elaborate catechism of apologetics in which justification and diversionary explanations for white malice could be derived even for those whites who claimed not to approve of such behavior."[41] A rhetorical lens decodes white supremacy's code. The rhetorical history of *Brown v. Board of Education* reveals the terms upon which segregation was defended, the reasons that white people remained silent, and the ways in which white Americans reconciled the contradiction between white supremacy and American democracy.

The language in the 1940s and 1950s used to refer to Black people offends in the twenty-first century, as it should. In some of the letters that the Warings received, white people were civil and polite. Even so, they defended segregation in the coded language of white supremacy. Other letter writers did not deign to code their language. They used racial slurs such as n——r. I did not include the word even in direct quotations. Instead, I substituted "n-word," not because I want to avoid the appearance that I tolerate bigotry, but because, as Michael Eric Dyson points out, it is unacceptable for a white person to say (or write) the word under any circumstances. At the same time, I do not want to erase how the word "condenses the history of hate and the culture of violence against black folk." The letter writers used the word as a container for "lynching, castration, rape, rioting, intellectual inferiority, Jim Crow, second-class citizenship, bad schools, poor neighborhoods, police brutality, racial terror, mass incarceration, and more" that Black Americans have endured—and still experience.[42] I ask readers to remember that when white people invoke the n-word, they are calling upon past violence to intimidate.

At its core, this book has three primary aims: recover texts, restore life stories, and revise history. Davis Houck explains that "textual recovery and discovery is the process of locating and evaluating primary source documents—in this case speeches—which have the *potential* to advance our knowledge of public address generally and significant persons, event, genre, and rhetorical situation more specifically." *Recovering* is finding a speech and confirming that a "speech already deemed significant does, in fact, exist." *Discovering* a speech involves locating *and* evaluating it: "it is to argue that a heretofore unknown speech demands attention."[43] This project recovers, discovers, evaluates, and reconstructs the Warings' public address. Of the more than thirty speeches that the Warings delivered from 1949 to1952 across the United States, the full text of only four is preserved. As a lawyer and judge, Waties had been trained in oratory. Away from the courtroom, he preferred what he called extemporaneous speaking, so he did not prepare traditional speech manuscripts. He thought of extemporaneous speaking as more informal, without the pomp of the courtroom.[44] Any full-text manuscripts of his speeches were transcribed from audio recordings.[45] Elizabeth disliked speeches that were read and preferred to deliver her speeches extemporaneously "with only notes at hand."[46] Two of her speech manuscripts are preserved. No manuscripts exist of the other speeches that the Warings delivered during their rhetorical campaign to end school segregation.

The archival absence raises a methodological dilemma in terms of textual recovery and discovery. Even as the Waring Papers at the Moorland-Spingarn Research Center brims with correspondence, newspaper clippings, and legal documents, manuscripts of the Warings' speeches are absent. I adapted Pamela VanHaitsma's method that she utilized to remedy the archival absence of speech transcripts for Sallie Holley, a nineteenth-century abolitionist. Like VanHaitsma speculated about Holley, I knew that the Warings delivered more speeches than those preserved. The event programs and newspaper clippings preserved in Elizabeth's scrapbooks at the Moorland-Spingarn Research Center are archival evidence that the Warings launched a rhetorical campaign at the same time that Black parents in Clarendon County were organizing to use the federal courts to resist white supremacy. In the archive I listed the dates, locations, and sponsoring organizations from the event programs and newspaper clippings. I supplemented this list from secondary literature such as Tinsley Yarbrough's judicial biography of Waties. Using these data, I conducted searches through ProQuest Historical Newspapers (Black and white press) and NewsBank (*The State*) available through university libraries. From the South Carolina State Library, I accessed Charleston's white newspapers, *News and Courier* and *Evening Post*. The State Library's ProQuest Black Newspaper Collection included access to more newspapers than the university. In addition, I paid for a subscription to Newspapers.com. Knowledge of where the Warings delivered their speeches was vital when searching this database because it is organized geographically. Newspapers.com yielded coverage of the speeches in smaller cities such as Providence, Rhode Island. In some cases, the database searches generated no results, so I turned to the sponsoring organization. For example, Waties spoke to the Congress of Racial Equality (CORE) in 1951 and 1952 for which there was no media coverage. However, CORE published a monthly newsletter available on microfilm.

Information from the archives and secondary literature proved useful in limiting the searches. Without the date, location, or sponsoring organization as a search term to include with the Warings' names, the searches resulted in hundreds of newspaper articles about Judge Waring's rulings from the bench. I was mindful that Black newspapers were often published weekly so did not limit searches to the specific day that the speech was delivered. In addition, I used variations of the Warings' names in the searches. For example, in 1950, white women were usually referred to as Mrs. Husband's Name so for Elizabeth, I tried "Mrs. J. Waties Waring," "Mrs. Waring," and "Mrs. Elizabeth Waring." For Waties, I used "Judge J. Waties Waring," "Judge Waring," and "Judge J. W. Waring."

I compiled the results of the database searches into a new digital collection consisting of newspaper articles that announced the speeches, quoted directly from the speeches, and interviewed the Warings. I transcribed the direct quotations from the newspaper articles into separate Word documents for each speech, comparing the quotations across sources for accuracy. I pieced together these fragments to carefully re-structure the speeches for which no full transcript was available.[47] Although not a collection or archive in the traditional sense, these digital surrogates facilitated indirect reading of the Warings' speeches. As such, the digital surrogates "can be read and analyzed like any archival sources."[48]

The speeches re-constructed through the digital surrogates provide information about the topics, appeals, and arrangement of the Warings' speeches. Even with the absence of speech transcripts, the recurring themes and phrases within the digital surrogates suggest what it is reasonable to assume about the Warings' speeches.[49] The manuscripts that are preserved substantiate these assumptions. This method uses digital surrogates located through systematic database searches to supplement archival materials. In fact, the digital data mining began with information from primary sources. Innovative recovery methods, such as reconstructing the Warings' speeches through digital surrogates, permit a fuller rhetorical history of *Brown v. Board of Education*.

The Warings' life stories and their multipronged campaign against segregation are examples of concealed stories. In *Storytelling for Social Justice*, Lee Ann Bell describes concealed stories as ones just beneath the surface "not so much unknown as constantly overshadowed, pushed back into the margins, conveniently 'forgotten' or repressed." If mentioned by historians, Elizabeth Waring is consigned to the role of That Woman who delivered That Speech. Waties is constructed as the white savior whose dissent in *Briggs v. Elliott* laid the legal foundation for *Brown v. Board of Education*. With a narrow focus on one speech, claims that Elizabeth acted out of revenge appear legitimate. An emphasis on Waties's dissent affirms the singular role of white morality in the Black Freedom Struggle. By restoring dimension to their lives and activism, this book provides a more accurate history that white people can draw upon "to think about and work for justice as equals with others." By unearthing the Warings' concealed stories, readers "learn about role models of white people who have fought against racism throughout our history and whose example could guide them today."[50] Despite the problematic aspects of Elizabeth and Waties's activism, they exhibited remarkable courage to publicly denounce white supremacy.

Although their strategies and rhetoric offer lessons in the modern day, Elizabeth and Waties were fallible humans with strengths and weaknesses that imbued their activism. Inflexible and radical, they pursued their goal with the passion and one-sightedness of the newly converted, leaving little opening for collaboration. Although they perceived themselves as allies, their privilege precluded an awareness that in their efforts to end school segregation, they reproduced the same biases as the white supremacists whom they condemned. They never articulated an awareness of their privilege as white people. At the same time, they said what others could not say. They took advantage of their privilege to gain access to platforms and audiences to oppose segregation. Due to their circumstances, they were insulated from repercussions. Neither of the Warings formally associated themselves with established organizations. Instead, they built a national interracial network of like-minded individuals. Even so, their allyship was fraught with contradictions and conflicts that demonstrate the fragile process of coalition building.

Another aim of this book is to disrupt the master narrative of the civil rights movement that functions as a stock story, "a set of standard, typical or familiar stories held in reserve to explain racial dynamics in ways that support the status quo, like a supply of goods kept on the premises to be pulled out whenever the necessity calls for a ready response."⁵¹ The master narrative focuses on large-scale demonstrations, court victories, and charismatic leaders that diminish other aspects of social activism. The movement is reduced to a campaign for legal rights with victories in court considered wins for the movement. The master narrative marks *Brown* as a triumphal moment within a larger narrative of American progress: good white people did the right thing when they learned of Black people's suffering.

The master narrative crafts racial injustice as resolved. In the present day, past legal and legislative victories are appropriated to advance color-blind conservatism. As Bell argues, "A myopic focus on the present through the haze of a fixed and glorified past also means that the broader society is bereft of the kind of deep historical knowing that could make genuine progress on racial matters possible."⁵² Jeanne Theoharis describes American democracy as a "self-cleaning oven." Once injustice is revealed, it is eliminated. She explains that this concept results in a national fable whereby "courage is inevitably rewarded, cases inevitably won, injustice inevitably vanquished."⁵³ The images of individual courage are fixed in a moment that removes the collective action that occurred in the years before Rosa Parks did not give up her seat or Martin Luther King Jr. had a dream. As a consequence, as Jacquelyn Dowd Hall points out, "the master narrative simultaneously elevates and diminishes the movement" because it prevents "one of the most remarkable mass movements in American history from speaking effectively to the challenges of our time."⁵⁴ Popular accounts and public memorializing of the movement evacuate the radical and political nature of the Black Freedom Struggle and miss "the staggering resolve and perseverance of small groups of people who actually pressed it forward, and in so doing attracted larger groups of people to their cause."⁵⁵ The national fable of the civil rights movement relegates racial injustice as a problem of the past that has been resolved and therefore, disconnected from the present day.

Often heralded as the impetus for the civil rights movement, *Brown* did not spring up in a vacuum. The case involved more than one little Black girl who had to walk past the white school to get to the segregated Black school. The decision encompassed five cases from Kansas, Virginia, Delaware, South Carolina, and the District of Columbia. Steven J. Crossland argues that *Brown* has received the glory, attention, and criticism with scant attention paid to the companion cases.⁵⁶ Even terming the cases "companion" indicates a subordination that belies the actual record. Winfred B. Moore Jr. and Orville Vernon Burton argue that most accounts of the civil rights movement emphasize urban experiences such as bus boycotts or lunch counter sit-ins, "but South Carolina's rural Clarendon County can legitimately claim to have initiated the modern civil rights movement."[57] The Clarendon County case, *Briggs v. Elliott*, was actually the first case filed in federal court to directly challenge the constitutionality of segregation. Yet, the rhetorical history of the case and *Brown* are largely unwritten. The rhetorical road converges with the legal road, resulting in landmark decisions that simultaneously reflect and constitute a new social order. The failure to account for all these elements creates a one-dimensional account of social change. The Warings' rhetorical campaign dispels the notion that the *Brown* decision was inevitable.

The Rhetorical Road to Brown v. Board of Education: *Elizabeth and Waties Waring's Campaign* interweaves the lives and words of two white allies with grassroots action and NAACP legal strategy. The Warings launched their rhetorical campaign to publicize race relations in the South to a national audience in order to shift public opinion. The speeches that they delivered from 1949 to 1952 are directly linked to the Clarendon County school segregation case, *Briggs et al. v. Elliott et al.*, that was decided in *Brown v. Board of Education*. Elizabeth and Waties Waring pursued a rhetorical course of action to influence the outcome of *Briggs*. Examining that campaign offers a different appreciation and understanding for how *Brown* came about. My purpose aligns with Robert Asen's rhetorical history of poor women in welfare policy debates to "reconstruct a useable past to help make sense of present debates." The Warings' multifaceted campaign and the response to it "offers an account of the historical tensions leading up to contemporary debates."[58] Those contemporary debates revolve around rights: the right to make reproductive health decisions, the right to refuse vaccine mandates, the right to vote without restrictions, and the right to a living wage. The debates are public and rhetorical. They concern the government's role in protecting rights and in some cases, infringing upon them, who is entitled to these rights, and who must demonstrate that they are worthy. This complex account of social change from the past can instill a sense of agency for those who seek to realize the ideals of American democracy in the present day.

Chapter 1

BAPTISM

With Japan's formal surrender in World War II on September 2, 1945, the United States faced the herculean task of demobilizing hundreds of thousands of troops and sailors from the Asiatic-Pacific theater. Transporting nearly eight million service members from four continents, Operation Magic Carpet returned 22,222 Americans back home on a daily basis for nearly one year beginning on September 5, 1945.[1] The order in which service members returned home was determined by an "Adjusted Service Card," a point system based on length of service and awards. Although the system was modified and revised, the critical score hovered at eighty or eighty-five points.[2] Veterans who were inducted into service after World War II began, like army Sergeant Isaac Woodard Jr., had a longer wait to return home. Woodard's score was forty-two, far short of eighty.[3] Four and a half months after Japan's surrender, Woodard began the long trek back home on January 15, 1946. Three weeks later, he was stateside.

On February 12, he was honorably discharged from the army at Camp Gordon near Augusta, Georgia. About eight o'clock that evening, still wearing his army uniform, Sgt. Woodard boarded a Greyhound bus headed for Winnsboro, South Carolina, where his wife had been staying while he was overseas. Along the route, Woodard and the bus driver exchanged words. The driver had a schedule to keep, and Woodard kept asking to stop so he could use the restroom. About an hour into the trip, the bus stopped in Batesburg, South Carolina, and the driver summoned law enforcement. The police chief, Lynwood Shull, arrested Woodard, beat him with a blackjack, and put him in jail. The next morning, Shull drove Woodard to the Veterans Hospital in Columbia because he could not see. The damage to Woodard's eyes was irreversible. He was permanently blind. Woodard remained at the Veterans Hospital for two months.

The contradiction between American democracy and white supremacy reached an apex in 1946 as violence against African American people escalated across the South. Black World War II veterans returned from serving their country overseas in war, invigorated with a sense of pride and citizenship. They were determined to claim their rights because "if they could serve their country and risk dying for it, they deserved to be treated equally."⁴ They were met by white southerners determined that "Jim Crow would not be a casualty of World War II."⁵ The violence perpetrated against Black people was an intimidation tactic to let them know that nothing had changed. White people were still in charge. Jim Crow devalued African American lives. When a Black man transgressed the white man's law or the white man's code, then he caught hell. The same was not true for white men. As a consequence, white people could beat, rob, kidnap, murder, and rape Black people with near impunity.

On February 25, 1946, Gladys Stephenson went to pick up her radio that was supposed to be repaired at a local department store in Columbia, Tennessee. Mrs. Stephenson, a Black woman, argued with the white clerk. Her son, a World War II veteran, stepped in to defend his mother from the clerk. The men fought and the clerk crashed through a window. Mrs. Stephenson picked up a shard of glass and struck at the clerk's shoulder. The police arrested the Stephensons, but not the clerk. Mother and son were released into the custody of African American civic leaders and returned to the Black section of town. That night and in the early morning of February 26, "the Ku Klux Klan, local police, and the National Guard terrorized the town's black citizens."⁶ Not a single Black-owned business was left unscathed. All were damaged in unwarranted searches. Law enforcement seized weapons and took over one hundred Black residents into custody. Twenty-eight were charged with attempted murder.⁷ They were eventually acquitted but only with the NAACP's intervention. Two Black people were shot and killed in police custody. Although the United States attorney general investigated the case, the Department of Justice did not secure any indictments for the murders.⁸

Newspaper advertisements invited readers to the Klan's first public demonstrations since the Japanese attack on Pearl Harbor. At Stone Mountain in Georgia on May 9, a gathering of more than seven hundred robed and masked Klansmen initiated five hundred new members while their wives and children watched. Visible for miles, a three-hundred-foot cross blazed at the peak of the boulder. Initially planned as a local meeting, five chartered buses shuttled Klansmen and their families from beyond the area to Stone Mountain. The grand dragon denied that the Klan was subversive. In the political arena, the Klan planned to "actively oppose anyone who differs with Klan principals. One of those principles is maintenance of white supremacy."⁹

On July 25, 1946, a mob of twenty armed and unmasked white assailants shot two Black farmers and their wives. One of the farmers, Roger Malcom, had just been released from jail for stabbing his white employer. Known as the Moore's Ford Lynching, the white men shot Malcom and his wife, Dorothy Dorsey Malcom, and her brother and sister-in-law, George and Mae Dorsey. On August 8, John C. Jones and his cousin, Albert Harris, were released from jail in Minden, Louisiana, after being arrested for loitering. A group of white people attacked the men and blowtorched Jones to death.[10]

While reports of violence filled newspapers across the United States, news of Isaac Woodard's beating in South Carolina did not surface until July. After Woodard's release from the Veterans Hospital, he returned to his home in the Bronx and contacted the NAACP's office in New York. The NAACP took his deposition on April 23, 1946, and actively investigated the assault.[11] Unfortunately, Woodard incorrectly identified Aiken, South Carolina, as the site of his arrest. In addition, he could not identify by name the officers who arrested him or the names of other bus passengers. The NAACP wanted to pursue justice for Woodard but had few details.

On May 6, 1946, Walter White, Executive Secretary of the NAACP, sent a letter to Robert P. Patterson, Secretary of War, and enclosed Woodard's affidavit. Patterson replied that since Woodard had been discharged from the army: "The War Department lacks authority to intervene officially where discharge from the Army is completed."[12] A month later, White wrote to Tom Clark, United States attorney general, again with Woodard's affidavit. Clark responded on July 25 that "an investigation is now being conducted," and added a handwritten postscript, "Any publicity concerning our investigation should not be permitted—for as you know, it affects the investigation."[13] The same month, the NAACP contacted Harold Boulware, an attorney in Columbia, South Carolina, to engage a private detective to investigate the matter.

Before receiving Clark's letter, White had contacted Orson Welles and requested a meeting "to get your help on certain steps we are taking or planning to take to publicize and get action on this case."[14] An actor, producer, and director, Welles's career began in radio with adaptations of famous literature and plays. During and after World War II, his *Orson Welles Commentaries* radio show on ABC featured political content and Hollywood gossip. On July 28, 1946, Welles read Woodard's affidavit in the first of five fifteen-minute episodes about the veteran's plight. Welles named Aiken as the site of the attack on Woodard. Residents and officials of Aiken were upset that their city was associated with Woodard's blinding. Welles refused to apologize to the City of Aiken, saying, "that if the occurrence did not happen in Aiken County then it was up to Aiken to prove where it did take place."[15] White Aiken residents did not agree.

Even with national publicity from Welles' radio show, the NAACP was desperate by August. The organization offered a $1,000 reward "to any person or persons supplying information which would lead to the apprehension and convictions of the sadistic Aiken, S.C. cops who used Nazi storm-trooper tactics on Negro vet, Isaac Woodard, who lost the sight of both eyes as a result of the outrage."[16] It placed an advertisement in the *Columbia Record* seeking information about the incident. In early August, 1946, Robert L. Carter wrote to Boulware, "Frankly, Boulware, we are over a barrel about this whole Woodard incident, and it is necessary that we get more definite information on where it occurred or else we will be placed in a very unhappy situation as well as those people who went out on a limb with us."[17] Despite the publicity in the newspapers and citizens' outrage, the NAACP did not have enough information to offer to the Department of Justice so it could pursue the case.

Lincoln Miller, a passenger on the Greyhound bus, saw the advertisement in the *Columbia Record*. Boulware was dispatched to get Miller's affidavit as well as the addresses of other passengers. In his affidavit, dated August 8, 1946, Miller reported that he knew Woodard in the Philippines, and both soldiers came over on the same boat to Camp Gordon where they were discharged on the same day. Miller identified Batesburg as the city where Woodard was beaten. The police came on the bus and took Woodard off, but Miller said: "Isaac Woodard was sitting near me and I did not observe him raising a disturbance on the bus." After they got off the bus, the police searched Woodard, then one of the officers struck him over the head with a nightstick. Miller also identified McQuilla Hudson of Lynchburg, South Carolina, as another passenger.[18] With trepidation, Miller signed the affidavit. Boulware wrote, "I was afraid at one time that he would not sign at all."[19] Later that month, Carter wrote that "Miller is very frighten [sic] and does not want his name used in connection with giving us this information."[20] Miller's identifying the city and another passenger aided the NAACP in following up with the Justice Department.

In response to the ongoing violence perpetrated against African American citizens across the United States, the NAACP and forty civil rights, labor, religious, and veterans' groups created the National Emergency Committee Against Mob Violence on August 6, 1946.[21] The newly formed committee sent a delegation to meet with President Truman on September 19, 1946. Less than a week later, on September 25, the FBI took Woodard's statement. A bench warrant was issued for Shull's arrest on September 26. Shull was charged with violating Woodard's civil rights and allegedly "did assault, strike and beat him about the head with a blackjack, thereby seriously injuring him and causing loss of eyesight and total blindness to Isaac Woodard, Jr."[22] Shull surrendered himself on September 28 and posted $2,000 bond for his appearance at the trial scheduled for November 4 in Columbia. After posting bond, Shull openly admitted assaulting Woodard and told newspaper reporters that "he struck Woodard across the front of his head when the soldier attempted to take his blackjack out of his hands as the officer was arresting him for allegedly causing a disturbance on a bus." Shull denied culpability, "I was no harsher than was necessary to complete the arrest."[23]

The case was originally assigned to Judge George Bell Timmerman Sr., but he was from Batesburg. The case was reassigned to Judge J. Waties Waring who recalled that Timmerman "knew Shull and didn't want to try the case. I don't think he liked that type of case anyhow. He asked me if I'd come to Columbia and take it, which I did."[24] An eighth-generation Charlestonian, Waties was born on July 27, 1880, into a family that had enslaved persons of African descent.[25] After he finished high school, Waties went to the College of Charleston and graduated in 1900. Because of his family's limited financial means, Waties read law instead of entering law school. He passed the bar exam, worked with a local lawyer, J. P. Kennedy Bryan, and became active in the local Democratic Party. In 1914, President Woodrow Wilson appointed Waties as assistant US attorney for South Carolina's eastern district, a position that he held until the end of Wilson's presidency. After his tenure under Wilson, Waties returned to private practice, forming a law partnership with D. A. Brockinton.[26] In the 1920s, the firm prospered, handling real estate, maritime law, and federal cases as well as defending large corporations in damage suits. During the Great Depression, the firm had difficult times, and in 1932, Charleston's mayor, Burnet Rhett Maybank, invited Waties to join the city's administration. The city council elected Waties as corporate counsel. He served in that capacity for the City of Charleston from 1933 to 1942.[27]

There was an unspoken family consensus that Waties would enter law, with his father calling him "judge."[28] In 1941, the family endearment became a reality when President Franklin Roosevelt nominated Waties to the federal bench. Waties recalled, "That being so I always had somewhere in the back of my head that someday I'd like to be a federal judge, and that while there was no particular campaign for the subject, I always looked to that with some hopes."[29] The nomination came from Burnet Rhett Maybank and "Cotton" Ed Smith, both of whom were firmly entrenched in South Carolina's Democratic Party.[30] When he was nominated in late 1941, "No one had cause to feel uneasy. Attorney Waring had always been conventional in his habits and conservative in his public life. . . . He showed none of the tendencies that sometimes crop out among fire eating radicals of the South."[31] For example, in his role as city attorney, Waties ensured that the army would enforce Charleston's whites-only mandate in the lease of Stoney Field. Septima Clark, a Black civil rights activist from Charleston, remarked that "when Waring was appointed U. S. Judge, he was considered a person who would protect the southern way of life."[32] White Charlestonians had no qualms about a descendent of the city's founding families serving as a federal judge. At sixty-one years old, Waties had reached the pinnacle of his legal career and enjoyed a respected social status. Hence, Judge Timmerman's willingness for Waties to preside over a racially charged case.

For the prosecution of Shull, the Justice Department sent Fred Rogers, "one of its crack civil rights lawyers," to assist Claud Sapp, the US attorney in Columbia. In October 1946, Rogers had assisted in the government's prosecution of a town constable in Florida who whipped a Black man and then forced him to jump off a bridge. The man drowned.[33] Sapp had served as chair of the South Carolina Democratic Party. He was a loyal supporter of Franklin Roosevelt's New Deal policies. Like Waties, Sapp's appointment as US district attorney came from Roosevelt. Filled with a strong sense of duty to both the Department of Justice and South Carolina, Sapp stood squarely between the department and the citizens whenever departmental policy, in his opinion, was not in the best interests of the citizens of his district.[34] Some white South Carolinians resented that the Justice Department side-stepped the grand jury and filed charges against Shull based on information. A legal maneuver permitted for misdemeanors, it had the same effect as an indictment. Sapp told reporters that Shull would stand trial for violating Woodard's civil rights under the Fourteenth Amendment of the US Constitution.[35]

After the case was assigned to Waties, the prosecution requested a continuance. Waties refused to grant it. He suspected that if the case was not tried until after the 1946 midterm elections, the public would forget the matter and the government would let it quietly disappear. Waties prepared a memorandum that he presented to the prosecution. If the government was not ready to proceed on the scheduled trial date, Waties would dismiss the case. In the memorandum, he questioned the prosecution's haste in bringing the case, and its unpreparedness to try the case more than a month after the charges were brought. He wrote:

> I am also aware of the fact that a national election is pending. But I do not believe that a criminal prosecution in the courts of this country should be influenced one way or the other by the desire of any of such parties for publicity and the resultant benefit to seek for public exhibitionism or for political preferment. . . . And I do not believe that

this poor blinded creature should be used as a football in the contest between box office and ballot box.³⁶

Faced with an outright dismissal of a highly publicized case that outraged voters across the country, the Department of Justice had little option except prepare for trial.

The trial began on November 5, 1946, with Waties presiding. During jury selection, Shull's attorneys used two of their challenges. They also requested that Waties ask each prospective juror if he belonged to the NAACP. The prosecution did not challenge any of the prospects, not even to ask if he belonged to any antinegro organizations like the Ku Klux Klan. The wooden bar that separated the observers in the crowded courtroom from the business of the trial also served as a color line. The prosecutors, Shull, his attorneys, the judge, and the jurors were all white men.

After opening statements in which Sapp mispronounced Woodard's name and said "Woodward," Isaac Woodard testified first. Riding alongside civilians, he and other soldiers were on their way home after serving overseas in World War II. When Woodard asked the white bus driver to stop so he could use the restroom, the driver cursed him. The soldier cursed him back, "Damn it, talk to me like I'm talking to you. I'm a man just like you." About an hour into the trip, the bus pulled into Batesburg. The driver summoned the soldier off the bus and told him there was "someone I want you to see." Shull was waiting for Woodard on the street at the bus door. When Woodard asserted that he had not done anything wrong, Shull slapped him on his head with the blackjack. Shull grabbed Woodard's left arm, twisted it behind his back, and led the soldier around the corner, out of sight of the bus. Shull then asked Woodard if he was discharged. When he responded "yes" instead of "yes sir," Shull hit him repeatedly with the nightstick, until Woodard grabbed the stick and wrung it out of Shull's hand. Then, a second policeman approached with his gun pointed at Woodard. He let go of the stick, and Shull continued hitting him, knocking him unconscious. When Woodard came to, Shull pushed him into the jailhouse and locked him in a cell. That was the last time Woodard remembered seeing anything.³⁷

During cross-examination, Woodard did not contradict any of his previous testimony. After the defense attorneys finished their questioning, the prosecutor asked Woodard to take off his sunglasses. The veteran turned towards the jurors. The twelve white men leaned forward. Woodard's eyes were nearly closed and shrunken back into his head.³⁸

The prosecution next called three physicians who all agreed that Woodard's eyeballs were ruptured. However, each testified that he had seen no other bruises, lacerations, or contusions on any other part of Woodard's body. The prosecution rested after one and a half hours of testimony from Isaac Woodard and three physicians. Franklin Williams, NAACP attorney, questioned Rogers about why Woodard's hospital records had not been subpoenaed. Those records would have shown that Woodard suffered injuries other than his eyes. According to Williams, Rogers's "answers to these questions were evasive and unsatisfactory."[39]

The defense called Shull, the bus driver, and the other officer who was with Shull on February 12. The bus driver and officer both testified that Woodard was abusive, profane, and drunk.[40] The defense presented three character witnesses, including Batesburg Mayor Quarles and a Black preacher, Archie Beecham.

On rebuttal, the prosecution called two witnesses, McQuilla Hudson and Jennings Stroud, both passengers on the bus. Hudson testified that he had not seen Woodard drunk or disorderly as the bus driver claimed. However, Hudson was not allowed to testify to having seen or heard anything that took place outside of the bus. According to some accounts, Stroud was taken off the bus at the same time as Woodard, questioned by the police, then allowed to return on the bus.[41] Stroud also was not allowed to testify as to what took place outside the bus.

Fred Rogers's thirty-minute summation was ineffective. He told the jury that "he knew how the jury felt in as much as he, himself, was a Texan. That he had come to Columbia at the request of the local District Attorney to 'assist' in the prosecution of the case."[42] He concluded by requesting a verdict of guilty. Sapp's ten-minute closing argument was largely apologetic. He told the jurors that he was only doing his duty by prosecuting Shull and that the government would be satisfied with any verdict that the jury would bring.[43] The defense attorneys relied on racial prejudice in their summations. One asserted that Woodard belonged "to that inferior race which South Carolina has always protected" and his "profane and vulgar" language was not "the talk of a sober South Carolina Negro."[44] The other defense attorney claimed that if Shull was convicted, the jury was saying "to the public officers of South Carolina that you no longer want your homes, your wife, and your children protected."[45] Waties tried to diffuse the racial prejudice in the case with a strong charge to the jury.[46] He asked the jurors to remember that they were not trying the case as between Black and white. Instead, the case was based on the fact that it is illegal to deprive someone of his civil rights.[47]

After the jurors left the courtroom to deliberate, it occurred to Waties that they would probably return a verdict in two minutes. He decided to go for a walk, "trying to give the thing a little more atmosphere of respectability."[48]

The jury could not come back with a verdict unless the judge was present. Waties left the courthouse and walked to the hotel to check on his wife, Elizabeth. She traveled with Waties to Columbia as she always did when he presided in jurisdictions outside of Charleston.

Born into a life of privilege in 1895, Elizabeth Avery was a direct descendent of John Alden, a Mayflower passenger.[49] Her maternal ancestors came from Litchfield, Connecticut, and included intellectuals, teachers, ministers, and lawyers. The Avery family's wealth came from her grandfather's lumber business in Maine which her father, John H. Avery, assumed after his father's death. Growing up, Elizabeth attended private schools including Liggett School in Detroit, Sacred Heart School in Paris, and Westover School in Middlebury, Connecticut.[50] Elizabeth made debuts in Detroit and Chicago. In 1915, she married Wilson W. Mills, a lawyer and board member of one of Detroit's largest banks.[51] Elizabeth and Wilson had three children: William born in 1917, David born in 1919, and Ann born in 1921. In Detroit, Elizabeth spent her time volunteering, promoting the arts, and socializing. A talented mezzo-soprano, Elizabeth was very prominent in the city's musical circles and appeared on numerous programs.[52] Her life while married to Mills was that of a socialite. As Mrs. Wilson W. Mills, her name graced the society page of the *Detroit Free Press* almost every week.

The Mills' marriage lasted nearly twenty years until Elizabeth unexpectedly divorced Wilson to marry Henry Hoffman, a wealthy retired textile manufacturer and antiques collector. She most likely met Hoffman while wintering in Ormond Beach, Florida. Hoffman was twenty years older than Elizabeth.[53] She went to Reno, Nevada for the Mills divorce and married Hoffman five days after it was finalized. Elizabeth's divorce from her first husband left her estranged from her family and children. She left Detroit and moved with Hoffman to Litchfield, Connecticut.

To escape the harsh winters in Connecticut, the Hoffmans traveled to Florida, stopping over in Charleston, South Carolina to break the long trek. By the end of the 1920s, Charleston had established itself as an ideal spot for rich northerners escaping frigid winters, either with an extended stay or as a layover before the final leg of their journey to Florida. Charleston boosters actively promoted the city's mild weather, historic architecture, and luscious flora within a setting that offered a chance "to slip back into the days gone by, recalling to the fabric of the history of this old city."[54] Rich, charming, and possessing social status, Elizabeth was a hit when she arrived in Charleston as Henry Hoffman's wife. Poppy Cannon described Elizabeth as "well-born, correctly schooled, couturier-gowned, socially graceful."[55] She was the toast of Charleston. Elizabeth's ties to the city were strengthened when her daughter, Ann, married Simeon Hyde Jr., a descendent of another Charleston founding family.

Because of the small social circle among the downtown group in Charleston, the Hoffmans likely encountered Waties and Annie Waring who often entertained in their home.[56] Waties married Annie Gammell in 1913.[57] Waties was one of Charleston's most eligible bachelors: good-looking, impeccable family, and prestigious career. Miss Annie, as she was called, was one of Charleston's own. In his marriage, like his career and politics, Waties had selected a suitable bride to take her place by his side in elite society. Shortly after their marriage, Waties and Annie moved to her house at 61 Meeting Street, south of Broad Street. Broad Street marks the line of social acceptability in Charleston. The downtown group was known as the SOBs because they resided South of Broad. Like the Warings, the SOBs were descendants of the families that settled Charles Towne in the late seventeenth century.

Miss Annie was devoted to Waties, proud of his position as a federal judge, and appreciated their prominent status in Charleston society.[58] Outwardly, their relationship appeared warm but "behind closed doors things were cold and somewhat aloof."[59] D. A. Brockinton Jr. observed that Miss Annie "worshipped the ground that Waties walked on, especially later when he became United States district judge. . . . But intellectually she didn't have the depth of Waties."[60] In a social circle concerned with appearances, Waties and Miss Annie may have continued the facade of a happy marriage until their deaths, especially since South Carolina did not have a legal provision to dissolve marriages. Any glimmer of a lifetime of marital bliss was extinguished when Waties met Elizabeth Hoffman.

In early 1945, Waties told his wife of thirty years that he wanted a divorce. According to Waties, "My first wife and I lived along pretty happily. . . . Then I met my present wife, and we fell in love. I discussed the matter very frankly with my first wife, and she agreed to a divorce and went to Florida and obtained it. Then I married my present wife. We have been in thorough accord."[61] While Miss Annie was in Florida, Elizabeth once again went to Reno, Nevada, to obtain a divorce from Hoffman. Waties and Elizabeth married on June 15, 1945, in Greenwich, Connecticut, barely a week after Waties's divorce from Miss Annie was finalized. Outwardly, it seemed as if he ended an ideal marriage so he could take up with some Yankee woman of questionable morals.

With their divorces and marriage, Elizabeth and Waties fueled the rumor mill in Charleston. Waties confessed "there was a good deal of ill-will based on" his divorce and marriage to Elizabeth.[62] The couple moved into Annie's house on Meeting Street, with Annie renting a small kitchen house less than one hundred feet from her former home. In his social circle it seemed as if Waties had abandoned his wife and set up Elizabeth in Miss Annie's bed and home. Septima Clark thought the white people South of Broad Street would have been okay if Waties had "gone next door and taken a woman," but the idea of "marrying a Yankee woman, that was a terrible thing."[63] Elizabeth's northern background and divorces did not endear her to Charleston society. White Charleston aristocracy cooled towards the Judge and new Mrs. Waring. People would leave the room when the couple entered. Few invitations were extended to them. Very few accepted their social invitations. With a near-extinct social life in Charleston, Elizabeth often traveled with Waties when he presided in other cities. Waties said that Elizabeth "was very much liked and very much admired, and taken up a good deal in the rest of the state."[64] For Elizabeth, trips with Waties offered a welcomed respite from the glacial social atmosphere in Charleston.

At the Shull trial, Elizabeth sat among the other observers. She heard the testimony. She saw Woodard's eyes when he took off the sunglasses. During his walk while the jury deliberated, Waties stopped at the hotel and found Elizabeth in tears. She told her husband, "I've never heard such a terrible thing and had no idea how bad the situation was." Waties said that the Shull trial was Elizabeth's "baptism in racial prejudice."[65] The trial was just as transformative for him. Ruby Cornwell, a Black civil rights activist who became Elizabeth's close friend, recalled, "You know, the judge's 'baptism of fire' was the case of the soldier who was blinded."[66] When Waties returned to the courthouse, the marshal greeted him with the news that the jury had been rapping on the door and was ready to come back into the courtroom.[67] The jury delivered its not guilty verdict immediately upon Waties's return. It had deliberated for twenty-eight minutes.[68]

The day after the Shull trial, Elizabeth visited with a Columbia matron, a white woman from the South. Elizabeth confessed to her friend that what Elizabeth had seen at the Shull trial shocked her. Woodard served as a living symbol of racial violence in the South. More than a newspaper account, Elizabeth saw Woodard's eyes that gave proof that the horrors in the South for Black people were not exaggerated. Although Elizabeth had lived in the South for over a year, she had never heard such a terrible thing. The woman responded, "Well, Mrs. Waring, that sort of thing happens all the time. It's dreadful, but what are we going to do about it?"[69]

The NAACP had been trying to do something about that sort of thing since its founding in 1909. The organization pressured Congress to enact a federal antilynching law. Until 1938, a flag emblazoned with "A Man Was Lynched Yesterday" flew outside its headquarters at 69 Fifth Avenue in

New York City. The NAACP had invested time and money to publicize the assault on Isaac Woodard. Thurgood Marshall, as Special Counsel for the NAACP, wrote a letter to Tom Clark, US attorney general, on November 14, 1946, to protest the Justice Department's handling of the case. Marshall wrote that neither Sapp nor Rogers "did as much as in their power to obtain a conviction." The prosecution failed to inquire about prospective jurors' affiliations with the Ku Klux Klan or other antinegro organizations. Marshall told Clark that when Sapp said the government would be satisfied with any verdict, he invited the jury to bring a verdict of not guilty. Marshall wanted it on the record that the NAACP objected "strenuously to the manner in which the trial was conducted by the agents of the Government of the United States."[70]

Waties agreed with Marshall's assessment of the government's performance. Woodard and other witnesses testified that the bus was full. The prosecution's failure to produce other passengers on the bus raised serious doubts for Waties about the government's intention: "That, to my mind, was quite a shocking instance of whether the Government was really prosecuting the case under pressure or sincerely, because it occurred to me that with all the facilities of the United States Government, and of the bus lines, certainly some of the passengers who were on the bus that day could have been found and brought to court to testify."[71] Waties did not blame the jury for not convicting Shull. Without testimony from other passengers on the bus, the jurors were faced with contradictory versions of what happened on February 12. One story from a "white man and a constable living in the community, twenty-five miles away from Columbia where the case was being tried" and another from a Black man from out of state, "an 'uppity Negro' because he'd asserted his rights."[72] In that time and place, the testimony of other passengers on the bus may not have made any difference, but justice required a more rigorous case from the prosecution. Marshall could protest all he wanted. He knew, as did everyone else, that nothing would change the outcome of the trial. No justice would be meted for Woodard's loss of sight.

With no answer to the matron's query "What are we going to do about it?," the Warings pursued their own course of study about the Race Problem when they returned to Charleston. In their living room each evening, Elizabeth and Waties read tomes like W. J. Cash's *The Mind of the South* and Gunnar Myrdal's *An American Dilemma*. Critics commended Cash for his ability to view his native South with detachment as he analyzed and criticized its faults. Ralph McGill, editor of the *Atlanta Constitution*, praised Cash and called for those who loved the South "to point out its weaknesses and try by patient effort to correct them."[73] Cash argued that the Civil War and

Reconstruction were the North's attempts to sweep the South into the main current of the nation. Instead, those efforts had operated "enormously to fortify and confirm" the white southerner's mind and will.[74]

Defeated and decimated in the Civil War, white southerners struggled to understand what it meant to be white and southern. For many, the answer could be found in the Lost Cause, the movement to honor the Confederacy. David Goldfield describes the Lost Cause as "an impressive body of intellectual alchemy that transformed a crushing defeat into a glorious crusade accompanied by heroism and sacrifice."[75] The phrase, Lost Cause, first appeared in Edward Pollard's *The Lost Cause: A New Southern History of the War of the Confederates*, published in 1866. Pollard offered "a full and authentic account" of Civil War battles, extolled the virtues of southern society, and condemned the North. Howard Dorgan explains that Lost Cause narratives function to soften defeat, purify causes, vindicate losers, and exonerate southern values. Overall, the Lost Cause turned an era of humiliation into an era of triumph, "and from there into a source of regional pride."[76]

Because South Carolina was the first state to secede from the Union, the first shots of the Civil War were fired in Charleston, and it was the last city from which federal troops were removed during Reconstruction, the city and state were uniquely focused on Confederate identity. The Lost Cause embraced a past in which the Confederate cause was just, slavery was benign, and Black people were racially inferior.[77] With the Lost Cause, the South became more than a matter of geography. It became "an object of pride, patriotism, and identification." Cash wrote that "The South in its entirety was filled with an immense regard for nostalgia; yearned backward toward its past with passionate longing."[78] Glorifying the mythic past helped southerners reestablish and maintain self-respect in the face of adverse conditions.[79] The past for white southerners became an object of worship.

According to Cash, Reconstruction served to strengthen southern whites' determination to restore slavery in all but name. This legacy created "a world in which the Negro was still 'mud-sill,' and in which a white man, any white man, was in some sense a master."[80] Waties agreed that the white man who does not do so well always likes someone to look down on; no matter how low the white person is, he is not Black.[81] For white southerners, maintaining superiority to the Black man was paramount in life. Cash observed that in their efforts, they formed "too great attachment to racial values and a tendency to justify cruelty and injustice in the name of those values, sentimentality and a lack of realism—these have been its characteristics in the past. And, despite changes for the better, they remain its characteristic vices today."[82] Waties called *The Mind of the South* a wonderful book that "gives you the ways and the thinking, the perverted and wrong method of thought, of those who have carried on the persecution of the Negroes."[83] As a federal judge, Waties had seen how this mentality manifested itself in the lives of African American people.

In the late 1930s, the Carnegie Corporation commissioned the Swedish economist Gunnar Myrdal to study the race problem in the United States.[84] Published in 1944, Myrdal's study extended to forty-five chapters in two volumes followed by over four hundred fine-printed pages of appendices, bibliography, and footnotes.[85] *An American Dilemma* painstakingly studied every aspect of race relations in America.[86] Myrdal proposed that a common social ethos and political creed created strong unity and stability in America. He called the creed "the cement in the structure of this great and disparate nation." Myrdal's concept of the American Creed encapsulated the American ideals of equality and liberty. The American Creed is an "explicitly expressed system of general ideals in reference to human interrelations." Myrdal explained that these ideals included the dignity of each human being, the fundamental equality of all men, and the inalienable rights to freedom, justice, and fair opportunity. Furthermore, "The ideals of the American Creed have thus become the highest law of the land. The Supreme Court pays its reverence to these general principles when it declares what is constitutional and what is not." According to the American Creed, race and color were not acceptable grounds for discrimination. Therefore, social segregation and racial discrimination were a challenge to it.[87] The dilemma of the white American was to uphold the creed on the one hand and betray it on the other with its treatment of Negroes.[88]

Writing more than seventy years after the Reconstruction Amendments, Gunnar Myrdal argued that "The region is still carrying the heritage of slavery."[89] With the horrors of Reconstruction neither forgotten nor forgiven, South Carolina had to protect itself against the possible recurrence of Black supremacy. While the Thirteenth, Fourteenth, and Fifteenth constitutional amendments abolished slavery legally, the habits, customs, and prejudices associated with it persisted in the region. Waties called *An American Dilemma* "a great monumental work" that "will give you all the facts and a true picture of what is happening."[90] Myrdal's assessment resonated with the Warings because it confirmed their increasing dissatisfaction with the racial status quo. For Waties and Elizabeth, the American Creed meant equality of all citizens.[91]

After reading Cash, Myrdal, and other treatises, Waties "began to understand the complexity of the thing and come to the conclusion that the solution was to get rid of the complexity, and adopt a simple doctrine that all people in this country are equal and should have equal opportunity, that they should have complete freedom of association." This was not only Waties's doctrine. In their study of race relations in the South, Elizabeth read aloud to Waties, and he recalled, "But in these racial matters we talked over the situation very much. . . . She had very little knowledge of the racial situation, or any feeling about it, until she began to see it closely, as I began to see it. We did a good deal of study together then."[92] To the Warings, the Fourteenth Amendment meant "entire equality for Negroes."[93] The system of racial segregation in the South mocked the precepts of the American Creed as the Warings understood it. Segregation was legally mandated in South Carolina. Because the separation of the races was legal and enforced, the Warings could not envision how the American Creed could ever be realized until segregation ended.[94] Based on the Jim Crow justice that they witnessed at the Shull trial and their readings, Elizabeth and Waties came to believe that racial violence was a manifestation of segregation.

The Warings were not alone in their belief that the South was unable or unwilling to protect the rights of African American citizens. One month after Shull's acquittal, President Harry Truman issued Executive Order 9808 which established his Committee on Civil Rights. The committee was one way—without Congress—that Truman could address the gruesome violence directed towards Black people and southern states' failure to protect their rights. Garth E. Pauley points out that Truman's civil rights initiatives were not solely motivated by political pragmatism or moral repugnancy, but a combination of the two.[95] Truman announced the formation of the committee in his State of the Union Address to a joint session of Congress on January 6, 1947. The committee was a necessary response to the "numerous attacks upon the constitutional rights of individual citizens as a result of racial and religious bigotry." In his address, Truman boldly told the joint session "I am not convinced that the present legislation reached the limit of federal power to protect the civil rights of its citizens." He called upon his belief that "the will to fight these crimes should be in the hearts of every one of us."[96] Truman appealed to the audience's sense of humanity. He transformed the South's problem into a national crisis. Instead of leaving the South alone to deal with Black people as they saw fit, Truman put the white South on notice that he was committed to ensuring that the federal government protected all citizens' civil rights.

Convinced that the federal government had the duty to act when state or local authorities failed to protect the constitutional rights of all citizens, Truman empowered his committee with the legal tools necessary to recommend federal legislation and other federal actions to ensure civil rights equality.[97] Referred to as "Noah's Ark" in the press, the committee consisted of two: corporate heads, labor representatives, Jews, Catholics, Protestants, college presidents, southerners, women, and Black people. None of the fifteen committee members had links to political parties or demonstrated any radical viewpoints.[98] From the South, Frank Graham, president of the University of North Carolina, and Dorothy Tilly, a white southern woman involved in the Southern Regional Council, participated in meetings, heard testimony at public hearings, analyzed evidence, and made recommendations in the committee's report.[99]

While the president's committee heard testimony and reviewed evidence, Elizabeth and Waties continued their study together. Elizabeth often read aloud because Waties's eyes tired easily. They stayed up late discussing what they read. At times, their discoveries were too disturbing. Elizabeth would close the book and they loaded into their car, driving miles and miles in the night through the deserted streets of Charleston.[100]

Chapter 2

IT ALL STARTED WITH A BUS

On the same day that an all-white jury acquitted Lynwood Shull, J. Strom Thurmond emerged victorious in South Carolina's gubernatorial election. In the primary held on August 13, 1946, the Democratic Party's slate for South Carolina governor included nine candidates. Just over 290,000 white South Carolinians voted in the August primary and more than 250,000 voted in the September runoff between Thurmond and James C. McLeod. In the general election, Thurmond ran unopposed. Only 26,326 people voted.[1] Black voters like George Elmore were excluded from the August primary and September run-off. The Richland County Democratic Party refused Elmore's request to participate on the grounds that he was Black, and membership in the party—what party officials called a private club—was restricted to white people.[2] The NAACP filed *Elmore v. Rice* in federal court against the Richland County Democratic Executive Committee and the election managers on February 21, 1947.

The *Elmore* suit landed on Judge George Bell Timmerman Sr.'s docket along with another case, *John H. Wrighten v. Board of Trustees of the University of South Carolina*. Wrighten, a Black man, sought admission to the University of South Carolina's law school because at the time, the state did not provide a separate law school for Black residents. Timmerman served as a trustee for the university so he could not preside over the Wrighten case. Like the Shull trial, Timmerman requested that Waties hear *Wrighten*. Waties explained to Timmerman that the *Wrighten* and *Elmore* cases were clearly interlocked so the same judge should hear both.[3] Timmerman agreed. He was a staunch segregationist and willing to let Waties take any race-related cases. On March 10, 1947, Timmerman informed the attorneys in the cases that he had disqualified himself and that Waties would hear both matters.[4]

Waties agreed to take the cases off Judge Timmerman's hands "after some pretty serious thought and considerable worry." He felt that someone had to face the issues of segregation and disenfranchisement for Black South

Carolinians. As a native white southerner, Waties also knew what was at stake. He explained to Elizabeth the terrible feeling in South Carolina about racial matters. They had seen it at the Shull trial. They had read about it. He told his wife that they may have to pay a penalty. Waties warned Elizabeth that "The Klan still rides in South Carolina." Elizabeth reassured Waties, "I'm with you start to finish. I think you ought to take it; we don't know what's going to happen if you don't."[5] The woman who had abandoned two marriages showed intense loyalty to her third husband when the stakes were much higher than being invited to parties. The downtown group in Charleston questioned Elizabeth's commitment to Waties. They whispered that she exerted her feminine influence and northern ways on her older husband. Yet, it was Waties who actively pursued a case that would transform South Carolina politics.

In the summer of 1946, John H. Wrighten applied for admission to the School of Law at the University of South Carolina. The university denied his application based solely on his race. Wrighten wrote a letter to the Chairman of the Board of Trustees to appeal the decision, to no avail.[6] He then filed a federal suit in January 1947, because South Carolina did not provide a law school for Black students and the state-supported university refused to admit him to the segregated white school. Shortly thereafter, the state legislature appropriated money to establish a law school at South Carolina State College, the state-supported Black college in Orangeburg.[7] Wrighten's case did not challenge South Carolina's constitutional provisions that required segregated institutions. Instead, the issue was whether the state offered law school facilities to Black students that were comparable to those provided to white students.[8] It was a separate-but-equal case that challenged South Carolina's failure to provide "equal" facilities as required under *Plessy v. Ferguson*.

The Wrighten case was fairly straightforward since it did not challenge South Carolina's constitutional mandate of separate schools for Black and white students. Waties offered the university three options: provide a law school for Black students comparable to the one in Columbia for white students, admit Black students to the law school at the university, or close the University law school to both Black and white students. In his order, Waties gave the state until the following year to provide a law school "on substantial parity." The legislature appropriated $200,000 for a building and $30,000 for a law library at South Carolina State College instead of admitting a Black student to the white law school. Wrighten enrolled in the fall of 1949 and graduated in 1952.[9]

The second case, the one that Waties requested from Timmerman, was not as straightforward as the law school case. Since Reconstruction, the South Carolina white power structure had effectively disenfranchised Black citizens. George Elmore's suit against the Richland County Democratic Party officials rekindled a long-dormant volcano. During World War II, as Allied troops battled Axis powers across multiple fronts, South Carolina Governor Olin D. Johnston convened an extraordinary session of the State General Assembly on April 14, 1944. Johnston called the session eleven days after the United States Supreme Court ruled in *Smith v. Allwright* that the primary was an integral element of the election process. Therefore, no citizen could be excluded from voting in primaries because of race. The objective of the South Carolina legislature's session was to launch the "most spectacular" plan to preserve the all-white Democratic Party primary.[10]

The *Smith* decision threatened to disband the Solid South, the region that had consistently disenfranchised Black citizens and clung to the Democratic Party to do so.[11] Politically, the Solid South meant one party. After Reconstruction, the Democratic Party was *the* political party in former Confederate states. The primary was the only election in South Carolina that voters could make any meaningful choice among candidates because whoever triumphed in the primary won the office.[12] Thurgood Marshall said that the all-white primary was the most effective and legal means to disenfranchise Negroes.[13]

At the extraordinary session, Johnston invoked the Reconstruction era and warned the General Assembly that unless white people protected themselves, history would repeat itself: Radical Republicans and Black people would govern the state. Johnston said that Reconstruction "left a stench in the nostrils of the people of South Carolina that will exist for generations to come."[14] He shouted to the Assembly that "White supremacy will be maintained in our primaries. Let the chips fall where they may."[15] The white politicians heeded Johnston's call. They repealed nearly 150 statutes that gave state support to the Democratic Party and passed more than a hundred laws designed to separate the Democratic primary from the control of the state government.[16] South Carolina's effort to circumvent *Smith* severed the political party from the state. As a result, the South Carolina Democratic Party was a voluntary association of citizens that could discriminate on the basis of race without encroaching on the Fourteenth or Fifteenth Amendments.[17] In November 1944, white voters approved an amendment to the state constitution that erased all mention of the primary in South Carolina. The Democrats formed private clubs, incorporating nearly all the repealed laws, as well as stringent membership rules, including being white.[18] Repealing all laws related to the primary meant that in effect, by statute, there was no primary.

Waties recalled that everybody in South Carolina knew exactly what had happened. The newspapers were full of it. Johnston was frank about his motives.[19] The NAACP also knew. Other southern states looked to the

South Carolina model to evade *Smith v. Allwright*. If left unchallenged in South Carolina, then other states would adopt the "club" model, nullifying the NAACP's victory in *Smith*. Franklin Williams contacted Harold Boulware seeking a plaintiff to challenge the South Carolina model. Boulware suggested George Elmore who agreed to serve as a plaintiff.[20]

Shortly before their second wedding anniversary, Elizabeth and Waties traveled to Columbia for the law school and primary cases. Waties handled the law school matter on June 3, 1947. The primary voting case stretched across the next two days. Despite assembling a team of the most highly regarded legal minds in the state, the Democratic Party failed to persuade Waties, as a matter of law, that it operated as a private club. In his ruling issued on July 12, Waties referenced President Truman's historic address at the NAACP's thirty-eighth convention held two weeks earlier on June 29. Truman was the first president to address the NAACP and the first president to define civil rights as a crisis.[21]

Standing before the Lincoln Memorial, Truman proclaimed that it was more important than ever that the United States guarantee freedom and equality to all its citizens: "When I say all Americans, I mean all Americans." In his remarks that were broadcast nationally on four radio networks and lasted twelve minutes, Truman stressed his conviction that the federal government must ensure these rights: "We must make the federal government a friendly, vigilant defender of the rights and equalities of all Americans."[22] Truman seized the responsibility of civil liberties from localities and designated the federal government as protector of Black citizens.

Waties answered Truman's call in the *Elmore* ruling when he exhorted "It is time for South Carolina to rejoin the Union. It is time to fall in step with the other states and to adopt the American way of conducting elections." Waties noted that the South Carolina legislature's extraordinary session "was wholly and solely for the purpose of preventing the Negro from gaining a right to vote in the primaries as granted under the doctrine of the *Smith v. Allwright* case."[23] He removed the legal barriers that excluded African American citizens from the electoral process with harsh language that set him on an irreversible course in opposition to white supremacy. Waties told Carl Rowan that he purposefully crafted the *Elmore* decision to "arouse the decent people of the state to a realization that democracy cannot survive if we continue to have first- and second-class citizens. I knew that it would take more than a dust-dry opinion to arouse them from a decades-old sleep." The animosity towards Elizabeth and Waties in Charleston spread to the rest of the Palmetto State. Throughout his native South Carolina, Waties became known as "the man who let the n-word vote."[24]

During July, the Black and white press reported on the *Elmore* ruling. The white press confirmed the South Carolina Democratic Party's intent to appeal to the highest court in the land and if unsuccessful, then explore other measures to preserve white supremacy in the primaries. In contrast, the Black press assured readers that the *Elmore* decision adhered to *Smith v. Allwright* and as such, marked the end of the all-white primary, not just in South Carolina, but in the South. On July 12, 1947, the Charleston *Evening Post* blazed with the headline "Right of Negroes to Vote in Democratic Primaries Upheld by Waring's Decision." Former Charleston Mayor Thomas P. Stoney was the only member of the South Carolina Democratic Party apparatus willing to comment on the record about the *Elmore* ruling. Just like Wade Hampton and Benjamin Tillman had preserved white supremacy in the past, Stoney was confident "thousands of others who will meet the test" of Waties's ruling. The newspaper noted that other white Democrats were "shocked" and "disappointed."[25] Two days later, Senator Burnet R. Maybank, Charleston's former mayor and Waties's former boss, said that the ruling was "clearly wrong" and "clearly without precedent." Maybank detached the South Carolina situation from *Smith v. Allwright*. The situation was different because according to South Carolina law, the Democratic Party was a voluntary association.[26] The Democratic Party was determined to upend the *Elmore* ruling.

Elsewhere in South Carolina, *The State*, based in Columbia, ran the Associated Press's report on the *Wrighten* and *Elmore* decisions. Alongside the AP report on the front page, *The State* published James Hinton's letter to William Baskin, chairman of the South Carolina Democratic Party. As president of the South Carolina State Conference of NAACP, Hinton asked that the party abide by Waties's ruling and "that any and all feelings and bitterness be forgotten."[27] Later in July, *The State* published the full text of the *Elmore* ruling.[28] Nationally, the *New York Times* ran the AP report on the front page, then an editorial on July 14 that offered lukewarm support.[29] The *Chicago Daily Tribune* and *Washington Post* also published the Associated Press report.[30]

The response from the Black press catapulted the sixty-seven-year-old white jurist from the South Carolina lowcountry onto the national stage. The major dailies and weeklies heralded the *Elmore* ruling as the end of the white primary. The *Atlanta Daily World* declared that technicalities and shibboleths would no longer be tolerated and hoped that "no further reviews will be granted to the false appeals to higher courts."[31] The *Pittsburgh Courier* reported the widespread opinion that Waties's ruling sounded the death-knell for the all-white primary across the South.[32] Walter White reminded readers of the *Chicago Defender* that the victory in *Elmore v. Rice* took more than thirty years. He predicted that if appealed, the case would almost certainly "be roundly trounced by the United States Supreme Court." White credited Waties with putting "an end, many lawyers and political observers believe, for all time, to the stupid efforts" to abolish primary laws as a means to evading *Smith v. Allwright*. White ended his column with a "special mete of thanks" to Waties "who rose above narrow sectionalism in the finest tradition of American jurisprudence."[33] The Black press praised Waties's courage and celebrated the end of disenfranchisement for Black citizens.

On the last day of its board of directors' two-day meeting in Richmond, Virginia, the Southern Conference for Human Welfare (SCHW) passed a resolution that hailed Waties's ruling as "a landmark in the South's struggle for honest democracy."[34] Founded by southern supporters of Franklin Roosevelt, SCHW's inaugural meeting was held in Birmingham, Alabama, in 1938. For ten years, SCHW espoused reforms in voting, racial violence, labor unions, and education.[35] For SCHW's efforts, the House Un-American Activities Committee branded the organization a "Communist-front" in 1947.[36] Initially established as an extension of SCHW, the Southern Conference Educational Fund (SCEF) became a separate entity in 1947. Unlike SCHW, SCEF focused exclusively on integration. SCEF's director, James Dombrowski, was convinced that no fundamental change would take place in the South until segregation was eliminated.[37] Dombrowski personally wrote to Waties less than a week after the *Elmore* decision: "Southerners who accept the full implications of the democratic way of life, and I firmly believe that includes the majority of us, will take satisfaction in your decision."[38] His letter articulated the belief among SCEF's leaders that more white southerners were sympathetic to SCEF's concern with racial equality than would openly admit their views.[39]

Waties received many letters even from white southerners who praised him and commended him for his courage. These letters and subdued response from white southern newspapers revealed a fissure in white supremacy's Solid South. Instead of unified denunciation of his ruling, Waties received affirmation from whites—and gratitude. Stephen Nettles, an attorney in Greenville in the upstate region, wrote: "So often in South Carolina an evil condition continues to exist simply because there is no leader with the mind and courage to speak out and lead the way." The private letters of support for voting rights belied the public outcry. They signified a glimmer of decency that confirmed Waties's belief that he was "not alone in this and there is a substantial stratum of sanity, decency, and liberality in our State."[40] In addition, the national publicity in the Black and white press indicated that beyond the South, an interested and informed constituency existed that viewed the region's Race Problem as a national issue.

After Waties issued the rulings in *Wrighten* and *Elmore*, he and Elizabeth traveled to Santa Barbara for an extended vacation. Without the demands of court, they continued their study of the Race Problem which extended beyond Cash and Myrdal. Intellectually curious, neither length nor complexity deterred them from studying works that less robust readers would decline to undertake. One such work was Rebecca West's *Black Lamb and Grey Falcon*. West's six-week journey through Yugoslavia in 1937 showed "the past side by side with the present it created."[41] Her linking past events to the contemporary global situation resonated with Waties, an eighth-generation Charlestonian awakening to the legacy of slavery in his native South. In 1947, West applied her writing talents and insights to the trial of more than twenty taxi drivers charged with kidnapping and murdering Willie Earle. Her article, "Opera in Greenville" published in the *New Yorker*, impressed Waties. He called it "magnificent."[42]

The lynching of Willie Earle was the first test of South Carolina's newly inaugurated governor, Strom Thurmond. At about five o'clock in the morning on February 17, 1947, a group of cab drivers kidnapped Willie Earle from the Pickens County Jail, where the twenty-four-year-old Black man was being held under suspicion of stabbing a white taxi driver. The men stabbed Earle in his chest, stomach, forehand, neck, and right thigh. None of the stab wounds was lethal. One driver shot Earle three times.[43]

In his statement to the press on February 18, Governor Thurmond called Earle's murder a disgrace to the state. He framed the lynching as an offense to the "law abiding citizens" who should not have to bear the infamy and shame of the crime.[44] Thurmond asserted that South Carolina would combat mob rule with the same determination that the United States defended democratic principles in World War II. To back up his declaration, the governor assembled a "whirlwind-dragnet" of city and county law enforcement, state constables, and FBI agents. By February 21, law enforcement officials had thirty men in jail and obtained confessions from twenty-six of them. Thurmond appointed a special prosecutor to assist the Greenville solicitor. As the state's prosecution team prepared its case against the defendants, more than 150 gas stations, barber shops, stores, pharmacies, and other small businesses across the Upstate, down to Columbia and even as far as Georgia, displayed glass jars to collect money for the taxi drivers' defense fund.[45]

The trial of the drivers began on May 5 and lasted over two weeks. The state's prosecution of white men for kidnapping and killing a Black man drew national attention. Dorothy Tilly traveled from Georgia to observe the trial and sat in the courtroom, like Elizabeth at the Shull trial. Unlike Elizabeth, Tilly was the prototype of the southern lady, wearing roses in her hats. In Greenville, she watched the jury make a brazen mockery of the trial, openly talking and cracking jokes back and forth.[46] Her experience spurred her to found the Fellowship of the Concerned. She determined that if the "good people" were in the courtroom and "bear silent witness," just their presence would safeguard justice. By "good people," Tilly meant white people of a certain class. Fellowship members were respectable white middle-class women "imbued with a spirit of Christian love and determined to bring out the goodness in all southerners."[47] Tilly was a devout Methodist who parlayed her faith and femininity to champion human rights.[48]

Along with interested observers like Tilly, journalists from across the nation descended upon upstate South Carolina including British-born Rebecca West. An outsider to the South, West artfully told without judgment how race impacted each aspect of the trial from the seating of Black journalists and Black observers in the balcony to the technical definition of lynching. She questioned how, while the small city of Greenville laid asleep, the sheriff failed to notice the taxi drivers' flurry of activity. West's evaluation of the prosecution echoed Waties's experience at the Shull trial. She wrote, "As the case was handled, the jury cannot be blamed for returning an acquittal. . . . The trial had not the pleasing pattern, the agreeable harmony and counterpoint, of good legal process, however much the Judge tried to redeem it."[49] The prosecution of the taxi drivers who murdered Willie Earle was poorly prepared. Like the Shull trial, the jury acquitted them.

In Santa Barbara while on vacation, Waties filled four pages with his sprawling handwriting in a letter to West. West's objectivity alongside her sympathy and courage struck him. He pleaded with her to write about "our South" as she did about Yugoslavia and "show us ourselves with truth which did not hurt because we know that you understood what brought about our sinning." Waties seemed deeply troubled and desperate for someone to reach his fellow white southerners. He ended his letter with "A clear voice might free them."[50] Waties's prevailing concern was the well-being of white southerners and how their bigotry eroded their souls. He turned to a stranger as one who could offer a clear voice. Waties's entreaty revealed his love for his native South and his belief that its people were not evil necessarily, but sick and fearful. His belief in the potential for white southerners' salvation points to an underlying conviction similar to that of Dorothy Tilly, that if they knew better, then they would do better. However, his earnest desire did not account for white southerners' unwillingness to listen to a clear voice. Waties turned to West seeking a cure for his beloved South. His plea was one of genuine sorrow for the region, not one motivated by revenge against those who shunned his second wife.

As 1947 came to a close, the Warings headed to Florence where Waties presided twice a year for about three weeks. One of the cases scheduled to be heard on December 3 was *United States of America v. John Ellis Wilhelm*. Wilhelm had employed James DeWitt and Robert McBride on his farm for about four years. In late 1946, the men quit because Wilhelm had not paid them and cussed them when they asked for their wages. After DeWitt and McBride found new jobs, Wilhelm obtained a warrant for the Black men's arrest charging that they had breached a labor contract. Wilhelm claimed the laborers still owed money to him because of pay advances. Wilhem visited the men in jail and offered to drop the charges if they worked for Wilhelm's father, James Wilhelm, at a lumber camp in Georgia. McBride and DeWitt refused. After arresting the men on trumped-up charges, the magistrate eventually released DeWitt and McBride.

A few weeks later, John Wilhelm kidnapped Dewitt outside of a movie theater, held him overnight, and then transported him to Georgia. DeWitt remained in Georgia for nearly a year, working for one dollar a day on the Wilhelm father's farm. The local authorities in Darlington County, South Carolina contacted the FBI. Based on their investigation, the Department of Justice invoked the Lindbergh kidnapping law. The federal grand jury returned indictments against the Wilhelm father and son for peonage and kidnapping. Peonage is a form of involuntary servitude based on alleged indebtedness.[51] Waties held a pretrial conference with the US Attorney, defendants, and their attorneys. In return for John Wilhelm's plea of guilty to violating the Civil Liberties Act, the government agreed to drop the charges against the father. Waties did not accept the plea agreement without first hearing testimony from DeWitt. In response to Waties's questions, the young man said he stayed in Georgia because "I was scared to go back to South Carolina."[52] Waties accepted the agreement and sentenced the son, John Wilhelm, to one year and one day in the federal penitentiary in Petersburg, Virginia.[53]

After Waties imposed the sentence on Wilhelm, a juror from Charleston came to bid his goodbye to Waties before leaving Florence. The juror, who Waties called a "first class citizen—who knew the difference between right and wrong," admitted to the judge that although he and the other jurors agreed that Wilhelm was guilty and should go to jail, they would not have rendered a guilty verdict. Waties called the case a matter of "common sense and decency" that did not entail any sophisticated legal judgment. But the jurors were unwilling to uphold their oaths in the face of community pressure to uphold white supremacy.[54] At the peonage trial, the Warings learned that local law enforcement would uphold illegal labor practices. They learned that the intervention of federal law could halt those practices. And they learned the extent of the pressure upon white southerners to comply with white supremacy. Even "first class citizens" bowed to threats. The juror's disclosure affirmed Elizabeth's insight about white southerners. They knew what should be done. They admired Waties for doing it, "but they admitted not one of them would have done it."[55]

The route between Charleston and Florence took Elizabeth and Waties through Clarendon County, a Black Belt rural area lying about fifty miles northwest of Charleston. Interstate 95 bisects the county with the dammed Santee River, now Lake Marion, serving as the southern boundary. In 1950, the county's total population was 32,221, with about 70 percent Black residents. Clarendon County relied on cotton as its industry and most Black people were agricultural laborers. Two-thirds of Black families earned less than $1,000 a year and as many as one-third of Black adults were illiterate.[56] Clarendon was one of the poorest counties in South Carolina which in turn was one of the nation's poorest states.[57] The county was ruled by what Waties characterized as "a small white minority very limited in their viewpoint and education."[58]

South Carolina's state constitution mandated separate schools for Black and white children. The law relied upon the doctrine of separate-but-equal set forth in *Plessy v. Ferguson*. However, separate was rarely equal. South Carolina allocated $395,000 for white schools and $282,000 for Black schools.[59] The NAACP reported that Black, school-aged children (five to fourteen years old) outnumbered white children nearly three to one in 1940 (6,292 Black children; 1,922 white children). Waties said,

> You could drive through Clarendon County, as I often did on my way to and from Florence, and see these awful looking little wooden shacks in the country that were the Negro schools. The white schools were nothing to be really enthusiastic about, but they were fairly respectable looking. In the towns they were generally of brick and some of them had chimneys, running water and things of that kind. The Negro schools were just tumbledown, dirty shacks with horrible outdoor toilet facilities.[60]

As bad as the schools were, what most concerned Black parents, at least in the 1940s, was their children getting to and from school. Black high school students had to walk nearly nine miles to Scott's Branch School. The Jordan section of the county often flooded, so children paddled a boat then walked the rest of the way to school. The parents' concern increased in 1947 when a young man drowned outside Society Hill AME Church. The local children used the same boat as he had. The boys and girls came and went to school each day across an arm of the newly created Lake Marion where the young man drowned. The children usually took the most direct route through fields that were barren during the school year, but on days when rain transformed the fields into muddy bogs, they walked along the roads barely wide enough for a school bus. White kids used Black children as targets, throwing bottle caps and spitting from their warm, dry seats on the bus.[61] The school board provided thirty-seven buses for white children in the county but none for Black students.[62]

As early as 1943, Black parents approached school authorities requesting transportation for their children. Their requests were denied. Realizing they were unlikely to get a bus from the school board, Black parents pooled their money and bought a used school bus in 1945. The bus was unreliable, often not starting in the morning or breaking down in the middle of the route. It finally broke down and was irreparable.[63] The parents scraped together enough money to buy another bus so by spring, 1946, students were again riding a bus to school. While more reliable, it was still costly to operate because the parents had to pay out of their pockets for gas and the driver. The parents, led by Reverend Joseph De Laine, principal at Liberty High School and African Methodist Episcopal (AME) pastor for the Pine Grove/Society Hill circuit, approached the school board for operating funds to transport their children to and from school. L. B. McCord, superintendent of schools and pastor of Manning Presbyterian Church, refused.[64]

After McCord's refusal, De Laine and other parents traveled to Columbia and met with Harold Boulware. He wrote several letters to the school board, which were ignored. Boulware then prepared a petition on behalf of Levi Pearson, father of three school-aged children. The petition, dated July 28, 1947, was directed to the State Superintendent of Education, County Superintendent of Schools, and chairman of the Board of Trustees for School District 26 in Clarendon County. The petition asserted that the county violated Pearson's rights under the Fourteenth Amendment because it provided transportation for white but not Black children.[65] In December 1947, Pearson addressed a letter To Whom It May Concern. In the letter, he indicated he was done talking with the trustees and officers. They could get in touch with his attorney. Furthermore, the school board assumed too much if they thought that Pearson was not interested in pursuing a lawsuit against the County. Pearson closed the letter by confirming that he would be in Columbia the following week to meet with Boulware. In a handwritten note, Pearson wrote on the copy to Boulware, "Don't wait on that. Go ahead with the case."[66]

With no response from the school board, Harold Boulware complied with Pearson's request and filed a complaint against the school board in federal court on March 16, 1948. The complaint named the school officials to whom Boulware sent the initial petition and stated that Pearson lived in District 26. The relief sought was a permanent injunction restraining and enjoining the defendants from "making a distinction on account of race or color in providing, establishing or maintaining adequate free bus transportation for white school children while failing or refusing to provide adequate free bus transportation for Negro children."[67] Thurgood Marshall and Edward Dudley, attorneys for the NAACP Legal Defense Fund, also signed the complaint as counsel for Pearson.

The case was scheduled to be heard on June 9, 1948, before Waties. However, at a pretrial conference on June 8, 1948, an error in the complaint forced Boulware, Marshall, and Dudley to withdraw the action. Pearson's house straddled the line between Districts 26 and 5. His children attended school in District 26, but he paid his taxes to District 5. Therefore, he lacked legal standing to bring a suit in District 26.[68] Reverend De Laine's son, Jay, speculated that the county officials gerrymandered the district line to nullify the lawsuit.[69] Waties recalled that "the thing was so messed up that it probably would have had to been thrown out unless it was changed, and so leave was asked to drop it and bring another case."[70] Whether manipulation on the part of the county officials or an oversight on the part of the attorneys, the case was dismissed. For De Laine, Pearson, and other Black parents in Clarendon County, they had spent time and money to bring a lawsuit that changed nothing. Pearson suffered severe retribution for his courage in agreeing to be a plaintiff in the case. He lost his credit at white-owned banks and businesses. His crops rotted in the field when white farmers refused to lend him equipment to harvest them.[71]

Although Black parents still had to pay out of their own pockets for school transportation for their children, the suit accomplished one thing. Waties now knew they were willing to commence legal action to get equal opportunities for their children. The district number error was unfortunate since, based on Waties's past decisions, he would likely have ruled in favor of Pearson. However, the case *only* addressed the bus transportation issue. With the dismissal, De Laine and the parents could bid a strategic retreat and marshal their resources to fight for more than buses from the local school board.

While Black parents in Clarendon County continued organizing to resist white supremacy, other southern states contemplated abolishing all state laws regarding the primaries as a strategy to evade the Supreme Court's *Smith* decision.[72] Thurgood Marshall opined that "virtually all of the pending white primary cases in the South were dependent upon the outcome of the South Carolina ruling."[73] The Supreme Court foiled the southern states' plans on

April 19, 1948, with its formal order refusing to review Waties's rulings in *Elmore*. The *New York Times* declared that the Supreme Court's denial "dealt a death blow" to the South Carolina plan.[74] However, pronouncements of the all-white primary's death were premature. In South Carolina, the Democratic Party had not drawn its last breath.

When the South Carolina Democratic Party convened its annual convention in May 1948, party officials tried to "devise some other schemes to force an all-white primary."[75] The Party exploited two loopholes in the original *Elmore* order. First, the ruling only applied to Richland County, not the entire state. Second, the ruling specified participation in the primary, not membership in the party. At the state convention, Party officials adopted rules that limited membership to white people. In order for African American citizens to vote, they had to take an oath that supported states' rights, separation of the races, and opposed the proposed federal Fair Employment Practices Commission. In addition, they had to swear that they were not a member of any other party. White voters were not required to take the oath.[76]

In early July 1948, the NAACP filed an action on behalf of David Brown from Beaufort, south of Charleston. Party officials ended up back in federal court before Waties in *Brown v. Baskin*. Waties issued a preliminary injunction on July 16 that prohibited any discrimination or exclusion from party membership or voting.[77] He ordered the registration books remain open until July 31. His impatience with the Party's evasive tactics was apparent. He chastised them for subverting his order and the Fourth Circuit Court of Appeals. He and many others had viewed *Elmore* as the end of the all-white primary. Waties warned the eighty-six defendants—all officials of the state party machinery— that "imprisonment awaited any party official who failed to comply fully with the spirit and letter of the decision." He also admonished the officials, "It's a disgrace and shame when you must come into court and ask a judge to tell you you are an American."[78] Waties closed the ruling with language designed to dispel any notion that he would tolerate further defiance from the Party:

> It is the intent of this opinion that the full spirit hereof, as well as the mere letter, be obeyed so that the Democratic organization of South Carolina and the primaries which it holds shall be freely open to all parties entitled to enter therein under the laws and Constitution of this country and State, without discrimination of race, color or creed. And any violation of the terms of the Order, or of the law as set forth in the opinion, by them or their successors in office, or those acting under them, will be considered a contempt and will be proceeded against and punished.[79]

The Party's attempts to evade the *Elmore* order exhausted his patience. Waties's language in *Brown v. Baskin* left no doubt that he saw through the Party's subterfuges.

South Carolina Democratic Party officials had to forego the party's national convention in Philadelphia to appear in court before Waties. In the South, the Democratic Party felt the pressure of a progressive tide led by Truman. The president's civil rights initiatives threatened southern states' policies and laws that retained slavery in all but name. To protest the Party's civil rights plank, southern Democrats walked out of the national convention in Philadelphia and then convened in Birmingham. Once dominant within national politics, "a group of disgruntled southern Democrats formed the States' Rights Democratic Party and chose Strom Thurmond as their presidential candidate." As they came to be known, the Dixiecrats sought to reclaim "their former prestige and ideological prominence in a party that had moved away from them."[80] The day after Waties issued a temporary injunction against the state party, South Carolina Governor Strom Thurmond told an audience of six thousand at the States' Rights Democratic convention in Birmingham that "There's not enough troops in the Army to force southern people to break down segregation and admit the Negro race into our theaters, into our swimming pools, into schools and into our homes."[81] Thurmond "emerged as the segregationist symbol of the 1948 Dixiecrat movement."[82] South Carolina's governor was the presidential candidate of a political party formed to maintain every aspect of Jim Crow.

When faced with the prospect of change in race relations, white supremacists engaged in political and legal maneuvers to delay, evade, and deflect. Unable to sidestep Waties's rulings that allowed Black South Carolinians to vote in the Democratic Primary, white supremacists attempted to initiate impeachment proceedings. On July 27, 1948, Representative W. J. Bryan Dorn of South Carolina introduced House Resolution 704 in order to "conduct a full and complete investigation of the conduct in office of Judge J. Waties Waring." According to Dorn, granting Black voters full participation in the Democratic Party's affairs was a "gross usurpation of the rights of the party." In his extended remarks, Dorn argued that Waties had practically set the rules for the primary of the Democratic Party. Dorn was not content to rely on Waties's supposed incompetence as a judge. He also accused Waties of using his position to exact revenge against white Charlestonians, "I am convinced, also, that he has tried to traduce the Democrats of South Carolina, and especially to humiliate the people of Charleston, his old friends, neighbors, and relatives, some of the finest people of that city, who, because of his ungentlemanly conduct in many respects in the past, have refused to associate with him, and even now treat him with silent contempt." In his frenzied plea, Dorn dragged Waties's personal life before Congress, declaring, "The people of that State would like to know how Judge Waring can obtain a separation from a lady to whom he had been married for approximately 30 years, remarry, and serve on the Federal bench in that great State."[83] Dorn exposed the circumstances of the Warings' marriage on the floor of Congress. He broadcast the widely held opinion among white Charlestonians, and now South Carolinians, that Waties opened the all-white primary to Black citizens out of spite. Waties was retaliating against the white people who shunned his second wife and using his power as a federal judge for personal gain. Therefore, he should be removed from the bench.

L. Mendel Rivers also attacked Waties in Congress.[84] Rivers broadened Waties's defects beyond the primary ruling. He called Waties's conduct "high-handed, unjudicial, ungentlemanly, outrageous, and deplorable." Rivers assured Congress that he was not complaining about Waties's "decision permitting Negroes to vote" but rather Waties's "clumsy handling of a delicate situation" that has hurt the case of the Negro in South Carolina. Just like Dorn, Rivers attributed the social ostracism in Charleston as the motivation for Waties's rulings from the bench. Rivers predicted that "Unless he is removed, there will be bloodshed. I prophesy bloodshed because he is now in the process of exacting a pound of flesh from the white people of South Carolina because through his own actions he has been ostracized from their society."[85] When asked for comment on Rivers's tirade, Waties said, "It should be unnecessary to comment on those silly, childish ravings."[86] Confident in his rulings and conversant with Rivers's tactics, Waties dismissed his fellow Charlestonian.

The NAACP had a stake in Waties remaining a federal judge and retaining his seat in South Carolina. Thurgood Marshall suggested someone track down the petition and see that it would not come up for consideration.[87] Leslie S. Perry spoke with members of Congress, including the Chairman of the Judiciary Committee and a member of the House Rules Committee. On August 6, Perry wrote Thurgood Marshall that Congress would take no action on this matter and "We don't have anything to worry about."[88] While this impeachment attempt died, it was not the last time South Carolina's elected officials would try to remove Waties from the bench.

Waties postponed his vacation to Santa Barbara until after the primary election on August 10. As he warned the party officials and white southerners, Waties sat in his chambers to ensure that he was available in case any Black voters were turned away from the polls. Despite Mendel Rivers's dire prediction of bloodshed, thirty-five thousand African American citizens voted with no mishaps.[89] Thurgood Marshall was in South Carolina on election day. He reported that there was "no evidence of any friction in the first voting of Negroes in South Carolina primary elections since Reconstruction time." Echoing Waties's *Elmore* order, Marshall said "the skies did not fall" when Black people cast their votes after a twenty-three year battle in the courts.[90]

The *Greenville News* praised Waring's ruling in *Brown v. Baskin*, and a number of white southerners wrote congratulatory letters. A woman from Montgomery, Alabama, wrote: "You make one less ashamed of the behavior of Southerners as a whole." From Virginia, a white hardware dealer condemned states' righters: "Thanks to men like Thurmond, Wright, Rankin, Bilbo, Long, Talmadge, and our Harry Byrd, the South has become a stench in the nostrils of the civilized world."[91] Curtis Karlson from Camden, New Jersey, unfavorably compared white Charlestonians to Waties, writing that "there are very likely many white people in Charleston who feel that your ruling was right and proper. The only trouble is that they apparently do not have the courage to back up their convictions with some sort of action."[92] P. B. Young, publisher of the *Journal and Guide*, called the 1948 decision "a breath of fresh air in a torrid desert."[93] The letters he received strengthened Waties's belief that although white supremacy's grip on the South was firm, it was not intractable. However, in order to loosen the grip, the sentiment expressed in the private letters needed public expression.

When Elizabeth and Waties returned to Charleston after their California vacation, *Brown v. Baskin* had to be decided on a permanent basis since the injunction that Waties issued in July was temporary. He scheduled a hearing for October 22, 1948, to rule on several motions filed by both the plaintiff and defendants. One of the matters was an affidavit of bias filed by John Stansfield, a member of the Aiken's Democratic Party executive committee, on behalf of himself and the other named defendants. In his affidavit, dated October 20, Stansfield asserted that Waties was biased in favor of the plaintiff and prejudiced against the defendants. As evidence to support his claim, Stansfield used quotes from a speech that Waties delivered to the New York City Chapter of the National Lawyers Guild.[94] Stansfield had read about Waties's speech in the newspaper. Both *The State* and *Columbia Record*'s articles included direct quotations. The next day, the headline "Bias and Prejudice Charged to Waring" splashed across the front page of the *News and Courier*, above the fold. At the hearing in Charleston on October 22, Waties denied Stansfield's charges of bias and refused to recuse himself.

The New York City chapter of the National Lawyers Guild welcomed Waties as a guest speaker at a luncheon on October 11, 1948. Judge John Knox of the Southern District of New York introduced Waties and lauded the southern jurist's decisions as "a great contribution to humanity and justice." Thurgood Marshall, William Hastie, and Judge Hubert Delaney, along with officers and members of the chapter, attended.[95] Delivered two years after his experience at the Shull trial, Waties's hour-long address in New York City refuted the long-standing misperceptions about outside interference and so-called inferiority of Black people.

Waties repudiated southern paternalism and gradualism when he asserted that the "Negro is an American citizen." He called upon rights, not favors, to be bestowed. Instead of more time for white people to adjust or Black people to change, Waties declared that at its core, "The problem was to change the feeling, the sentiment, the creed, of the great body of white people of the South that a Negro is not an American citizen." It was the white person's image of the Black person that needed to be remedied: "My people have one outstanding fault—the terrible fault of prejudice. They have been born and educated to feel that a Negro is some kind of an animal that ought to be well-treated and given kindness, but as a matter of favor, not right. That's not the kind of conception that we should show to the world."[96] By placing responsibility for the problem upon white people, Waties summoned full citizenship rights for Black people, not as something they should have to earn or wait to be conferred, but instead as something they already possessed and should be able to exercise freely without fear of violence.

Waties likened white supremacy to a "southern fog." While the present situation was pretty dim, he believed it would improve, "sunlight is going to come in. But I don't believe that the windows are going to be opened voluntarily." White people in the South were too frightened to publicly praise his primary decisions: "Not one man in public life has dared support these decisions. . . . The few people in public life who have communicated with me have done so in letters marked 'strictly confidential.' That's pretty bad."[97] By sharing the "strictly confidential" letters, Waties emphasized the need for help from outside of the South. He called upon the audience, "men and women of your caliber," to let in the light. Waties exhorted the audience to interfere, even as he qualified his call for outside help with "be careful with your methods." On the other hand, "don't stay away," because "The situation has to be handled gently but firmly."[98] The confidential letters that Waties received offered a glimpse of hope that white southerners could be redeemed.

Waties received threatening letters that pointed to why those who supported the primary decisions marked their letters "strictly confidential." The day after the *Brown v. Baskin* hearing in Charleston, several newspapers including the *Washington Post, Chicago Tribune, News and Courier,* and major Black newspapers published an Associated Press report. The night before—the same day as the hearing—Waties received a typed letter postmarked in Columbia and sent special delivery.[99] Signed by the Knights of the Ku Klux Klan, the letter asked that Waties give due consideration to his decision in the white Democratic primary because, as a white citizen, he must realize "the fearful racial hatred that will follow any adverse decision that you may render." The entire letter was published in the AP article along with Waties's response.

Waties insisted that the Klan letter would not affect any decision. Still, he wanted the people across the nation to know about the Klan's "attempt to threaten and influence a United States judge in his judicial decisions."[100] Waties did not say it outright, but his incredulity at the Klan's audacity to threaten a federal judge seeps throughout his statement. The Klan's bold letter indicates an underlying belief in the group's ability to escape retribution. The threat was another example of white supremacy's lawlessness. Faced with upholding the constitution or white supremacy, Klan members resorted to menacing a federal judge. Because of the wide circulation in state and national newspapers, the Klan's attempts to intimidate a federal judge reached readers across the United States.

Although the *News and Courier* minimized the Klan letter by placing quotation marks around the word "threat," the letter was the culmination of increasing visible Klan activity in South Carolina in the late summer and early fall of 1948. In an editorial for the *News and Courier* published on September 6, William D. Workman described the third Klan parade in less than a month. Automobiles formed a procession. When nearing a town, they began blowing horns and even sirens. The lights inside the automobiles were turned on so spectators could see the hooded Klansmen, usually riding four to a car. Workman claimed that the presence of cars with sirens was evidence that "peace officers" were members of the Klan. He also attributed the revival of Klan activity in South Carolina to the group's strong presence in Georgia.[101] Workman reconfigured "outsider" in this situation to place blame onto Georgia for Klan activity in South Carolina.

Elizabeth was aware of the Klan parades in South Carolina and the murders of Black men who defied white supremacy. After Elizabeth married Waties in 1945, she collected newspaper articles and preserved them in scrapbooks. At first, the clippings consisted of news about Waties and the trials he presided over outside South Carolina. In 1947, the subjects she deemed worthy of clipping started to expand. Along with the primary cases, she assembled articles about local, state, and national politics. Elizabeth informed herself about current politics and issues through a variety of sources. By 1949, she included articles from John McCray's *Lighthouse and Informer* and other

Black newspapers. From 1946 to 1962, she filled seventy-two scrapbooks with newspaper clippings. The articles about attacks on Black people with impunity for white assailants confirm two points that Will Maslow and Joseph B. Robison of the American Jewish Congress made in 1947. First, African American citizens had to "run the gauntlet of election officials who refuse to register him, apply discriminatory and character tests and often resort to intimidation to prevent him from exercising his rights under the Fifteenth Amendment." In addition, the absence of either legal or social consequences for violence against African American citizens validated a paradox. For white people to condemn the violence while, at the same time, comply with all other aspects of white supremacy was to ask the impossible.[102] Those articles confirmed Elizabeth's experience at the Shull trial. A dual system of justice and citizenship existed in the South. Violence against African American citizens was rampant and went unpunished.

President Truman aimed his civil rights initiatives at the classes of citizenship wrought by white supremacy. Waties's rulings in the primary cases drew the attention of Truman, who invited the judge to the White House on December 1, 1948. During his visit to the nation's capital, Waties also met with Supreme Court Chief Justice Fred M. Vinson and Attorney General Tom C. Clark. Reporters speculated that Waties was being considered to replace Judge Morris Soper on the Fourth Circuit Court of Appeals.[103] Waties insisted the trip was to congratulate Truman on his election victory and tell him that Waties voted for him. While in Washington, Waties called the poll tax "stupid" and said lynching cases should be tried in federal court. He went on the record to say, "I believe Negroes should be treated as American citizens. I believe that the Federal Government should protect all its citizens in their civil rights and should see that they are treated as Americans."[104] The meeting with Truman offered Waties the opportunity to express his belief in Truman's civil rights initiatives. He and Truman shared the conviction that "when the people really understand issues they can be thoroughly trusted to do right."[105]

In his letter thanking Truman for the meeting, Waties reiterated his belief in the need for federal action: "The people in this state will <u>not voluntarily</u> do anything along the lines suggested by you. It therefore is necessary for the federal government to firmly and constantly keep pressure." But he assured Truman that many people were "ripe and ready for your program," yet fear and timidity kept them from supporting it. Waties closed the letter by assuring the president: "I am more than willing and anxious to answer any call you may wish to furnish information at any time."[106] Although Truman's response was brief, he assured Waties, "I wish we had more Federal Judges like you on the bench."[107] Waties wrote to Thurgood Marshall that he had "a very delightful interview with the President" and spent one and a half hours with Chief Justice Vinson, "I may assure you that both interviews were very helpful to many things that you and I agree on."[108]

It is hard to overstate the significance of this correspondence because two things are clear. First, Waties was corresponding with NAACP attorney Thurgood Marshall outside of official business. Second, Waties had the ear of the president of the United States and chief justice of the Supreme Court, men who had the power to end school segregation and implement civil rights legislation. As early as 1948, Waties was campaigning to further his agenda and reassuring Marshall that the NAACP had a sympathetic jurist in South Carolina.

Despite the public outcry opposing the primary decisions, Waties had received a great many letters that commended him but expressed their views as "confidential." Elizabeth recognized that the damning Waties received was public. She curated the letters he received, "great packages of them," so she possessed firsthand knowledge of how people felt about white supremacy.[109] The letters verified the existence of a cadre of whites who welcomed change in the South. For Waties, that was the crux of the problem: "Many men in the South feel that the Negro should be given his rights—but are unwilling to say so in public."[110] John McCray, editor of the *Lighthouse and Informer*, said that "The South is yet dominated by a lot of loud-mouthed racists who, like jackasses, 'bray in public.'" McCray lamented that white people who were reluctant to join white supremacy's crusade against minority groups did not dare come out in the open. He claimed that white people opposed to the regimes and tactics of white supremacy were "more thoroughly channeled than are our Negro residents, against whom there can be no stringent social penalties, nor any worse economic pressures."[111] White politicians' denunciation of Waties and their impeachment attempt created the impression of unanimity of opinion that functioned to silence more moderate opinions among white southerners.[112] The public and persistent message revealed to the Warings that even when the Constitution was at stake, the politicians would subvert federal law to garner favor with their white constituents. The pressure for conformity effectively minimized public dissent.[113]

Charleston was very cool to the Warings after their marriage, but the ostracism intensified and spread throughout the state with Waties's rulings in the primary cases. Once socially accepted in cities other than Charleston, the Warings became social pariahs in the entire state of South Carolina. Waties declared, "And when I say complete, I mean not one break in the white population of South Carolina." Because of Waties's belief in the American

Creed, he saw that he had two options: "Either you were going to be entirely governed by the white supremacy doctrine and just shut your eyes and bowl this thing through, or you were going to be a Federal judge and decide the law. That was the issue."[114] At this point, cut off from family and friends in Charleston and vilified in the rest of South Carolina, Waties and Elizabeth did not appear to have much left to lose in publicly opposing white supremacy. Isabella Finnie, Elizabeth's friend from Detroit, pointed out that "It is a strange turn of fate that Waties's 'ostracism' on account of his marriage has really strengthened him for public service because there is nothing more that public opinion can do to him—all the bricks have been thrown already."[115] However, the South was not done throwing bricks at the Warings, and the Warings were not done with the South. Discontent was brewing in Clarendon County, and because of it, another case would come before Waties. He and Elizabeth were preparing to throw their rhetorical bricks.

Chapter 3

I HOPE TO MAKE MORE FRIENDS

James Hinton served as president of the South Carolina NAACP State Conference of Branches from 1941 to 1958. Like other members and officers, Hinton maintained full-time employment to support himself as he battled white supremacy. In Columbia, he built a successful career with a Black-owned insurance company based in Augusta, Georgia. In 1949, he traveled to Augusta on company business.[1] Few hotels served Black guests, so Hinton obtained lodging at a rooming house. At about ten o'clock on the night of April 21, two men knocked at the door. The men grabbed Hinton, who was clad in his pajamas and standing behind the landlady when she answered the door. The men pushed Hinton into their car, told him to lie on the floor, then sped out of town. After a ten-mile ride, the driver stopped the car, hauled out Hinton, and flashed a light in his face. Evidently, they grabbed the "wrong n-word." They let Hinton go and told him to get back to Augusta the best he could. In his pajamas, Hinton walked for two hours in the rain before he flagged down a passing bus. The driver took Hinton back to Augusta.[2] When Hinton arrived in Columbia after his wild ride, enthusiastic supporters crowded two blocks as he made his way to his home. Earlier in 1949, Hinton had received an invitation from the Klan to a cross-burning ceremony on the State House grounds with Hinton "on top of the cross."[3]

The threat against Hinton and the abduction served as "a clear sign that the forces of lawlessness are still doing business as usual" across the South in 1949.[4] A Klan motorcade paraded through West Columbia with sirens screaming and horns blowing in early January.[5] Further south in the state, twenty miles or so across the Georgia border, a cavalcade of forty-five automobiles, many with Georgia tags, meandered through Ellenton. Packed with hooded Klan members, the cars honked their horns, the lead car blew a siren, and the second car carried a lighted cross.[6] A forty-five automobile caravan descended upon Orangeburg shortly after nightfall on January 15. Like the parade in Ellenton, one car displayed "a large burning cross, fiery symbol of the klan."[7] In Denmark, the Klan held a foot parade. Bamberg

County residents lined the streets with an atmosphere "seemingly free of any sense of oppression" as 656 Klan members walked through town. The hooded group converged at the train platform in the heart of town and ignited an eight-foot wooden cross that blazed as the grand dragon of the Klan addressed the crowd.[8] The Klan targeted Orangeburg and Denmark, where South Carolina State College and Voorhees College, both historically Black institutions, are located.

Newspapers in major cities across South Carolina reported on the Klan's parades and motorcades. Hooded to cloak their identities, the members traipsed through the main thoroughfares of towns as darkness fell. Under cover of night, they perpetrated their violence. Elizabeth clipped the articles—lynchings, kidnappings, beatings—and preserved them in her scrapbooks alongside the articles reporting on the acquittals of white men who had committed violent acts against Black people.[9] The reports confirmed Waties's claim that "the Klan still rides in South Carolina."[10] They also reinforced Elizabeth's experience at the Shull trial and contributed to her realization that Jim Crow manifested as more than segregation or disenfranchisement. Under Jim Crow, Black people had no protection. Viewed as less than second-class citizens, they had no recourse. For Waties and Elizabeth, Klan activity and Jim Crow justice subverted the Constitution. White supremacy fostered a climate of violence.

Jim Crow was the reason that Black people in the South were denied their human dignity and constitutional rights. Segregation was not a symptom but the root of the evil of racial prejudice.[11] Therefore, segregation had to end and end immediately because the immediate end to segregation was the only way to change the white person's image of Black people. Elizabeth and Waties clearly defined their goal, but their means to accomplish it were severely constrained. How could a federal judge and his wife transform an oppressive and violent system that squelched dissent?

Elizabeth and Waties could not view with any optimism that the executive and legislative branches would solve the Race Problem in the South. President Truman exercised the extent of his authority by issuing executive orders, including establishing the President's Committee on Civil Rights. The committee's report, *To Secure These Rights*, was published on October 29, 1947. Simon and Schuster published a pamphlet of the 178-page report and sold it for one dollar.[12] The title of the report reflected a belief in existing rights already possessed by Americans. The report framed the protection of civil rights as a national problem, not isolated to the South. The committee also asserted that neither its members nor Americans could "avoid the knowledge that the American ideal still awaits complete realization."[13] The committee made several recommendations for concrete actions to protect the rights of all Americans and realize the American ideal.

Truman presented the committee's recommendations in his message to Congress on February 2, 1948. He introduced his ten-point plan with an assertion that, contrary to American ideals, "Not all groups of our population are free from the fear of violence. Not all groups are free to live and work where they please or to improve their conditions of life by their own efforts. Not all groups enjoy the full privileges of citizenship and participation in the government under which they live." To rectify these flagrant exceptions, Truman proposed a number of initiatives to transform the ideal of American democracy into lived reality. He recommended federal legislation against lynching, the poll tax, and interstate transportation segregation. Truman also wanted a permanent Fair Employment Practice Commission, Joint Congressional Committee on Civil Rights, Commission on Civil Rights, and a Civil Rights Division in the Department of Justice. In his address to Congress, Truman invoked the burgeoning Cold War when he concluded, "If we wish to inspire the peoples of the world whose freedom is in jeopardy, if we wish to restore hope to those who have already lost their civil liberties, if we wish to fulfill the promise that is ours, we must correct the remaining imperfections in our practice of democracy."[14] Truman claimed American democracy as the better alternative and appealed to American exceptionalism as the motivation to correct its imperfections. His message to Congress, Americans, and the international community was one of federal commitment. The ending, "We know the way. We need only the will," served as a clarion call to African American citizens in South Carolina.

At its national convention in the summer of 1948, the Democratic Party's platform included a strong civil rights plank committing the Party to its belief "that racial and religious minorities must have the right to live, the right to work, the right to vote, the full and equal protection of the laws, on a basis of equality with all citizens as guaranteed by the Constitution."[15] To protest the plank, southern Democrats formed the States' Rights Democratic Party. The Dixiecrats' scheme was to dilute the electoral college so that no single candidate, and especially not Truman, won the requisite number of electoral college votes. If no candidate accumulated the required electoral college votes, the election would be decided in Congress, where southern Democrats held the majority. The Dixiecrats, "limited in number but loud of voice and clamor," called themselves "states' righters." But Senator Hubert Humphrey called them "states' wrongers" because "they seem to have forgotten their history and failed to have done their home work in American constitutional government." Voicing the Warings' conviction, Humphrey declared,

"The people of these United States are not only citizens of their respective states but also citizens of the United States of America."[16] Citizenship rights under federal law took precedence over so-called states' rights to impose laws and policies that circumvented Black and white American citizens' rights under the Constitution. The Dixiecrat plan failed. Truman handily won the 1948 presidential election with Democratic control of both Houses of Congress.

Truman failed to pass any meaningful civil rights legislation in 1948. His efforts to pass legislation in 1949 were just as fractious. Alan Brinkley points out that, "The South, in short, held a crucial balance of power in Democratic politics, and because of that it had almost always been able to prevent any federal initiatives that might have threatened its conservative institutions or its hierarchical social structure."[17] In his 1949 inaugural and State of the Union addresses, Truman laid the success of global democracy at the feet of domestic programs. Because the world looked to the United States for leadership, Truman again proposed to the 81st Congress the civil rights program that he proposed to the 80th Congress. Before considering Truman's civil rights initiatives, Congress debated its filibuster rules. The filibuster remains a parliamentary procedure that a congressional minority may utilize to stall or block objectionable legislation. Constraints on the right to filibuster would seriously diminish the minority's ability to prevent legislation. Southern Democrats decided to "filibuster to the limit of their power against any sharpening of the rules against filibusters."[18] They used the filibuster to foil any modification to the filibuster rules and forced a compromise. As a consequence, southerners retained the filibuster to wield against Truman's civil rights proposals.[19]

By the middle of March 1949, "there was no issue of more importance at the moment than the civil-rights question" to the "average [white] Southerner."[20] With the filibuster at their disposal, southern Democrats achieved their goal of forestalling civil rights legislation because "little hope of favorable action" remained in the 81st Congress.[21] Northern Democrats and some Republicans joined forces with the southerners—a genuine bipartisan effort to hinder Truman's agenda. Senator Hubert Humphrey charged that "a determined and organized minority of Senators" kept the Senate from taking any action by "refusing to stop talking," and that "in most cases the talk is not even pertinent to the issues."[22] The *Pittsburgh Courier* editorialized that the "shadow-boxing, sham-battling, double-talking exhibition in the United States Senate" made it "virtually impossible in the future to enact all or even a part of the civil rights program." The *Pittsburgh Courier* also pointed out that "if there had been widespread revulsion against the [Senate's] actions, they would not have voted as they did, and we might as well face that fact."[23] The persistent issue was how to trigger "widespread revulsion."

Waties's primary rulings catapulted him onto the national stage, so he gained a platform to generate "widespread revulsion" against Jim Crow and southern Democrats' obstruction tactics. Throughout 1949, the Warings' burgeoning network and lived experience informed them as they formulated a strategy to dismantle Jim Crow. As animosity towards the Warings increased in South Carolina, accolades increased across the nation. Several organizations presented awards to Waties. In the national spotlight, Elizabeth and Waties encountered other white and Black people who shared their determination to end Jim Crow. The Warings made the most of the positive response to Waties's primary rulings to cultivate a local and national interracial network of activists. They drew upon their deep study of race relations, their experience at the Shull trial, and their interactions with other activists to develop a rhetorical campaign that called upon the force of public opinion and federal law to extinguish segregation.

Waties threw the first rhetorical brick at white supremacists in early 1949. The National Lawyers Guild named him the recipient of its Franklin Delano Roosevelt Award of 1948 for best exemplifying the ideals of its namesake. Waties delivered "The Struggle for Negro Rights" on February 20, 1949, when presented with the award at the Guild's Ninth Annual Convention held at the Book-Cadillac Hotel in Detroit. Although he spoke to the Guild's New York chapter in October 1948, only excerpts of it are available. The February 1949 speech was Waties's first public speech delivered after the primary rulings that is preserved in its entirety. Waties's address to the Lawyers Guild is significant for several reasons, not least of which is that the full text is preserved. In letters to Donald Harrington, Waties indicated that he liked to speak extemporaneously or informally, "the way that I always address meetings."[24] Waties wrote notes on the back cover of the program for the convention.[25] The audio transcript indicates that Waties spoke from his scribbled notes. Because he did not formally prepare his speeches, there is no handwritten or typed version of the entire speech other than the transcript prepared from the audio recording. As a lawyer and judge, he had many occasions to address audiences. Therefore, it is plausible that he delivered speeches without a full manuscript. "The Struggle for Negro Rights" rehearsed the points that Waties and Elizabeth would refine and circulate in 1950.

"The Struggle for Negro Rights" marked the demise of Waties's gradualist tendencies and birth of his burgeoning radicalism. The speech offers glimpses of Waties's increasing impatience with white southerners' rationalizations for denying African American people their constitutional rights as citizens of the United States. Moreover, "The Struggle for Negro Rights" defined the race problem as he saw it and also offered his rhetorical solution to the problem. Waties saw the need to open discussion about racial equality, cultivate public opinion against white supremacy, and pressure elected officials to pass meaningful civil rights legislation. In the months after receiving the Roosevelt Award, Waties's stance on segregation and race would differ drastically from other white southerners agitating for change. The Lawyers Guild address offers a glimpse at a transitional identity for Waties. He was not an avowed gradualist but not quite radical—yet.

The National Lawyers Guild (NLG) was a racially and ethnically diverse bar association that admitted Black attorneys. In the mid-1940s, its membership peaked at five thousand and hit an all-time low of five hundred in 1955.[26] Founded in 1937 as an "association of progressive lawyers and jurists," its work in the late 1930s and early 1940s dealt mostly with labor unions such as the United Auto Workers and Congress of Industrial Organizations. At the height of McCarthyism, Guild members represented Julius and Ethel Rosenberg and others accused of communist activities. Robert W. Kenny, the NLG's president in 1949, was one of the group's founders. His clients included William Schneiderman, head of the Communist Party in California.[27] In 1950, the House Un-American Activities Committee targeted the Guild and officially designated it as a "subversive organization."[28] The audience in Detroit consisted of two hundred delegates, their spouses, and dignitaries from England, France, and Cuba.[29] In a letter dated February 25, 1949, Thurgood Marshall expressed concern to Robert Silberstein, executive secretary of the NLG, about the lack of publicity given to Waties's speech at the banquet. The Guild had scheduled a press conference but then canceled it.[30] Unlike the speeches that Elizabeth and Waties delivered in 1950, Waties did not publicize his speech or the award, most likely because of the Guild's reputation.[31]

The Guild selected Waties for the Roosevelt Award because of his "judicial integrity and courage." The banquet program described Waties as a "vigorous foe of racial and political intolerance, fearless advocate of social progress and expanded democracy, and effective executor of the constitutional mandate against discrimination."[32] The criteria for the Roosevelt Award and description in the program affirmed the Guild's selection of Waties. The speakers used honorific language to reinforce Waties as worthy of an award named after Roosevelt. By way of introduction, Clifford Durr and Thurgood Marshall paid tribute to Waties. Durr asserted that democracy depends upon the courage of its members. He clarified his statement: "I do not mean the courage of the battlefield, as magnificent and important as that is." Instead,

Durr referred to "A courage of a greater and rarer kind is required to face the disapproval of society in defense of a basic democratic principle.... Loneliness can be more painful than the wounds of battle, and few are willing to risk it."[33] Durr pointed out that Waties's courage consisted of two dimensions. First, because of his judicial duty, Waties opposed "deep seated folk-ways" of those with whom he lived. Second, Waties's language in the primary rulings constructed his decisions as morally right.

Waties had a choice in the primary rulings. He could have excused his primary rulings by saying that he had no other option because he would have been reversed on appeal. The excuse would lay the blame for Black people voting onto the Supreme Court—it was out of his control. Instead, Waties followed the Supreme Court's precedent in *Smith* and then supported his decision with claims of decency, morality, and American democracy. Because Waties chose the latter option, his ostracism spread from Charleston to the entire state. His marriage to Elizabeth was a social scandal within Charleston. His primary rulings were a political scandal that struck at the core of white supremacy. As a result, Waties became an island within a sea of opposition. Therefore, Durr reasoned that Waties was not "able to draw upon the courage of his fellow men."[34] Waties's primary rulings were ground-breaking, but for Durr, Waties deserved recognition because of his willingness to make those decisions knowing that he would stand alone.

Thurgood Marshall said that Waties and Elizabeth "are in a category where you can just cannot find words to describe them." After criticizing the hostility of some white southern judges, Marshall called Waties "the new type of judge" who "is willing not only to rule as he believes the law to be, but to rule with courage and sufficient firmness that everybody will not only respect the ruling as is but respect the ruling in all its ramifications" (5).[35] Marshall reinforced Durr's judgment when he called Waties "a tremendous light coming out of the dark" and "person of courage and determination" (10).

Marshall shared the private conversations he had with white southerners, which were similar to the letters that Waties had received. The NAACP attorney conceded that the audience may find it difficult to believe but insisted that "In private talk, they [white people] feel the same way you and I, and will talk that way." But something stopped them, "they are afraid to stand up." Marshall speculated, "Sometimes it might be fear, it might be politics, it might be personal favor, or it might be social ostracism. For those reasons, they stay underground" (5). Marshall validated Elizabeth and Waties's conviction that a faction of white Americans existed who believed as Marshall, the Guild audience, and Warings, that white supremacy was a scourge on American democracy. They remained silent out of fear.

Neither Durr nor Marshall named Elizabeth as the reason for Waties's rulings in the primary cases. However, they both gave her credit for supporting Waties so he would have the courage to issue the orders. In his remarks, Durr referred to Elizabeth as a "source of courage" for Waties, along with his own conscience. Marshall called Elizabeth "a true lady in every sense of the word and an important factor in the honor that is being bestowed tonight" (6). By characterizing Elizabeth as a true lady, Marshall contradicted most white South Carolinians' opinion of her. When she met Waties, she had already divorced one husband and then divorced another to marry him. Beyond white Charleston society, Elizabeth impressed Black and white activists as a courageous and lady-like white woman. She performed the role of loving and supportive wife to a husband upon whom white supremacists heaped their animus.

The theme of courage permeated all the speakers' remarks, including Waties's. They highlighted Franklin Roosevelt's courage in leading the country out of the Great Depression and to victory in World War II. Roosevelt genuinely served the people because he made unpopular decisions even when publicly criticized because of them. Waties demonstrated the same conviction with his primary rulings. For a white southerner to threaten other white people with imprisonment in order to protect African American citizens' right to vote without restraint was a near-blasphemous infraction. Once the Supreme Court ruled in *Smith v. Allwright* that the all-white primary was an integral element of the electoral process, Waties had no supportable legal options because if he had ruled otherwise, he would have been reversed on appeal. However, it was more than his decisions that earned his fellow South Carolinians' ire. He condemned his home state's continued subversion of constitutional principles and made it clear that he was willing to put the Democratic Party officials in jail if they defied his order. He upheld the constitution and federal law.

In the "Struggle for Negro Rights," Waties described a progression from dark, secret, and shame to light, open, and clean or a process of "becoming." He spoke of himself and the South moving from a dark past to a dim present to a bright future. He did not unfavorably compare the South to the North. Instead, he envisioned the South becoming one with the promise of American democracy. Just as Waties was in the process of "becoming," he expressed confidence in the South's ability to achieve its bright future but only if it relinquished its past. Waties relinquished his past with the condemnatory language in the primary orders. Doubtful that white southerners could move from the dark to the light on their own, he called upon people outside the South to facilitate the process. Overall, his tone was realistic and optimistic but lacked the venom of the 1950 speeches. Even so, "The Struggle for Negro Rights" portents the Warings' 1950 rhetorical campaign in the way it defined and proposed to solve the Race Problem.

Waties established common ground with his audience in the first paragraph of the speech when he expressed his admiration for Franklin Roosevelt, a sentiment likely shared by the audience since the Guild named its most prestigious award after Roosevelt. The speakers who preceded Waties also praised the late president. Waties said, "We miss him." He called Roosevelt "the greatest American of our generation." He then pressed the audience "to live up to his memory" and to steer the nation according to Roosevelt's "wise, able, and courageous chart." He called the evening "a magnificent tribute" (11). Then, he told the audience that it was difficult for him to express how much the award meant to him because it was named after Roosevelt, who appointed Waties to the federal bench. Waties fostered identification with the audience by emphasizing the Guild's ties to Roosevelt.

Waties confessed to the audience that his ancestors were slaveholders and that his family had been in South Carolina a long time (12). Waties's description of the dark past related to both his past and the South's past of slavery. He linked this past with inadequacy in the Declaration of Independence because it did not abolish slavery. It took the Thirteenth, Fourteen, and Fifteenth Amendments to abolish slavery legally, but the Amendments did not abolish "habits, customs, prejudices, and subterfuges" (12). These habits were part of "a system that has just been there" (12). The "indecencies" and "injustices" had been "allowed to live and to survive and to flourish" (14). Ridding the South of segregation required opening the white southern mind, speaking of the problem openly, and pressuring representatives.

Waties dismissed the gradualist notion that white southerners needed time to adjust to Black people no longer being enslaved. Gradualism's "postponement and appeasement and soft talk are not ever going to get you any place" (16). More time would not change white southerners' attitudes and beliefs about African American people. Such change would come about only when white southerners were forced to acknowledge African American people as equal citizens under the law. Such an acknowledgment would never come about as long as state laws required segregation. Furthermore, local customs and traditions were inadequate to justify or defend white southerners' repeated subversion of American democracy. Progress for Waties meant that Black people would be able to freely exercise their full citizenship rights guaranteed under the Constitution without fear of recrimination or violence.

Waties declared that the great problem was not a Negro problem but a white problem. This turn-of-phrase came from Donald Harrington's sermon,

"What Negroes Can Do About the White Problem," delivered on October 27, 1946, at the Community Church of New York. The Warings visited the Church when they were in New York City and formally became members in 1954.[36] Elizabeth also mentioned this sermon in her speeches. Interestingly, Waties did not cite Harrington as the source for the phrase in this speech. To attribute his ideas about race to a northern liberal would have diminished Waties's credibility as a native white southerner. In his sermon, Harrington wrote that the problem of race relations stemmed "from the attitudes and prejudices of white people more than from the actual condition of the Negro."[37] By transposing terms from one cultural sphere to the other (Black inferiority to white prejudice), Waties defamiliarized the world as previously understood by white people. He presented a perspective by incongruity or a shift in emphasis that unsettled prevailing wisdom.[38] The problem was white southerners' unreasonable racial prejudice. Instead of an external origin (African American people), Waties claimed an internal cause, white southerners' sickness. With this shift, he turned dominant beliefs about race relations inside out and upside down.

Throughout the speech, Waties commended the progress that had been made and was continuing to be made (14). However, to this constituency, Waties decried, "I know that those things take time, but, after all, we have had almost one hundred years to do it" (14). Waties was impatient. He was not willing to wait "a thousand years from now" to have "truth and justice and beauty and sweetness" (13). He acknowledged his own mortality: "I am afraid I will not be here to see it. I would like to see and taste some of it" (14). Waties equated truth and justice with beauty and sweetness. He infused the abstract ideas of truth and justice with embodied senses. Just as he referred to the Constitution as a "living, vital thing" (16), Waties did not conceive of truth or justice as elusive ideals but as tangible and concrete.[39]

As American citizens in a democracy, African American people were entitled to rights, and bestowing those rights as a matter of charity was "not one of the pillars of the American way of life" (16). Even though African American people had better housing and more job and educational opportunities, those opportunities had "come mostly as a matter of charity and not as a matter of right" (16). Waties perceived charitable endeavors as a way to appease and postpone change. They also reinforced the stereotype of Black people as childlike and needing the guidance of white people. Such endeavors were a subterfuge because they did not address the core issue: "If a man is entitled as an American citizen to certain rights, I do not want to see them handed to him by a charitable institution" (16). Waties deployed an image of African American people as citizens to displace the image of formerly enslaved persons. White people needed to recognize Black people as fully fledged citizens.

Waties argued that the so-called inferiority of African American people resulted from a lack of opportunity, not an inherent biological characteristic. He conceded that the majority of the Negro population in his part of the country was "underprivileged, uneducated, inefficient" (17). White supremacists attributed these qualities to biological inferiority. Waties asserted that with better homes, education, and jobs, "they will be as good as any other citizens" (17). The issue was not one of inherent inability or inferiority but rather opportunities, or lack thereof (18). Black people with access to opportunities comparable to white people "measure right up on an equal basis with everybody else. I see it in my court" (17). To support his assertion, Waties offered the example of NAACP Legal Defense Fund attorneys Thurgood Marshall and Edward Dudley, who presented cases before him. He called Marshall "as good a lawyer as any lawyer in this country" (18). He said that Dudley's "mind clicked so fast" that Waties sat up and "had trouble keeping up with him" (18). Waties followed Harrington's advice and tried to "dispel the white mists of false legendry" about Negroes' inferiority. Waties, like Harrington, declared that the issue was not one of ability "but of white repression and denial of opportunity."[40] He called it an "old caste system" which kept a "poor, ignorant, and unprivileged group of people working for them [white people] on starvation wages" (18). The problem was not Black people's inferiority. The problem was white people's image of African American people as inferior. Segregation enforced the image and stereotypes of Black people as less than white people. The image prevented white people from recognizing the rights of their fellow Americans (19).

Waties envisioned full equality for all American citizens. He believed that the American Constitution

> not only gives you those rights that it enumerates, but it gives you the right to live as a decent citizen; it gives you the right to ride on a street car or in a bus; it gives you the right to eat dinner in a dining car on a railroad train; it gives you the right to get a fair wage, and, if you are good enough to qualify for a job, to get the job and keep it. I do not care whether you are blonde, brunette, or redheaded, or dark-skinned. If you are an American and an American citizen, you are entitled to no more than that, but no less. (16)

He described equality as more than voting—it was the right to "live as a decent citizen." By redefining citizenship in this way, Waties departed from gradualism. Whereas gradualism sought to make separate-but-equal more equal in a material sense, Waties insisted that full citizenship rights for Black people was impossible with segregation. He reasoned that segregation precluded life as a decent citizen because of the badge of inferiority attached to it. For Waties, the term "American citizen" meant "justice and fairness and equality in every respect" (20).

In Detroit, Waties explained that the problem of minority groups "is not really discussed openly and fully and freely as it should be . . . come down to my state and you do not talk about it openly. That is the sadness and pity of it all" (13). White supremacy effectively silenced dissent. But Waties knew from the letters he had received that some white people opposed segregation. He lamented their lack of courage. "The proper democratic way" to solve problems was to meet on common ground and discuss them (13). Of course, such discussion did not take place in the South. Instead, the open and free exchange of ideas was smothered by white supremacy. Waties reasoned that without such an open discussion, race relations would not change. The issue was how to create a climate in which people would feel free to express their opinions.

Waties was impatient and convinced that change would not come voluntarily. Therefore, others must intervene. To achieve his vision of full equality for American citizens, then segregation and economic exploitation must end. For that to happen, his audience must act. The Guild audience consisted of those who could perform the task because "you are willing to go ahead, study problems, express your opinions, and think new thoughts" (12). Waties expressed his high regard for his audience, calling them "men and women of your caliber" (14). He respected the audience because they were "not afraid to think and not afraid to express your thoughts. . . . I am for any man or woman who has the courage to express his honest, clean opinions" (14). Waties constituted the Guild audience as individuals of integrity, good will, and American citizens. Furthermore, he outlined what they could do to achieve his vision. The audience needed to apply "continuous and continued pressure of public opinion and of thinking men and women of this country—decent thinking men and women of this country—that your representatives in any branch of the government are going to do anything about this hideous problem that we have had" (14). Waties asked the Guild to summon the courage to speak out against segregation which would hopefully create an arena where others would vocalize their objections against it. If public opinion turned against segregation, then elected representatives and the Supreme Court would fulfill their responsibilities and intervene in the South.

Waties reminded the audience of Franklin Roosevelt's iconic statement "We have nothing to fear but fear itself." The national press, civil rights advocates, and even some white southerners, at least privately, praised Waties's courage for opening the all-white Democratic primary in South Carolina. He told the audience in Detroit that "the white people of the South are afraid to do justice. They are looking over their shoulders to find out what the other fellow thinks of them. There are not any political leaders that as yet have had the courage to come out with this in the open" (19). Waties knew that he and Elizabeth were not alone because they had received confidential letters and whispered agreements of support. But he also knew that the consequences for speaking out against white supremacy were severe, and most white southerners were unwilling to take a public stand. He told the Guild members that "There are a great many people ashamed of what is happening who believe in fairness and right and justice and humanity and the soundness of this cause, but they have no leaders and they do not have the courage" (19). Waties bemoaned their fear. His courageous stance had the potential to loosen the clutch of fear because as more people publicly denounced white supremacy, others might feel inspired to do the same. Waties invited the Guild audience to enact his rhetorical remedy to remove the barriers that silenced those who privately disagreed with white supremacy.

Waties minimized his actions in the primary cases because the cases that Marshall and Dudley argued before him were straightforward, and so his rulings in them were a matter of "simple justice" (17). What he did in the primary cases was a "little job" and simple (19). It was a simple thing to write an order that he knew was right: "After all, it is not only a simple thing, but it is an awfully comfortable thing to be able to face your conscience and not be ashamed of each other" (15). He had a clear conscience because he adhered to the Constitution, not local tradition. He assured the audience that with the courage to speak out and act upon their convictions, they could excise the material manifestations of racial prejudice, such as segregation. He offered the audience a vision of the outcome:

> When the people see how easy it is to be fair and just and live under those circumstances, how much more comfortable it is to know that you are not cheating or wronging or taking advantage of someone else, how much more comfortable it is for the man and the woman who have been doing this wrong *to have the wrong taken away*, they will begin to wake up and see that, after all, this is right and this is better and this is what we want. (20, emphasis added)

Segregation had to end to free white southerners from racial prejudice. However, Waties was convinced that only with help from outside the South would state laws requiring segregation be eliminated. He clearly announced his stance on state laws that required segregation: "I do not believe the state has a right to tear up the Constitution of the United States" (20). Hence, his exhortation to the Guild audience to pressure their elected representatives.

Waties radicalized the means-end equation. For some gradualists, the means was equal-but-separate with the end goal of preparing Black people for eventual citizenship. For other gradualists, white southerners needed more time to adjust their attitudes. For both groups, eventual citizenship meant voting, never social equality. Both strategies consisted of Black people changing by and through the means determined by white people. Waties's end goal was full citizenship rights for Black people—now. As long as the law required segregation, the white southerners' image of Black people would never change. Segregation reinforced the image of African American citizens as inferior. Therefore, legally sanctioned segregation had to end.

Maligned by white supremacists and exalted by Black citizens, Waties captured the attention of groups that figured prominently in the 1960s, like the Southern Conference Educational Fund. Under James Dombrowski and Aubrey Williams' leadership, SCEF became a small but "militantly antisegregationist organization."[41] Dombrowski invited Waties to address a gathering of like-minded activists at the Gramercy Park South home of public relations tycoon Benjamin Sonnenberg. Although Waties had declined Dombrowski's invitation to serve on SCEF's board of directors, he agreed to speak to the group at Sonnenberg's home. Former first lady Eleanor Roosevelt went to the meeting and wrote in her syndicated newspaper column that Waties "made a plea to those in the North and who originally came from the South to come back and help those who live there." She also wrote that after hearing him, she reconsidered her hesitancy to interfere in the South.[42] For a national audience, Roosevelt linked Judge Waring with herself and other prominent white southerners who publicly advocated for change in the South. The column demonstrated that Waties's rulings from the bench were more than the "letter of the law" but also a personal conviction. In addition, Roosevelt revealed the persistent struggle among those who desired change but remained silent or inactive because they were afraid to interfere. Their fear originated from concern that interjecting would do "more harm than good" to both the issue and those on the ground agitating for change.

In his remarks to the Sonnenberg group, Waties likened states' rights to the old spirit of secession and compared segregation to slavery. As a staunch anticommunist, Waties was particularly mindful of how racial inequality damaged the United States' international standing. He told Sonnenberg's guests that as the leading democracy in the world, racial prejudice could seriously harm the United States. The Sonnenberg get-together was likely a fundraising opportunity. As an invited speaker, SCEF would have paid Waties's traveling expenses. However, Waties graciously waived them.[43] While in New York, Waties and Elizabeth also visited the NAACP Legal Defense Fund's office.[44]

Throughout the summer of 1949, Aubrey Williams and Waties corresponded after meeting at the Sonnenberg mansion. In his letters, Waties reiterated that he was convinced that "we needed outside help." Waties repeated many of the same sentiments from "The Struggle for Negro Rights." His private correspondence reveals a man deeply troubled and genuinely concerned about his native South:

> We all agree that the South is sick and I have long thought that the only way to cure its Cancer is to open it wide and call in good diagnosticians. If the people of this country and of the world can only once see and understand the disease which has long lingered hidden under a scab of romance and wrapped in the Confederate flag, they can and will find a way to restore to health our poor pitiful people whom you and I love and weep for.[45]

In this passage, Waties affirmed the Lost Cause's hold on his region. His letter to Williams echoed Waties's 1947 letter to Rebecca West after the Willie Earle lynching when he wrote, "I have lived all my life in Charleston and try to see over the fog of prejudice which engulfed that land of ours since the fall of the Confederacy, the horrors of the Reconstruction period and the years of blindness that have resulted."[46] Because of the depth and breadth of the racial prejudice, outsiders needed to cure the South. White southerners could not or would not cure themselves. As a federal judge, Waties was in a better position than most to remedy the situation. However, he had to wait for cases. He could not initiate them himself. Racial prejudice could not be removed if the law mandated separate schools for Black and white children. Therefore, he needed African American parents in Clarendon County to persist with their actions against the school board.

Black parents had not given up on the school board providing bus transportation for their children. On March 8, 1949, Harold Boulware wrote to Reverend Joseph De Laine that Thurgood Marshall and NAACP staff would be in Columbia on March 12 "for the purpose of mapping out plans for our school action."[47] De Laine, Reverend J. W. Seals, and members of the Pearson family traveled to Columbia and met with Marshall. De Laine was determined not to lose momentum and wanted the NAACP to refile the case. The *Pearson* dismissal in June 1948 was a severe blow to the African American parents in Clarendon County. They had revealed their willingness to resist the white power structure and then suffered repercussions for their temerity—all for naught. At the meeting, Marshall delivered devastating news to the group. The Legal Defense Fund would no longer pursue bus transportation cases.[48] The Clarendon County activists could not believe that after all they had been through, the matter was dead. The Summerton group cajoled and entreated Marshall to do something. The situation in Clarendon County was precarious. A backward county with authority vested in a small white minority, the NAACP debated the wisdom of filing suit there instead of a larger southern city or a border state. Although concerned about raising money for the lawsuit, Marshall acquiesced, but he would only take the case if the New York office approved and twenty families signed the petition. Having twenty plaintiffs would ensure the case would survive the disqualification of one, a harsh lesson learned in *Pearson*. Also, Marshall indicated that the suit needed to be brought in a district with both a white and Black school in order to create as much parity as possible when comparing the two.[49]

At the end of March, Eugene A. R. Montgomery, the South Carolina NAACP executive secretary, met with about 150 people in Clarendon School District 26 and 250 people in District 5. At those meetings, fifty possible plaintiffs were secured in five districts. Committees were appointed to work in each district to get more plaintiffs. On April 20, W. Lester Banks, the executive secretary for the Virginia NAACP, traveled to Summerton and participated in conferences all day to lay the groundwork for legal action in educational facilities lawsuits. That night, Banks spoke to over two hundred people at a meeting in Summerton. For the next two days, Banks and Montgomery visited the Black and white schools in six districts. On May 12, Montgomery attended a meeting of 150 people at St. Mark AME Church in Summerton to receive the authorization papers from parents for the legal action. In his report to James Hinton, Montgomery wrote: "From the responses shown at the several meetings I have attended in Clarendon County I am certain that we can begin action with[out] any fear of support from the people."[50] In just two months, local organizers in Clarendon County fulfilled Marshall's directives. They had secured permission from enough parents to proceed with legal action.

Eight months after the meeting with Marshall in Columbia, Reverend De Laine finally received the petitions from the New York NAACP office on November 11, 1949. That night in Harry Briggs' home, twenty-four families with children attending school in District 22 signed the petition asking for educational advantages and facilities equal to those provided to white children. The petition outlined the gross disparities between the Black and white schools, such as higher teacher-to-student ratio, inadequate facilities, no running water or heat, and no bus transportation. The petition ended with a request for immediate action and that the petitioners be allowed to present their complaint to the County Board of Trustees and School Board. Three days later, Montgomery wrote to De Laine that the petition had been mailed to the school officials. If the county did not reply to the petition within thirty days, then the parents would file a complaint in federal court.[51]

The white power structure in Clarendon County responded but not in any official capacity. Instead, Harry Briggs lost his job at the Carrigan Service Station in Summerton, where he pumped gas, repaired tires, and greased cars. Harry's wife, Eliza, worked for a motel on Highway 15 in Summerton for six years. Her boss told her he was under a lot of pressure to get her name off the petition. She informed him that she did not sign it; her husband did. Her boss gave her a week's notice, and she lost her job. Harry left the state to find work to support his family, who remained behind in Summerton. Reverend De Laine, his two sisters, and his niece lost their jobs. Petitioner Annie Gibson and her family were dispossessed from their home on Christmas Eve. Lucrisher Richard and her family were evicted. Lee Richardson and his family were evicted. Henry Scott was evicted at harvest time after working for most of the year to bring in a good crop. "None of the farmers could buy seed for crops, get cotton ginned, or use credit at the stores they formerly frequented." Wholesalers refused to sell, and delivery men refused to deliver goods to Mary Oliver, who owned a café.[52] The Black community sustained each other as they resisted white supremacy, "Realizing that no one person could do this alone, they decided to band themselves together."[53] The local white power structure's efforts to intimidate the parent-plaintiffs failed.

On March 12, 1949, the day after Thurgood Marshall met with the Black activists in Columbia, John McCray delivered a speech to the Omega Psi Phi fraternity at Allen University in Columbia. McCray was the editor of the weekly Black newspaper, *Lighthouse and Informer*, and founded the Progressive Democratic Party in 1944. Outspoken and uncompromising, McCray would unleash his sharp tongue onto white people and Black people. He rebuked Black people for accepting less than they were entitled. At the chapter meeting, McCray announced confidentially that at the fraternity's upcoming Sixth District meeting in Charleston, Judge Waring would be granted "a special award in behalf of the Negroes of South Carolina, which will mark the first time remembered that Negroes in this state have ever publicly honored a white man for being a good citizen, and having rendered a service they appreciate."[54]

The Sixth District of the Omega Psi Phi Fraternity held its three-day conference at Morris Street Baptist Church in Charleston. On April 30, 1949, the District presented a plaque to Waties that recognized "his contribution toward insuring justice for all in our democracy."[55] Dr. Benjamin E. Mays, president of Morehouse College, addressed more than one thousand people in attendance, with hundreds more unable to enter because of space limitations. In an article published in the *Pittsburgh Courier*, Mays wrote that he called Waties a free man because true freedom was not just physical freedom but also moral and spiritual freedom. Mays referred to Elizabeth as Waties's "charming wife" and declared that both of them had achieved "true freedom." And only with that type of freedom can one have peace of mind.[56] Waties expressed the same conviction in "The Struggle for Negro Rights." Segregation was the "wrong" that needed to be taken away so that white southerners could experience the same moral and spiritual freedom.

In his twenty-minute address at the Fraternity's district meeting, Waties commended African American leaders such as Ralph Bunche, Walter White, and Thurgood Marshall. He also repeated some of the themes from "Struggle for Negro Rights." Waties attempted to instill a sense of citizenship and entitlement when he said, "negroes should not want charity, but first class citizenship and all that citizens are entitled to receive." He also framed civil rights as citizenship rights: "American citizenship must mean freedom and justice to all. Leaders must see it is brought to all." His remarks included his vision for America and the South as exemplars of democracy whereby all citizens were equal, regardless of skin color. He compared that vision with the reality. The United States and his native region were not fulfilling the promises of democracy for all its citizens. He commended the audience's activism and recognized that there was more to do: "Continue to do outstanding work to make this country the land of the free." The audience responded to his address with "the greatest ovation ever accorded here." Elizabeth was included in the ceremony. Upon being presented with a bouquet of American roses, she told the audience, "This is the greatest privilege of my life to know you, and I hope to make more friends in Charleston."[57]

Unbeknownst to Black parents in Clarendon County, Elizabeth and Waties were formulating a plan that would take advantage of their national platform to transform public opinion about white southerners and segregation. An element of their plan was networking with other advocates. The Sixth District Omega Psi Phi meeting widened the Warings' network beyond members of national organizations. At the Morris Street Baptist Church event, the Warings met local African American activists. Elizabeth cultivated these relationships by corresponding when she was away from Charleston. She also invited them to her Meeting Street home, violating the taboo against white and Black people socializing in each other's homes. As privileged white people living in Charleston, Elizabeth and Waties were deeply immersed in the particular political and social climate of the city. They were receptive to developing relationships with African American people in South Carolina while Waties was in the national spotlight because of the primary rulings. Although the couple's advocacy does not correspond with traditional ideas of grassroots organizing, their extensive network offers a link between local and national levels of resistance to white supremacy.

Elizabeth's relationships with local African American women resulted in an invitation to the Ninth Annual Harvest Tea on November 27, 1949, at Calvary Episcopal Church, sponsored by the Women's Auxiliary. Printed on the program was "Address Mrs. J. Waties Waring," and handwritten on the bottom was "Address—Judge J. Waties Waring."[58] The Church was founded in 1847 to serve enslaved people, so more than likely, the Warings' audience was middle-class African American women. The Tea was the first time Elizabeth had "ventured in the speaking arena," and she planned to continue.[59] Elizabeth's remarks impressed Rose Huggins, who suggested to Septima Clark that they invite the judge's wife to speak at the Coming Street YWCA's annual meeting scheduled for January 16, 1950.[60] In November 1949, Clark extended the invitation. When Elizabeth accepted, she let the Committee know that "she didn't deliver 'apple sauce' speeches," and asked what type of talk they wanted. The Committee wanted a talk "which would put the people to thinking."[61] At the Sonnenberg gathering earlier in the year, Mrs. Roosevelt mused that Charleston being what it was, it was likely the last place to see improvement. Elizabeth remarked that while true, perhaps Charleston would be the best place to strike a brave blow.[62] Septima Clark's invitation was Elizabeth's opportunity to strike the first brave blow in her and Waties's rhetorical campaign to end segregation.

Chapter 4

BRICKBATS AND BOUQUETS

After they witnessed Jim Crow justice first-hand at Batesburg police chief Lynwood Shull's trial, Elizabeth and Waties Waring began a truth-seeking journey. They carefully studied W. J. Cash's *The Mind of the South* and Gunnar Myrdal's *An American Dilemma* and learned about slavery's legacy in the South. Although some white people denounced Waties's rulings in the primary cases, others applauded them. His popularity outside of the state rose in direct proportion to animosity towards him in South Carolina. Beyond the Palmetto State, journalists clamored to interview the white federal judge who threatened to jail Democratic Party officials if they excluded African American voters from the polls. An eighth-generation white Charlestonian ruling against white southerners made good headlines. Civil rights organizations reached out to Waties. Elizabeth established relationships with the African American community in Charleston. Septima Clark's invitation to speak at the Coming Street YWCA arose from Elizabeth's efforts to cultivate a local and national network of activists and journalists. As white southerners' hostility intensified against the Warings, this network, along with the couple's travels outside the South, sustained them.

Elizabeth and Waties's contacts with key figures in the NAACP and local activists in Charleston kept them informed of developments in Clarendon County. The Warings knew that Black parents in Clarendon County had the courage to use the federal courts to challenge the local school board's white supremacist policies. A few days before the Coming Street YWCA annual meeting, Waties wrote to his daughter and son-in-law, "Things are getting a good deal stirred up here and Negroes, at least some of them, are beginning to pick up a good deal of courage and beginning to insist that they be treated as citizens."[1] Waties corresponded regularly with Thurgood Marshall. In April 1949, Waties assured Marshall that the judge was eager to be of assistance: "Do not hesitate to call at any time as I do not mind being interrupted if I can be of any use. Unfortunately, at present I feel pretty helpless, but I am always, as you know, 'standing by.'"[2] The Warings also frequently socialized with Walter White and his wife, Poppy Cannon. White served as Executive Secretary of the NAACP. In Charleston, Elizabeth opened her home to African American activists such as Ruby Cornwell and Septima Clark. Waties and Elizabeth knew that Black parents in Clarendon County had not given up.

With the situation intensifying in Clarendon County and the Dixiecrats frustrating Truman's attempts to enact his civil rights program, the time was ripe for an aggressive assault to generate public pressure on white people who opposed segregation to publicly voice their position. In a letter to John Hammond and Palmer Weber dated January 4, 1950, after she had accepted the invitation to speak at the YWCA but before she delivered the speech, Elizabeth wrote, "The Negro Cause will drop into oblivion in this period unless the NAACP GET TOUGH and faces facts that ideological and Congressional approach is hopeless and only FORCE will work" (emphasis in original).[3] To the Warings, force meant the law, "orders signed by the president and the courts."[4] A strategic rhetorical attack could alter the public conversation and transform the political climate. For Elizabeth, the Coming Street YWCA's annual meeting presented an opportunity that may not recur and the moment she decided to speak. *Kairos* is the moment in which rhetorical action is most advantageous.[5] A situational kind of time, *kairos* is the principle of right timing and proper measure or "something close to what we call 'opportunity.'"[6] Elizabeth acknowledged the significance of timing in the speech: "This invitation to me to speak on Achievement came at a particularly auspicious time and seems like an answer to my prayer—my prayer to reach you and many others through you with the GOOD TIDINGS I have to bring you" (3). Elizabeth's speech to the Charleston Black YWCA was the centerpiece of the Warings' rhetorical campaign to provoke white supremacists and arouse silent white people across the country.

The Warings encountered a rhetorical situation in which threats of loss of social standing, economic insecurity, and violence squashed dissent. Elizabeth and Waties were insulated from potential repercussions. Because federal judges receive lifetime appointments and salaries from the federal government, the Warings were immune to financial threats. The social ostracism in Charleston as a result of their divorces and marriage infected the rest of South Carolina when Waties quelled the Democratic Party's repeated maneuvers to exclude African American voters. Already socially cut-off from white society and financially independent, they were uniquely situated to deploy a rhetorical campaign that said the unsayable. Their public denunciation of white supremacy had the potential to infuse courage into other white people to publicly condemn segregation.

After the Charleston *Evening Post* published the notice on January 11 announcing that Elizabeth would speak at the Coming Street YWCA's annual meeting, the white women from the Society Street YWCA chapter protested. They told Septima Clark, "Judge Waring himself was a controversial issue, that Mrs. Waring was a northern-Yankee and out of line with Charleston customs, and that her message would do no one any good."[7] Clark pointed out that Black members coming to hear Elizabeth at the Coming Street Y would not know anything about her divorces and social ostracism. But, "They [Society Street women] hated her. They didn't want her to speak."[8]

Nationally, the Y was approaching a true interracial organization that moved beyond parallel but separate chapters. However, on a local level, especially in the South, segregation still dictated the structure and leadership of the chapters. In Charleston, the white YWCA chapter on Society Street and the Black chapter on Coming Street had separate leadership with a mutual joint interracial committee of Black and white women.[9] On January 12, the interracial committee met, but the women could not resolve the situation. Until the night of the speech, various Y members pleaded with Septima Clark to rescind the invitation, dictate the speech's content, postpone the meeting, or ban reporters. The opposition attempted to obtain a copy of the speech.[10] The Society Street chapter delicately suggested "that it might be bad financially to do anything that might be offensive to those who control financial sources."[11] A woman less courageous than Septima Clark may have bowed to pressure. However, Clark summoned the separateness of the two branches and insisted that the Coming Street's leadership chose the speaker for its annual meeting. Clark insisted that the Charleston YWCA chapters did not function as "a total association therefore each group makes its own plan." The Coming Street chapter "asked her to be our guest speaker" (emphasis in original).[12] Rose Huggins, the Coming Street director, had signed the invitation to Elizabeth. The white Society Street members wanted separate chapters until the Coming Street chapter asserted its autonomy.

In the midst of the conflict, Clark and another Society Street member visited Elizabeth at her home. They "begged her not to listen to the current controversy if contacted by the whites and to let the chairman know if any colored members asked her not to be our guest speaker."[13] Elizabeth knew Charleston's segregated YWCA chapters defied the National YWCA's Interracial Charter adopted in 1946 that called for the inclusion of Black women and girls in the mainstream of Association life.[14] She telephoned the national headquarters in New York for support. Elizabeth told a newspaper reporter, "They tried to stop me from making the speech . . . the White Trustees of the YWCA told the separate Negro organization not to let me speak. But the Negro members stood right up to their decision 100 per cent with the backing of the national YWCA."[15] Elizabeth needed a public forum to reach a national audience. She exerted her influence to ensure that Clark could withstand the Society Street members' bullying.

Elmer W. Henderson wrote in 1951 that in regard to segregation, "Frank and objective discussion of the subject in public meetings by whites is rare, and speakers sympathetic with the abolition of segregation are seldom invited to speak to public gatherings and have difficulty obtaining large audiences for themselves."[16] The white southern press and radio censored news content and editorial policy to maintain the illusion of consensus about segregation. As a consequence, there was little, if any, challenge to segregation in white southern media. Few opportunities existed to shift white public opinion against segregation and thereby, create a favorable environment for it to be declared unconstitutional. Elizabeth's speech at the Coming Street YWCA could remedy the persistent silence among white people about segregation. However, she needed to reach an audience beyond those physically present at the annual meeting.

Just as Elizabeth pursued assistance beyond Charleston to support the Coming Street YWCA, Waties called upon his ties with the news media beyond the city to ensure that his wife's speech circulated to a national audience. The Warings enjoyed nearly unfettered access to the media due to Waties's ground-breaking decisions from the bench. The speech at the Coming Street YWCA's annual meeting offered the opportunity to address the target national audience without appearing to manufacture an artificial situation.[17] Waties believed that "no newspaper reporters or radio men in Charleston could be relied on to furnish even a semblance of a true report."[18] He contacted Paul Hansell, chief of the Associated Press's Charlotte bureau, and requested that a representative cover his wife's speech. Instead, Hansell asked Charleston's *News and Courier* to send a reporter. The Associated Press bureau did not want to antagonize Judge Waring, who was on good terms with the United Press. To maintain a working relationship with Waties, Hansell informed the *News and Courier* that the Charlotte AP Bureau would obtain a copy of the speech from the Warings.[19] Because Waties was personally acquainted with the Associated Press bureau chief, he ensured that representatives from the Associated Press and United Press had advance notice of Elizabeth's speech. On January 17, 1950, Elizabeth sent a clipping of her speech to Thurgood Marshall with a note: "The higher-ups of the Associated Press forced the hand of the *News and Courier*."[20]

The Warings' rhetorical strategy involved turning the civil rights struggle into a nationwide cause and thereby prod the federal government into exerting its considerable power to overturn the system of white domination in the South.[21] Elizabeth believed, "We've got to turn the spotlight of the world on them. Only force from the outside will help. We've got to get Congress to pass the civil rights program and make them live up to it."[22] Transforming civil rights into a national issue meant capturing the attention of people outside of the South. The Warings successfully manipulated the local wire services so that Elizabeth's speech to the Black Charleston YWCA circulated to a national audience. The *New York Times*' report of the speech was from the Associated Press, and the *Washington Post*'s was from the United Press.[23] Because of their behind-the-scenes maneuvers, the speech was not confined to the local audience at the Coming Street Y or even buried in the local newspaper. The objective of Elizabeth's speech, "Freedom Is Everybody's Job," was to ignite a national firestorm.

Despite the threats and exchanges between the Coming Street and Society Street YWCAs, Elizabeth delivered her speech without restraints or limitations on January 16, 1950, to an audience of approximately two hundred people who filled the small building. Fearful of interference from the KKK, Waties suggested that men stand at the light switches because "the first thing the trouble-makers do is turn out the lights."[24] In the first line, Elizabeth revealed the circumstances of the speech: "My very dear friends, it was brave of you to invite me to speak, and brave of all of you to come to hear me, for the White 'Powers that Be' have done everything underhanded in their power to keep me from speaking to you Negro people, even to defaming Judge Waring's and my character" (1).[25] She set herself and Judge Waring in direct opposition to the white power structure. She implied that the Society Street women were cowards "for it is apparent to everyone what their real motive is in not wishing me to speak—FEAR of the Judge and me" (1). Elizabeth's rhetorical assault was calculated antagonism whereby a speaker seeks "to force his listeners to reveal their deep-seated prejudices by exposing the rationalizations they use to cover their views."[26] She attacked white supremacy so its supporters would feel compelled to defend it. Their rationalizations would unmask Jim Crow as tyrannical and antithetical to American democracy.

Elizabeth's antagonism towards white southerners exuded throughout the speech, mainly in the opening and closing sections with prickly barbs sprinkled throughout. She did not differentiate between white southerners and white supremacists. In the first paragraph, she claimed that the "White 'Powers that Be'" were stupid, fearful, and guilty. She exposed the euphemism "Southern way of life" when she called it "SELFISH AND SAVAGE WHITE SUPREMACY WAY OF LIFE" (emphasis in original, 1). Her scorn for white southerners intensified near the end of the speech when she called "Whites down here" a "sick, confused, and decadent people" (9). Elizabeth cast white southerners as evil rather than benevolent protectors of southern civilization. She bared their seemingly benign concern with preserving the white race as racial oppression: "the White Supremacists try to keep submerging you in laws and etiquette to keep you from rising" (2). Instead of courageous defenders of southern civilization, Elizabeth disparaged their motives and characterized them as "full of pride and complacency, introverted, morally weak, and low . . . destroying and withholding" (8). They were self-centered and isolated from the rest of the world. White southerners represented exclusion, separation, isolation, and disintegration, not inclusion, wholeness, unity, and brotherhood.[27] Her language did not align with the norms of prudent conduct. The message was unpleasant and objectionable. But, because it was all those things, it attracted media publicity. It "stirred up a hornet's nest in the South" and "made headline news all over the nation."[28]

Elizabeth further violated the public vocabulary of Jim Crow when she unfavorably contrasted white southerners with Black southerners. Whereas Black people were in the "springtime of your growth," white supremacists "have sunk back into a slough of despondency and fallen asleep, if not quite dead, on the imagined laurels of their ancestors" (9). African American citizens were "building and creating," and white supremacists were "destroying and withholding" (9). Black people were active and creative, while white southerners were passive and stagnant. She turned the racial hierarchy upside down with African American people as the superior race, not white people. The reversal challenged the bedrock of white supremacy, namely the indisputable superiority of the white race. Elizabeth intentionally denied the white race's superiority in order to provoke white southerners.

Elizabeth ended the speech by describing a placard from the Charleston buses "where you Negroes sit in shame, segregated to the rear." The placard read, "Respect the rights of others," but Elizabeth insisted, "bear this in mind, in the deep South where no one practices—least of all the bus companies, Christ's command 'TO DO UNTO OTHERS AS YOU WOULD BE DONE BY.'" Along with "respect the rights of others," the placard had a picture of Pilgrims in prayer giving thanks for the freedom they found in coming to the United States. Elizabeth described the placard, "Among other things, this placard admonishes 'FREEDOM IS EVERYBODY'S JOB.' Let's follow the bus company's admonition—and right now. YES! FREEDOM IS EVERYBODY'S JOB!!" Her closing likened the Black Freedom Struggle to the Pilgrims who fled England because they were persecuted for their religious practices. By inserting the sacred covenants of American democracy as represented by the Pilgrims, Elizabeth underscored the legitimacy of extending full citizenship to all Americans. Elizabeth provoked the audience into questioning its reality by presenting hers: Black people were citizens and entitled to the same rights and freedoms under the Constitution as white people. Furthermore, she insisted that everyone participate in the cause. She and Waties could not end segregation by themselves. The parents in Clarendon County could not do it alone. The NAACP could not win the case by itself. Without the support of Black and white people from the rest of the United States, legal segregation would continue. Elizabeth's speech was a battle cry for everyone to mobilize and vocalize.

After Elizabeth delivered "Freedom Is Everybody's Job," Waties hugged his wife to wide applause from the audience. Then, he handed a typed copy of the speech to the reporters and said, "I want every word printed just as she said it. Don't change one word of it."[29] Newspapers from New York to Tallahassee to Chicago printed excerpts or mentioned the speech so Elizabeth achieved her goal of an audience beyond those physically present on January 16, 1950. While Elizabeth received national media coverage of the Y speech, not all newspapers published the entire manuscript. Some only published the most incendiary paragraphs. Out of nine double-spaced, legal-sized pages of text, the one sentence that was invariably printed was "They are a sick, confused and decadent people." The newspapers also included the phrase that white southerners were "introverted, morally weak, and low." Many white people only read those fragments. Whether due to space limitations or editorial decisions, the condensation of Elizabeth's speech to a pithy indictment of white southerners made it more palatable for readers outside of the South and more likely to provoke white readers inside the South.[30]

"Freedom Is Everybody's Job" was neither impromptu nor an isolated rhetorical event. The concerted effort to reach an audience outside the South demonstrates a thoughtfully designed strategy. Elizabeth intended the YWCA to be a shock treatment to penetrate the wall of silence: "We have been handling the Southerner with KID or even VELVET gloves with no hand of iron, even under the gloves, as is recommended" (emphasis in original).[31] The steel hand underneath the velvet glove was the meat ax of brutal frankness. Elizabeth explained, "BUT AS SOUTHERNERS WON'T DO ANYTHING EXCEPT EXCUSE, EXPLAIN, ANALYZE AND POSTPONE WITH GRADUALIST METHODS ONE CANNOT WAIT FOR THE MILLENIUM" (emphasis in original). A vocal collective that opposed segregation had the potential to balance the lopsided public conversation about racial equality. Because the speech was printed in the press, Elizabeth addressed two audiences simultaneously. She spoke to the limited audience physically present on January 16, 1950, and a broader group who read the text in newspapers.

The Warings took purposeful action to ensure that the speech "would hit the headlines and so intended it and were prepared for even worse personal persecution as a result."[32] Even so, a few people responded favorably, most often remarking on Elizabeth's courage.

The volume of letters that she received indicates that Elizabeth provoked a conversation. She anticipated swift response to the speech: "I decided to take the full force of their propaganda and place myself at their mercy, as a Northerner interfering with the attending propaganda of 'HATE' and 'LACK OF UNDERSTANDING'" (emphasis in original).[33] If Elizabeth wanted to penetrate the wall of silence about race relations in the South, she succeeded. Mrs. Parker, from nearby Summerville, accurately assessed the situation in her letter: "It's marvelous to think how much you have stirred up this staid and sluggish old Charleston but I fear they are all too stupid to have any proper reactions and many will have strokes or exceedingly high blood pressure."[34] Elizabeth had publicly disclosed what white people had written in their letters to Waties. She circulated the first public declaration to loosen the dam so that the waters of an unfettered open discussion would burst free. Waties remarked on the need for an open discussion in his speech, "The Struggle for Negro Rights," and repeated this belief to Aubrey Williams: "As a matter of fact, you know I advocate bringing these matters out as openly as possible."[35] Elizabeth was convinced more people agreed with her than disagreed. If those who opposed white supremacy publicly condemned it, then Truman's proposed civil rights initiatives would become law. Not to mention, Black parents in Clarendon County remained committed to their goal of equal educational opportunities for their children.

Four broad themes emerged among the negative letters that Elizabeth received in response to the speech: Good Southerner, Outsider to the South, Outsider to White Femininity, and Threats. The Good Southerner response masked the tyranny of segregation. Two themes exploited Elizabeth's status as a divorced woman from Detroit. She was an outsider to the South and an outsider to white femininity. Casting her as an outsider, opponents evacuated her rhetoric of its political potency. Elizabeth also received threats that made no attempt to hide the racism of white supremacy. More than iterations of the Lost Cause, the negative letters attempted to smooth the rupture of dissent created by Elizabeth's speech. The positive responses praised Elizabeth's courage for saying what others were afraid to say publicly. These responses confirmed Elizabeth's belief that others railed against the incongruity between the ideals of American democracy and the lived reality for Black people in the Jim Crow South.

On January 14, 1950, two days before Elizabeth addressed the Coming Street YWCA, the *Saturday Evening Post* published "Just Leave Us Alone" by Hodding Carter. Most white southerners considered Carter a racial liberal. As editor of the Greenville (MS) *Delta Democrat-Times*, Carter received the 1946 Pulitzer Prize for his editorials about racial intolerance in the South. Carter believed that the solution to the South's Race Problem had to come from within the region. His articles in the *New York Times* opposed a federal antipoll tax and antilynching laws because federal interference ignored "the achievements and democratic progress" made in the South.[36] He defensively claimed that the region had served as a "whipping boy for the public conscience, its role that of a petulant, backward, ragged and sometimes cruel child."[37]

Carter was the exemplar of a Good Southerner because even as he seemingly criticized the region, he refused to countenance any change other than that prescribed by white southerners. In the *Saturday Evening Post* article, Carter insisted that "The white South does have a historic and present-day basis for suspicion and fear. The Southern contradiction of democracy is the only one in the nation against which an aggressive demand for full, abrupt and forcible revision is continuously directed." The South was the only region constantly told that the dominant majority is "unqualifiedly evil in its behavior." Because more white Southerners were actively working to improve the South, they did not need a "sensational crusader from the North."[38] He praised the so-called progress in the South and attributed it to white southerners. As a consequence, he contributed to the illusion of consensus because he stopped short of offending white southern sensibilities. In their responses to Elizabeth, letter writers drew upon the acceptable public vocabulary in Carter's article.

Mild in tone, the Good Southerner response performed white supremacy using the language of *noblesse largesse* that masked overt racism. In a period of escalating and visible Klan violence, the Good Southerner invoked the language of what Jeanne Theoharis calls "polite racism." While the Good Southerner may condemn violence against Black people, they, nevertheless, used coded language that obscured their racism.[39] The Good Southerner asserted the inferiority of Black people, progress in the South, better race relations in the South, and the consent of Black people. The seemingly well-intentioned authority of white paternalism rationalized the inconsistencies between American democracy and Jim Crow by constructing the Black race as inferior and, therefore, requiring white southerners' protection and guidance. Mrs. Raymond Moore's letter to the editor typified the Good Southerner: "With all respect to the negro people and their progress and their achievements since the days of slavery, let it be said that they have progressed not through the weakness of white people, but by their help."⁴⁰ The Good Southerner believed that without the benevolence of white people, Black people were incapable of progress or achievement. As a consequence, the Good Southerner did not recognize Black people as citizens.

The Good Southerner praised the progress in race relations in the South: "things are getting better, slowly, but surely." Elizabeth was out of patience. At the Coming Street YWCA, she told the audience, "a NEW DAY IS DAWNING—IT IS HERE." (8). For the Good Southerner, any change in the South needed to come from white southerners. Those trying to change race relations in the South needed to do so in a way that would not offend white people—the "right way." The "right way" was gradualism as Mrs. Simms claimed, "In time, I believe segregation will be modified, but not all of a sudden," because "you must have the foundation, Southerners' willingness, but not all of a sudden." For Elizabeth, white southerners had had enough time: "DON'T LISTEN TO THOSE TIMID ONES WHO SPEAK OF <u>TIME</u> . . . IT IS AT HAND AND <u>YOU</u> MUST MAKE THE FINAL PUSH NOW OR NEVER" (emphasis in original, 8). Mrs. Simms implored Elizabeth to "help us, if you must, but in the right way."⁴¹

Elizabeth's way, "the modern revolution of a COLD WAR TO ATTAIN THE RIGHTS YOU ALREADY LEGALLY HAVE, TO ENFORCE THOSE RIGHTS," was the wrong way (emphasis in original, 9). A writer from Augusta, Georgia, accused Elizabeth of causing "a lot of fine Negroes being killed. . . . Yes you are hurting them."⁴² Other writers claimed that because she insisted upon full citizenship for Black people, Elizabeth was "asking for civil war between the races which could only mean bloodshed, death and destruction for the negros."⁴³ The letter writers who denounced Elizabeth's call for a revolution embraced Jim Crow storytelling. Elizabeth Gillespie McRae explains that Jim Crow storytelling celebrated enlightened race relations within segregation. Any possible reforms would come from "educated, liberal white supremacists, not mean reactionaries." White people of a certain class would control segregation and mitigate its worst abuses.⁴⁴ The Good Southerner characterized any call for change as a call for riots because their delusion of harmonious race relations belied the reality. As Carter wrote in the *Saturday Evening Post*, white southerners would remedy the situation in their own way and in their own time. Because the South was making progress in race relations, the Good Southerner perceived themselves and the region as a "morally responsive society." As such, Elizabeth's militant response to racial inequality was unjustified.⁴⁵ Rather than being reasonable, Elizabeth's call for a revolution was a call for violence. The

Good Southerner left unsaid that any violence would likely originate from white people.

The Good Southerner contrasted the North with the South to reinforce the benign nature of Jim Crow and magnify the good will of white southerners. As a northerner living in the South, Mrs. Munn shared her epiphany, "I have had my eyes opened to the fact that the negroes live better and are treated better, here, than they are in the north" (emphasis in original).[46] "Magnolia White" wrote that "the negro knows the South is his best friend."[47] A writer from Florence reasoned that "Evidently the negro is more contented with the opportunity the South offers because the majority of them are still here."[48] Race relations in the South were better than they were in the North, Mrs. Clifton from Bluffton declared when it comes to downright helpfulness and cooperation.[49] In an editorial, *The Statesman* from Hapeville, Georgia, offered that the "relationships between the races are better than at any time since the War Between the States."[50] The false image of the South being a more tolerant and hospitable region than the North was repeated numerous times. The Good Southerner reasoned that Black people did not oppose segregation; otherwise, why did so many Black people live in the South? The claim reinforced the appearance of unanimity, not just among white southerners but also among Black people. It also disguised the oppressive nature of segregation.

Indeed, some letter writers invoked their superior knowledge of Black people in order to repair the fractured consensus created by Elizabeth's speech. A belief that white southerners knew Black people best because they had lived side by side for hundreds of years underpinned the letter writers' condescension. Mrs. Turner of the Women's Society of Christian Service, a biracial board in Columbia, wrote, "I also believe that our wise Christian Negroes will agree with me that the prejudice which we are trying to erase will be greatly aroused by your caustic remarks."[51] Mrs. Duncan from Summerville agreed, "I am sure that the better class of colored people can judge right from wrong and do not appreciate such interference."[52] Mrs. Moore insisted, "But the truly educated and refined negro does not want to push himself past the laws of etiquette into the social realm of white people."[53] Mrs. Gates's letter to the editor of the *Atlanta Journal* repeated the women's belief. She insisted that Elizabeth had "lost the respect of the white people, and we are sure she is disgusting to the better class of colored people."[54] In the *Lighthouse and Informer* on January 21, 1950, editor John H. McCray wrote of the phone calls he had received from white people, imploring McCray to tell Elizabeth that Black people did not "appreciate such vicious denunciations of your white friends."[55] The Good Southerner paternalistically spoke for

Black people to assert their consent to Jim Crow and the benevolent nature of segregation. Segregation was not an oppressive institution imposed upon Black people. Instead, both white and Black southerners consented to the practice. The insistence on interracial accord about Jim Crow restored the appearance of unanimity.

The morning after the Coming Street branch's annual meeting, the Charleston *News and Courier* printed nearly the entire transcript of the speech. The South Carolina Legislature sat silently while Representative Schumacher of Oconee read the manuscript to his colleagues. The white men dismissed Elizabeth's speech as the utterings of a northerner who knew nothing of the relationship between Black and white people in the South. Governor Strom Thurmond said that Elizabeth was "beneath comment." South Carolina Representative Joseph F. Wise Jr. insisted, "We need no words such as hers from a Damnyankee."[56] Congressman L. Mendel Rivers stated that Elizabeth's speech was no more than "what could be expected from an individual completely uninformed on a very complex and trying subject" and that Elizabeth attempted "to discuss a situation about which she knows nothing."[57]

The politicians' unified perfunctory response drew upon persistent myths about Reconstruction. Hodding Carter described Reconstruction as a time when the South was assaulted by "circling buzzards who swooped down upon the prostrate body, by the cotton thieves and political plunderers, the tax ghouls and berserk comminglers, exploiting not only the prostrate Confederacy but the bewildered Negro."[58] Elizabeth anticipated this response in her speech: "The phobia and frenzy aroused by mention of carpet baggers and scallawags as a reason for White Supremacy is like the Versailles treaty propaganda of the Germans as an excuse for Hitler's later atrocities" (9). Because the white politicians employed terms like "Damnyankee" and "local matters," Elizabeth became the northern aggressor butting into the harmonious South. According to Lost Cause mythology, white people who had lost their wealth, their land, and their men during the Civil War then had to endure a "carnival of pillage and corruption." Some white people lost the vote, and "the ignorant and illiterate Negroes, led by unscrupulous carpetbaggers and scalawags" were in control.[59] Elizabeth embodied the horrors during Reconstruction. Her outburst against the white people of the South "was not only ill advised but also unintelligent—unwise and untrue."[60] The politicians' rejoinders branded Elizabeth as uninformed and irrelevant. After all, the South restored white rule after military occupation in the nineteenth century. She was of little concern. Therefore, she could be dismissed.

Pointing to Elizabeth's status as a person not from the South functioned in two ways. It reinforced the person criticizing Elizabeth as a Good Southerner.

It also dis-authorized her speech because, as an outsider, she did not have knowledge of the region to speak of it. In his letter to the editor of the *News and Courier*, Mark Anthony Brown of Florence explained the beliefs underlying the Outsider response. More than spouting a rapid-fire "outsider" label, Brown enumerated the ways in which Elizabeth's criticisms were unfair. First, the "established customs and traditions of the past . . . law and order, good sense and fair play for both white and colored to live in peace and harmony with other." These customs "established by great [white] Southerners of the past" served as the "cornerstone of good racial relationships for the past, the present and the future." Elizabeth's statements were "unfair to every Southerner," and she had "failed to study and understand the racial problems of the South which are typically Southern." The problem was not white southerners but "hot heads and rabble rousers" who "constantly aggravate both races into open hostile camps creating bloodshed and confusion."[61] Brown conflated resistance with riot. The confusion he referred to was any criticism because it would disturb the impression of harmony. Elizabeth deserved the label of hothead or rabble-rouser because she was a dangerous interloper.

The Outsider was a troublemaker: uninformed, unwanted, and dangerous. Mrs. Scudder from Florida wrote to Judge Waring, "Too bad your wife wasn't a good Southerner and understood the Negro race better."[62] Mrs. Duncan from Summerville charged that "The people in the South always got along with the colored people until an element from the North came here with one purpose in mind: to stir up strife."[63] Elizabeth was a Yankee agitator who did not know anything about the situation in the South and was causing more harm than good. The Outsider response attributed any racial unrest to nonsoutherners. The situation was fine as long as no one stirred up trouble. By dis-authorizing Elizabeth's speech, the letter writers evacuated her propositions of their political potency, which restored the artifice of unanimity.

George H. Lackey retorted that white southerners "were healthy enough both physically and morally and got along OK with the southern negro until people like you came here without an invitation to stir up something that <u>does not</u> concern you."[64] Ned Holland echoed Lackey in his letter: "We got along very well without her for many years and I am sure we can get along better for many years to come without her and others like her."[65] The letter writers' claims that Black and white people got along fine and everyone was happy erased the dehumanizing nature of Jim Crow. Upholding the appearance of good race relations was a matter of survival for Black people. Any hint of resistance or defiance could result in white violence against them. Elizabeth refused to perpetuate the lie. Since she did not go along with the lie, she was not a Good Southerner. The Outsider label stigmatized Elizabeth. It marked her as someone who did not belong to the white ingroup. It devalued her and delegitimized her speech.

Elizabeth was not only an outsider to the region. Letter writers turned to her gender and race to label her as an outsider to white femininity. Elizabeth tore asunder the sexual foundations of white supremacy. Because white women served as the repository of white racial legitimacy, white supremacy protected them, often with lethal methods. A respectable white woman accepted the mantle of protection. Elizabeth refused it when she condemned white supremacy. A white woman's public opposition to segregation placed her beyond the bounds of white respectability. A woman from Savannah wrote, "You are beneath the contempt of decent people."[66] A "True Southerner" from Texas called Elizabeth "white trash."[67]

Letter writers discredited Elizabeth by questioning her race. From Florida, "A True Southerner" expressed disbelief that Elizabeth was white: "Your speech to the Negroes gave me such a shudder to think of a white? Woman."[68] Mrs. Means from Texas read the article about Elizabeth's speech "with extreme horror" and was incredulous that "a white woman could have been fool enough to do such a thing."[69] Mrs. Means charged that Elizabeth "had better find out more about the negro before you try to push him on an equal basis with respectful white people."[70] Of uncertain race, Elizabeth was unworthy of respect for these letter writers. As Mrs. Gates from Georgia wrote, Elizabeth had "lost the respect of the white people."[71] Her public opposition to segregation rendered her nonwhite and no longer entitled to membership in the white ingroup. Labeling Elizabeth as an unrespectable white woman branded her. She failed to perform white femininity. As the letter writers removed Elizabeth's whiteness, they also removed the protection afforded to white women.

Because she failed to perform white femininity, Elizabeth was subject to abhorrent sexual stereotypes. White supremacists believed that Black women were promiscuous and accessible.[72] In the Jim Crow South, discussions of race necessarily involved questions of sex—they were one and the same. The specter of interracial sex was the *raison d'être* of white supremacy. Jim Crow was supposedly implemented to prevent contact, incidental or otherwise, between the races because such contact could lead to sex between Black men and white women. Elizabeth exposed herself to sexualized attacks, including the charge that she was a n-word lover. Letter writers reduced Elizabeth's advocacy for racial equality to sexual desire. An unsigned letter called Elizabeth an "old hussy" and suggested, "Maybe you are just hungry for a Negro buck. Looks like you could find one."[73] More than one letter writer suggested that one of Elizabeth's former husbands was a Negro.[74] Other letters were more graphic. One from New York City included a newspaper clipping of the speech with a handwritten note: "Here's hoping you're <u>raped</u> by a <u>diseased n-word</u>" (emphasis in original).⁷⁵ In her call to end segregation, Elizabeth erased the distance between Black and white bodies which threatened white womanhood, the core of white supremacy. The accusation that Elizabeth's activism was because of illicit sexual desire debased her and rendered her unrespectable to white supremacists. It further dis-authorized her speech. If Elizabeth was disqualified and dis-authorized, then her disruption could be dismissed and the appearance of unity restored.

Letter writers and newspaper editors deployed ad hominem attacks that jabbed at Elizabeth's divorces, remarriage, and social ostracism in order to discredit her. A respectable, proper *white* woman would not have extramarital affairs and divorce two husbands. They turned to her gender to delegitimize her rhetoric, a practice that persists to the present day for women. In comparison to Miss Annie, Elizabeth Waring fell short. The first Mrs. Waring was a lady, according to a writer from Augusta, Georgia, who knew her: Miss Annie was "one of the sweetest ladies you would want to meet."⁷⁶ A writer from Charleston wrote that Elizabeth used a n-word trick to steal Judge Waring.⁷⁷ "Magnolia White" accused Elizabeth of breaking up a "Southern woman's home, by taking her husband away." But, Miss Annie didn't lose much "by his being taken by you."⁷⁸ An unsigned letter from Tampa called Elizabeth "a calloused, barnacled old wart-faced Yankee" that the Judge had "such ill-luck and misfortune" to pick as his wife. The letter closed with advice for Elizabeth: "The best you can do hereafter is to keep that big mouth of yours shut."⁷⁹ These letter writers perceived Elizabeth's gender and marital history as legitimate points of attack. The comparison to the first Mrs. Waring intensified Elizabeth Waring's unrespectability, pushing her further outside white femininity. By stigmatizing her, they silenced her and restored the appearance of unanimity.

Letter writers classified Elizabeth's rhetorical attack on white southerners as revenge against those who socially banned her. The *Tallahassee Democrat* rejected Elizabeth as a legitimate advocate: "Stupid as her remark was, why be angry about it? She is just the girl who didn't get invited to the party and she had to say something catty about the hostess."⁸⁰ Hodding Carter classified Elizabeth's trouble as "social in the narrow meaning of the word" because the Warings were shunned in Charleston. Carter described Elizabeth as "the youngish, thrice-married Connecticut wife of elderly U. S. District Judge J. W. Waring of Charleston, S.C." After outlining the circumstances of the Warings' divorces and remarriage when Charleston was not "nice to Mrs. Waring back in 1945," Carter continued with "whatever their inner convictions, there can be no doubt that the judge and his wife are also intent upon getting even."[81] Someone mailed Carter's article to Elizabeth with the handwritten note "Too bad you didn't keep <u>quiet</u>! It would have been better to accept your <u>local</u> snubbing than to be a national joke and aren't we laughing!!!"[82] Elizabeth's motives were impure. After relegating her to the role of the spiteful woman, white southerners could reject Elizabeth's propositions about race relations.

Some letter writers did not use the coded language of "polite racism." They resorted to overt racism and threats. "A Southerner" who read of the speech in the Asheville (NC) *Citizen-Times* angrily responded that "The n-word is all right in his place, and that is right where we are going to keep them. I'm speaking for all good southerners, it makes our blood boil for the n-word loving white to try to force the n-word on us. Let well enough alone!"[83] White southerners were not weak or low because "what is any lower than the n-word loving whites?" "A Southerner" conceived of the Good Southerner as a person who reveled in the subjugation of Black people. A Good Southerner did not question or criticize the system. The letter writer intensified the supposed inherent superiority of white people by using derogatory labels for those who disagreed with them. From Laurens, a letter writer ominously predicted that if Elizabeth and her husband continued with their "beloved work," they would find themselves "way down <u>below</u> the negroes, in fact you may even get a coat of black paint you negro lovers. So you had better take <u>warning</u> (Mrs. Waring) you may have to swallow that word (decadent)."[84] The Grand Dragon of the Carolinas Associated Klaverns "promised to answer Mrs. Waring later."[85] White supremacy was the law of the South and there to stay. Because she denounced white supremacy, Elizabeth was subject to its violence. These letter writers threatened force to silence Elizabeth. The threats were intimidation tactics directed toward silencing Elizabeth *and* other white people. Once muzzled, the impression of racial harmony could be restored.

The responses to the speech attested to better race relations in the South, better treatment of Black people in the South, and the consent of Black people to segregation. More than a defense of the South, the responses smoothed the rupture in the illusion of unanimity. The appearance of unified consent to Jim Crow masked the tyranny of segregation and rendered criticism of it as rabble-rousing.

While the majority of the letters decried her toxic characterization of white southerners, Elizabeth also received affirming letters, flowers, and even a box of candy.[86] Immediately after the YWCA speech, members of the audience who attended that evening sent simple, heartfelt letters of thanks. Unlike the anonymous damning letters, these writers signed their names along with "and family." The Glenn and Byrd families sent notes telling Elizabeth that they enjoyed hearing her speak.⁸⁷ From Aiken, Mary Miles and her family thanked Elizabeth for her beautiful address.⁸⁸ Mrs. Brice and Mrs. Johnson, both of Winnsboro, also thanked Elizabeth for the speech.⁸⁹ Since the writers were physically present when Elizabeth delivered the speech, they were most likely middle-class African American South Carolinians. They sent brief, handwritten expressions of gratitude.

Other letter writers expressed their appreciation for Elizabeth's speech and the Warings' advocacy for racial equality. George Gramblin of Aiken wrote, "I am writing to express my appreciation for that wonderful speech you made in the YWCA meeting a few days ago. My family sends many thanks to you all, and may you both live long and keep up the good work."⁹⁰ Reverend and Mrs. J. H. McKissick also sent a note of encouragement, "We want you to know that we highly appreciate the attitude you have toward our race and for the many worth while things you have said and done. We assure you that we will do all we can to build on the foundation you have laid."⁹¹ Mrs. E. L. Wheeler Sr., secretary of the Pendleton, South Carolina NAACP branch, assured Elizabeth, "Our branch of the NAACP here . . . is doing its best to train our folk to be good citizens. I believe we are doing a good job, therefore you can depend on us to do our part."⁹² These writers understood that the fight for racial equality was a long-term endeavor that required white allies. They informed Elizabeth of their resistance to white supremacy and assured her of their support as she supported them.

The central theme of those who responded favorably to Elizabeth remarked on her courage. She broke the silence so that others could also speak out. Timothy Tyson argues that Southern white liberals failed to make the most of the moments of possibility after World War II in part because the "violent coercion that marked the everyday politics of race in the South and the slim chance of recruiting other supportive whites silenced most potential 'race traitors.'"⁹³ Mr. and Mrs. H. R. Scott, a Black couple who read the speech in the *Augusta Chronicle* (GA), realized the need for white people to speak out: "In our efforts to break down segregation and discrimination, it is heart-warming to know that there are other citizens who are able to analyze the race problem, see its ugliness, and openly do something about it."⁹⁴ From Duluth, Mr. and Mrs. F. Taylor, a Black couple, wrote that "In this Democracy we need more people that will up hold what they believe in. And will not be a coward in the cause of human justice."⁹⁵ Mrs. Alma Illery, speaking for eight thousand members of the National Achievement Clubs, said, "May God send us more people like you who are courageous so that we may have life and have it more abundantly."⁹⁶ An editor for the *Atlanta Daily World* proclaimed, "What a great change would come over the entire

Southland in a short while, if only others with similar influence and spiritual leadership would come out and take a positive stand for justice and equality!"[97] The *Pittsburgh Courier* saluted Elizabeth for her "courage to point out the right road to the South."[98] These writers recognized the need for other white people to publicly speak out in order to transform the repressive rhetorical culture of Jim Crow. Judge Waring said, "The wall of segregation crumbles only when somebody swings a hammer."[99] The letter writers and news media that praised Elizabeth for her courage recognized the barriers that silenced other white people from speaking out against segregation. Eliminating the legal sanction for segregation required collective action among Black and white people.

Just as her speech was not confined to the physical audience present on January 16, the letters that Elizabeth received did not remain private. Her strategic circulation of the responses served two purposes. The negative responses and threats lent credence to her claim that white southerners were "sick, confused, and decadent" and, as a group, sustained white supremacy. Circulating the affirming responses had the potential to prompt white people to publicly voice their opposition to Jim Crow. Because of the letters that Waties received after the primary rulings, Elizabeth knew that a dormant collective of white people existed who opposed white supremacy.[100] Elizabeth maintained that her speech, what she called her "shock treatment," broke "the conspiracy of silence on the mistreatment of Negroes in the Deep South."[101]

Elizabeth circulated the letters to create an imagined community—people dispersed through space, strangers to one another but connected through common beliefs and values.[102] Although the letters were addressed only to her, once she circulated them, the letters addressed indefinite others. Elizabeth hoped that the body of strangers would find themselves in the letters and organize as a public collective.[103] Circulation of the letters prompted awareness among oppositional white people that others thought like them. A man from Missouri articulated the primary obstacle to social change: "God bless you, lady for having character, strength, and bravery enough to speak your mind, in this country of ours where most people think, but are afraid to speak, for fear of ridicule."[104] Beyond whispers within a small social circle, Elizabeth exposed antipathy towards Jim Crow as more prevalent among white people than the public conversation indicated. The circulation of the positive responses to "Freedom Is Everybody's Job" shattered the illusion of unanimity among white southerners.

When Elizabeth sent the newspaper clipping of her speech to Thurgood Marshall on January 17, she wrote, "Also many threats coming over the telephone—harassing me 'Get Out of Town' splendid for the Cause!"[105]

Elizabeth's glee at being harassed indicates that she anticipated and welcomed the response. The Black and white press reported on the flood of telephone calls that Elizabeth received the morning after the speech. The callers told her to get out of town, called her a n-word lover, and "other insulting and vicious statements during the assault."[106] John McCray's articles in the *Lighthouse and Informer* and *Pittsburgh Courier* described how Elizabeth was "the target of vicious hate groups here this week."[107] The *Chicago Defender* included extensive quotes from the speech along with Elizabeth's reassurance that "she could not be intimidated by abuse and demands that she 'get out of town.'"[108] She dismissed the threats just as white supremacists dismissed her. Furthermore, her public disdain undermined the claim that her speech was motivated by spite against white society. *Time Magazine* reported on the brickbats "wrapped in white rage" and the telegrams of praise that Elizabeth received. She calmly responded, "I realize that if one has a cause, one has to be willing to suffer for it."[109] Her resolute stance in the midst of the barrage accentuated her courage.

Walter White wrote that the *News and Courier* miscalculated the response to its publication of "Freedom Is Everybody's Job" because along with threatening phone calls and letters, Elizabeth also received "admiring letters from many Negro and white Southerners who thanked God that one person had the grit to speak the truth."[110] McCray insisted that "everytime a word of disapproval is spoken against what she believes and advocates, it produces a new convert."[111] While Elizabeth foresaw the censure from white supremacists, "there was even more pronounced jubilance on the liberal side."[112] The *Chicago Defender* editorialized that Judge and Mrs. Waring's courageous actions "inspire us to believe that Dixie may yet be redeemed in the years to come." The Warings represented a "growing army of sane citizens in the mad land and we wish them Godspeed."[113] The editorial reiterated Elizabeth and Waties's belief that other white southerners agreed with them.

John McCray believed that white people in the South were "as enslaved to avenues of speaking as are Negroes to jimcrow seating." He expressed that "not only is she inspiring and encouraging the suppressed, but she is enlivening the hearts of other white citizens who feel the same as she; and they are right here in South Carolina."[114] Elizabeth agreed. The threat of repercussions silenced those who dissented which maintained the false impression of unity. The affirming responses circulated in the press fractured the image of cohesion among white southerners. Elizabeth's open defiance of white supremacy's rhetorical boundaries could lead to "further words and acts of daring."[115] Elizabeth's strategy depended upon other white people feeling emboldened by the discovery, through the circulation of the positive responses, that others felt the same as they did about white supremacy. Their public opposition to Jim Crow could negate the vocal white supremacists.

A few weeks after Elizabeth delivered "Freedom Is Everybody's Job," she and Waties went to New York City for Waties to preside. In New York, Elizabeth sorted through the letters that she had received in response to her speech. She had difficulty keeping up with the correspondence but tried to answer each letter personally. Elizabeth circulated the responses privately within the fledgling network she nurtured. The positive letters supported Elizabeth's declaration in "Freedom Is Everybody's Job" that "all the world is behind you now to establish the rights and equality that is already yours, but only needs enforcing" (3). From Pennsylvania, Dr. Laurence Frank wrote to Elizabeth and enclosed copies of his letters to *Time Magazine* and Governor Thurmond. In his letter to Elizabeth, Dr. Frank confessed that he was not often stirred to act in "purely altruistic" causes but that Elizabeth had a way of projecting some of her "fiery indignation" onto others. Dr. Frank hoped that his letters would "help a little bit to win the war, eventually."[116] Since Dr. Frank referred to racial equality as an altruistic cause, he was most likely a white man. His letter confirmed Elizabeth's claim that there was "a tremendous rising up of people all over the country, as a united body, white and Negro, to take this matter into their own hands and see that Justice is done" (3). Elizabeth transcribed Dr. Frank's letters—all three of them—on her manual typewriter and then mailed them to Ruby Cornwell.[117] Elizabeth asked Cornwell to show the letters to other Black activists in Charleston, such as Septima Clark and Susan Dart Butler. With Cornwell as the channel, Dr. Frank's letters reached Black leaders in Clarendon County and Charleston. Those letters signaled that other white people supported their resistance to white supremacy.

The bombardment against Elizabeth continued in the weeks after she delivered "Freedom Is Everybody's Job" culminating on February 8 with a petition to impeach Waties. The petition charged that Waties "has openly, through his wife, advocated dissension, on the part of Negro citizens against the white citizens of South Carolina."[118] The four men who initiated the petition were from Aiken County. John Stansfield, who filed the petition of bias against Waties in one of the primary cases, was also from Aiken. The county borders Georgia—a hotbed of Klan activity. The men denied "that the Ku Klux Klan has anything to do with it." They also claimed that out of one thousand signatories, only two criticized "Judge Waring's decision letting negroes into the Democratic party." Instead, they objected to what his wife had been saying and then saying that she was speaking for him.[119]

In his press release in response to the circulating petition, Waties pointed out the inconsistency between American ideals and white supremacy: "I understand that the petition attacks my fitness as a judge because I do not believe in white supremacy. I welcome that explanation. I think that any judge or other Federal or State official who attempts to pass upon the rights of American citizens blinded by color prejudice is an unfit public servant." Waties welcomed "the comparison between these views of mine and those of the proslavery or white supremacy groups as voiced by their spokesman of the Ku Klux Klan. The more light shed on this campaign of prejudice the better."[120] Since the *Elmore v. Rice* ruling, Waties persistently decried white southerners' continued subversion of American democracy. He invoked his authority as a federal judge to contrast rights guaranteed under the United States Constitution with the denial of those rights in the South. Waties did not have to respond to the petition, but the response from him was newsworthy, increased circulation of the negative reaction to Elizabeth's speech, and offered another example of courage for silent white southerners.

The Warings' rhetorical strategy depended upon a response from white southerners. And they responded. Waties said it was unpleasant "to have your telephone ringing day and night with anonymous messages." But the Warings re-circulated the impeachment petition, harassing phone calls, and threatening letters to disclose the depth and depravity of white supremacy in the South. The predictable response fueled the Warings' determination. It also generated more publicity. Waties surmised that the attacks on them "aroused the nation greatly."[121] As animosity towards the Warings increased in the South, so did admiration for the couple's courage surge beyond the region. With each speech and media interview, the Warings received more letters—both positive and negative—that they circulated to a wider audience. Elizabeth's letters to Cornwell were filled with optimism and enthusiasm: "It should encourage you as it has me this avalanche of response of an aroused people all over this country.... Yes, darling Ruby, the world is aroused and going to do something soon—keep up hope" (emphasis in original).[122] In the coming months, the Warings would repeatedly deploy the reaction to "Freedom Is Everybody's Job" to bolster their call for outside help to cure the South.

Chapter 5

ONLY FORCE WILL WORK

To activate the branches of the federal government and circumvent the southern white political structure, Elizabeth and Waties proposed to galvanize the public with their speeches. The American public was silent when the Dixiecrats' roadblocks first weakened the Democratic Party's strong civil rights plank in 1948 and was silent again when southern Democrats blocked federal civil rights legislation. No one protested! A shift in the voting public's attitudes could modify or alter the federal government's ineffective course.[1] The Warings' rhetoric could provoke white people to publicly condemn segregation. Their goal was to remove the barriers that silenced people so they would talk. *Any* public response could further expose the hypocrisy of democracy in the South. With each attack on the Warings, white supremacists exposed the contradiction between American democracy and white supremacy.

Elizabeth and Waties had little faith in the possibility that the executive or legislative branches would effect change. Southern representatives in Congress retained the filibuster, which diminished the potential that federal legislation was a viable vehicle for change. After Truman's victory in 1948, it never occurred to Elizabeth that Congress would not go ahead with his civil rights program.[2] Elizabeth believed that the Truman administration and Republicans appeased the Dixiecrats. She thought that the NAACP had given the administration plenty of time, so much time that the association's patience was perceived as a sign of weakness. Elizabeth reasoned that with this proof of Truman's betrayal, it was time for "rough methods ONLY."[3]

The southern Democrats' success in preserving the filibuster proved that Elizabeth's impatience with the executive and legislative branches was not unreasonable. *To Secure These Rights* was published in 1947, and Truman delivered his civil rights plan to Congress on February 2, 1948. Despite the NAACP's decades-long efforts, Congress had not passed a federal antilynching law or eliminated the poll tax. With persistent inaction from Congress and the president, Elizabeth and Waties looked to the force of public opinion and federal law to support the forthcoming school segregation case from Clarendon County. Even with the national publicity and heated response to Elizabeth's Charleston YWCA speech, one speech was insufficient to arouse public opinion to the degree necessary to abolish segregation laws. The Warings launched a rhetorical blitzkrieg of nine speeches delivered from February 11 to April 30, 1950. Remarkable consistencies exist among the speeches delivered over an eleven-week period. Elizabeth's speech to the Black Charleston YWCA was not an isolated incident. Waties's rulings from the bench were not his only advocacy for racial equality. The Warings' prolific rhetorical activity in 1950 points to a purposeful campaign designed with the specific objective of removing barriers to speech so that white people would publicly oppose segregation.[4]

Elizabeth was *the* controversy in January 1950 and a guaranteed ratings draw. The way she spoke of the South, white southerners, and Black people identified the Charleston YWCA speech as a happening the news media could ill afford to ignore.[5] Excerpts from the speech were printed in the *Atlanta Journal, Chicago Defender, New York Times, Time Magazine, Washington Post, Afro-American, Pittsburgh Courier, Kansas Plain Dealer,* and Charleston's *News and Courier*.[6] The press coverage of her shock treatment at the Charleston YWCA garnered her an invitation to appear on NBC's national television show, *Meet the Press*, on February 11, 1950.

Meet the Press first aired in 1945 as a radio program on the Mutual Broadcasting System. The innovative format, developed by Lawrence Spivak and Martha Rountree, moved to television on NBC in 1947, "before there were even 1 million sets in the nation."[7] On the February 11th show, Spivak served as moderator and assembled a panel of journalists from the southern and northeastern United States: May Craig of the *Press-Herald* (Portland, Maine), Mary Cottrell, Washington correspondent for the *Charlotte Observer* and *The News* (Greenville, South Carolina), Edward Jamieson of the Houston *Chronicle*, and Louis Lautier of the *Atlanta Daily World*. The panelists' questions focused on the YWCA speech and delved further into Elizabeth's stance on civil rights. Cottrell first asked how Elizabeth came to the conclusion that "whites down here are a sick, confused, and decadent people."[8] Elizabeth replied that she reached that conclusion by living in the South and observing them: "Any people who enslave the minds and bodies of another people are bound to destroy their own souls."[9] She refuted the concept that segregation's deleterious effects were limited to Black people. Elizabeth planted the idea that segregation harmed white people.

In the first few minutes of the show, Elizabeth had to explain what she meant by revolution, likened the Deep South to the Soviet Union, and proclaimed herself a southerner despite living in Charleston for only five years. She called Hodding Carter a "Southern parlor liberal" who was more dangerous than white supremacists (564–65). Furthermore, she described the "deep South press" as a "propaganda organ for the Dixiecrat movement," calling out the *News and Courier* by name (568). Craig tried to discuss political matters like the Fair Employment Practices Committee (FEPC) and Truman's civil rights program, but Elizabeth deftly turned the conversation with responses like "I can't speak for President Truman. I don't pretend to be on the inside and understand his mind," or "I have not frankly read the law." In response to one question, Elizabeth impatiently said, "I'm afraid the political aspect of it wouldn't interest me very much. I'm absorbed in the civil rights part."[10]

In the Charleston YWCA speech, Elizabeth did not directly address interracial sex. On *Meet the Press*, she did not hesitate when Craig asked if Elizabeth wanted civil rights or social integration for Black people. Elizabeth told Craig, "I want the whole thing. I want him to go through the same door, and so does the Judge. I want him to be an equal citizen. I want him to have the same opportunity, exactly the same. There's nothing in our Constitution that made it possible for white men to decide those things" (565–66). Elizabeth spoke of equal rights in terms of democracy and the Constitution. When Craig asked if Elizabeth saw "a distinction, however, between civil rights and social integration," Elizabeth interrupted her before Craig could finish the sentence, "I see none." Civil rights meant the right to vote. Social integration meant (sexual) contact between the races. For white supremacists, social equality inevitably led to Black men's sexual access to white women. For Elizabeth, the domino theory was without foundation.

Just as most of her YWCA speech was ignored because of her virulent tirade against white southerners, the press and public honed in on Elizabeth's response to one of the last questions from the panel. Cottrell referred to the photograph of Walter White and Poppy Cannon in the Warings' home. White was the Executive Secretary of the NAACP. He divorced his first wife to marry Poppy Cannon, a white woman. Cottrell asked, "Does this mean that you favor inter-marriage of the races, which is illegal in South Carolina?" Without hesitation, Elizabeth answered, "I certainly do. My husband is a U. S. Judge and we believe that our state should be a part of the U.S. and not have separate laws. I see no reason if they choose to marry why they shouldn't" (568). Then and there, Elizabeth admitted that there was nothing wrong with interracial marriage. And, it should not be illegal in South Carolina. Her unambiguous response aligned with Gunnar Myrdal's recommendation in *An American Dilemma*: "to have an open and sober discussion in rational terms of this ever present popular theory of 'intermarriage' and 'social equality,' giving matters their factual ground, true proportions, and logical relations."[11] In his letter to the Warings, R. T. Ashurst from California wrote, "The big smoke screen in the equal rights issue is that equality means intermarriage 'Would you want your daughter to marry a n-word?.' That's all hogwash.... It's only egotism of the white man that leads him to think all the dark-skin races are panting for intermarriage."[12] Elizabeth recalled, "This apparently was the South's never-never region, and the storm wasn't long in breaking."[13] It was the South's never-never region in more ways than one. With her responses on *Meet the Press*, Elizabeth knew she was setting herself up as the brunt of "THE FOUL AND OBSCENE FILTH OF SLANDER THEY SPREAD ABOUT ANYONE WHO CRITICIZES THEM" (emphasis in original).[14] However, as the foul and obscene filth circulated in the press, it provoked more conversation and publicity. With her declaration, Elizabeth plunged into a labyrinth of politics, myth, sex, and race—all wound tightly and ready to explode like dynamite.

In *An American Dilemma*, Myrdal explained that "Sex and race fears are, however, even today the main defense for segregation and, in fact, for the whole caste order." The persistent preoccupation with interracial sex and marriage was rationalization. At the core, "*what white people really want is to keep the Negroes in a lower status*" (emphasis in original).[15] Instead of openly voicing a demand for difference in social status between the races, white supremacists relied on racial purity as their defense. Until the interracial sex defense was exposed, race relations could not be transformed. Based on Myrdal's recommendation to have an open and sober discussion, the Warings determined to start that discussion. The rhetorical dilemma was that an argument based on reason was inadequate to dispel the emotionally charged and deeply entrenched myth of white racial purity. Milton Mayer wrote that "The segregationists say that the issue is sexual intercourse of Negroes with whites and the consequent amalgamation of the races.... As long as the integrationists go on saying that the issue is nothing but civil rights, they will be talking to themselves."[16] Elizabeth commanded attention because she did not avoid the issue of interracial sex. The question "Would you want your daughter to marry a n-word?" effectively silenced dissenters. Elizabeth did not run from the issue but retorted, "Why shouldn't she be free to marry whomever she chooses?" She slung the segregationists' grenade of interracial sex right back at them. Her goal was not to convince white supremacists of their racism. Instead, she provoked them to defend the indefensible and, thereby, expose the white racial purity defense. Either one was a full citizen or one was not: "Anything in between was simply delusion and evasion of the fundamental essence of American democracy."[17] For the Warings, full citizenship was not possible with separate-but-equal because separate simply could not be equal.

On February 12, in the first line of its article, the *News and Courier* reported that Mrs. J. Waties Waring spoke "in favor of complete breakdown of separation of the races in the South and intermarriage among whites and negroes."[18] Elizabeth confirmed the white South's worst fears about desegregation and subjected herself to detestable letters *and* more media attention. The tone in the letters Elizabeth and Waties received after the YWCA speech was revolting, but it pales in comparison to the crudeness and misogyny pouring from those received after *Meet the Press*. Marion Wright of the Southern Regional Council explained, "But the overwhelming majority of these hundreds of anonymous missives reek of the livery stable. Yankee. Divorce. N-word loving. These are the central ideas. But sex and the bodily functions are the vehicles for developing these themes—words usually reserved for the backyard fences and public toilets."[19]

According to James W. Vander Zanden, by the turn of the twentieth century, the miscegenation doctrine had been elevated to a cardinal position in southern society. The taboo against sex between Black men and white women was invested with mystical properties. As a result, white supremacists believed that the fate of humanity and society was inextricably bound with obedience to the taboo.[20] Mrs. Ernest Wood's letter reflected white people's outrage. When Elizabeth said, "let them marry if they want to," Mrs. Wood would have spit in her face if she had been near the judge's wife.[21] Elizabeth had said the unspeakable. Just as Dorothy Tilly, Anne Braden, and Sarah Patton Boyle were accused of desiring Black men, Elizabeth was charged with illicit sexual yearnings—again. Elizabeth was even more vulnerable to the charge because she was twice divorced. She wanted sex with Black men: "when a white person has fallen as low as you have. Yes—you belong to a big Black n-word."[22] One writer suggested, "Perhaps you are well fortified with the sex knowledge of a n-word. . . . Did a n-word ever hold you tightly . . . May be he has something you really want."[23] After Elizabeth failed to comply with white supremacy's "normative demands" of chastity, frailty, and graciousness, she "forfeited the claim to personal security."[24] When she violated the taboo against interracial sex, Elizabeth lost the shield of whiteness to protect her.[25]

More than one letter writer commented that since Elizabeth believed in divorce, why didn't she get one from the judge and marry a Black man since she loved them so much. Mrs. Robert Martin from Detroit suggested, "If you like n-word so well, I advocate your obtaining a divorce from the Judge, and marrying a nice fat oily juicy and I might add, smelly, black man."[26]

Mrs. Martin's suggestion was not unique or creative. Another "True Southerner" wrote, "Since you believe in marriage between negroes and whites, and also are a believer and a participant in divorces why don't you divorce your husband and marry a negroe, and make yourself the perfect example . . . believing so strong as you do????"[27] A letter "From one who used to know you very well, socially," warned Elizabeth, "If you continue your practice of breaking up homes, and getting divorces, it would surprise no one if your next husband would be a negroe."[28] "Your friend" was more explicit in his suggestion: "To show that you are acting in good faith I suggest that you divorce the old Judge who is getting old . . . as you made him divorce his wife of 30 years. . . . I suggest you pick a nice black negro young enough to give you what you want. . . . I hope you can still have several black children."[29] A "couple of white decent and respectable people" asked, "Are you getting tired of your white husband, that you want to change to a black color."[30] Those who slung this insult considered it the worst thing that they could say about Elizabeth. They intended to debase her. After white supremacists called Elizabeth an n-word lover, they could dismiss her.

Although the letters after *Meet the Press* turned vulgar, Elizabeth also received a number of missives thanking her for her courage, just as she did after the Charleston YWCA speech. John Panks from Atlanta pointed out, "We, as Americans, need more people like you each day to help America to stand for the basic principles for which it was founded."[31] From New Jersey, Fred Colvin assured Elizabeth and Waties that they were not alone: "It takes courage to do the work you both are doing and it may help a bit to know that many people are with you in it."[32] Someone sent a telegram thanking God for Elizabeth's courage and forthrightness that would inspire thousands to help in her efforts for human rights.[33]

While the obscene letters outnumbered the encouraging ones, Elizabeth ensured that the supportive letters reached an audience other than herself. Just like after the Charleston YWCA speech, Elizabeth transcribed the letters and sent them to Ruby Cornwell. A Black man from Georgetown, South Carolina, explained that he understood why the white man did not speak for Black people because "the sacrifice is so great." He was grateful that "someone has spoken for us and spoken effectively."[34] Two letters from white men, both originally from the South, praised Elizabeth. One approved of her "shock treatment" for the "sick, harmful persons" in the South who perpetuated the "decadent, poisonous system" that mocked true democracy.[35] Elizabeth shared the letters to encourage Cornwell and other Black activists. The positive letters confirmed Elizabeth and Waties's belief that other white people opposed white supremacy.

With Elizabeth's responses on *Meet the Press*, South Carolina had had enough! On February 14, 1950, the South Carolina legislature adopted a joint resolution to purchase two one-way tickets for Elizabeth and Waties "to any point of their choice provided they never return to the State of South Carolina." The resolution allocated "the necessary funds to erect a suitable plaque to Federal Judge and Mrs. Waring in the Mule Barn at said [Clemson] College."[36] The South Carolina legislature's grandstanding demonstrated that elected representatives played a role in maintaining the illusion of consensus about segregation. The white men ridiculed the Warings by including the plaque at the mule barn. At the same time, their attempt to run the Warings out of the state affirmed Jim Crow storytelling that race relations were harmonious as long as no one stirred up anything. The resolution became public knowledge because numerous letter writers referred to "your 'one way ticket' would be gladly paid."[37]

For the Warings, segregation was not an effect of racism. It was the cause. Legal segregation reinforced the erroneous belief in the inferiority of Black people. They witnessed Jim Crow justice and received letters that spewed vile lies about Black people. In his *Reminiscences*, Waties explained, "I think that the fight in the South is primarily a fight of law, and I iterate and reiterate over and over again—I intend it that way—the fact that when you have crystallized bias, in this case racial bias, into law, you have made it very difficult to make any change in the feelings of the people. You can't wait for the sentiment of people to change if it's unlawful for them to change."[38] The Warings had no interest in dictating that Black and white people socialize. However, because segregation fossilized the belief that Black people were inferior, white people refused to view them as citizens entitled to rights guaranteed under the US Constitution.

After Elizabeth's *Meet the Press* appearance, Elizabeth and Waties traveled across the United States and addressed eight associations. They repeated the same points and arguments in their speeches. First, they bolstered the Truman administration's claim that continued discrimination and violence against Black people diminished the United States' standing on the world stage. Second, they railed against the lack of an open discussion about the Race Problem, acknowledging people's fear of repercussions if they spoke out. Elizabeth had rallied the audience on *Meet the Press*: "I am afraid our government seems to be failing to do it along the usual procedure of the Congress and Senate, and if they fail to, the people are the ones that are going to take it up. And if my letters that I received from all over the U.S. and even further are an indication, the people are going to pick the ball up and insist."[39] The speeches and interviews in the spring of 1950 were crafted to get people "to pick the ball up." The Warings' repeated references to the affirming letters revealed the existence of white people who agreed with them. Because of the deadlock in Congress, Elizabeth and Waties encouraged audiences to publicly voice their opinions and pressure elected representatives.

Waties delivered two speeches in February 1950, the first on February 21 to the Harlem Lawyers Association and the second on February 26 to the Harlem Interracial Platform. The *New York Amsterdam News* included multiple photographs of the Harlem Lawyers Association Dinner.[40] Waties's speech, "Civil Rights and Segregation in the Deep South," to the Interracial Platform received extensive coverage in the Black press. The Platform organized a reception for Elizabeth after its meeting.[41] The next month, on March 17, Elizabeth and Waties accepted citations from the American Council on Human Rights (ACHR) in Washington, DC. Elmer W. Henderson, the plaintiff in a railroad dining car case, served as director of ACHR. At the end of March, the Warings traveled to Chicago and Minneapolis. Waties was the principal speaker at the twenty-fourth annual meeting of the Minneapolis Urban League at Coffman Memorial Union. In Chicago, Waties addressed white and Black members of the Cook County Bar Association at a luncheon. That evening, the Warings were guests of honor at a dinner party before Waties delivered "The Birth of a New South" to nearly one thousand people gathered for a public mass meeting at Tabernacle Baptist Church. In early April, the Warings returned to Washington, DC, where the city's chapter of the National Lawyers Guild honored Waties. On April 2, Elizabeth addressed more than two hundred persons in Amalgamated Clothing Workers Hall at the invitation of the Richmond Committee on Civil Rights. Waties also made brief remarks in Richmond. Their call in Richmond for "force" triggered L. Mendel Rivers, who crusaded for Waties's impeachment—again. On April 30, Elizabeth closed the National YWCA's week of celebration with "Priorities at Home," delivered at Tindley Temple Methodist Church in Philadelphia.

In the midst of their speaking engagements, Elizabeth and Waties granted several interviews with journalists. From February 19 through the end of March 1950, the news media published six interviews with the Warings: two with Waties, three with Elizabeth, and one with both of them. Before delivering the speeches in Harlem, Waties gave an interview to the *Sunday Compass*, the weekend edition of the *Daily Compass*. George Kenney's interview with Elizabeth for the *New York World-Telegram* on February 22, 1950, was distributed through the Associated Press and published in the *Richmond Times-Dispatch*.[42] For the *New York Post*, Tom Poston wrote an extensive article about Elizabeth.[43] The *Afro-American* published James Hicks's interview with Waties on March 4, 1950. James Booker met with Elizabeth at

Essex House for his article in the *New York Amsterdam News* on March 11.[44] In March 1950, Lillian Scott, a reporter for the *Chicago Defender*, wrote "The Warings of South Carolina: South's Most Courageous Couple."[45] An Associated Press article about the Warings by Sam Summerlin, published on April 20, 1950, coincided with *Collier's* article that featured Elizabeth and Waties in their Meeting Street home. The *Collier's* article included a photograph of the couple hosting a gathering of Black guests at their dinner table.

After World War II ended, the tensions between the United States and the Soviet Union reached an apex as the two powers sought to gain influence over states that had achieved autonomy or outright independence from European colonial rulers. The Truman Administration grew increasingly concerned in the 1940s and 1950s that as formerly colonized nations gained independence, Soviet-supported communist parties might achieve power in the new states, thereby shifting the international balance of power in favor of the Soviet Union.[46] The Warings were cognizant of the international dimension of domestic racial violence, disenfranchisement, and discrimination. Both remarked upon the hypocrisy of the United States promoting democracy on a global scale. In Richmond, Elizabeth said, "White supremacy and the politicians are like Russia. They coerce with lynchings and threats. We can never prove democracy that way."[47] Waties was more emphatic about the outright duplicity of the United States promoting itself as the beacon of equality: "How can the United States face the world and demand justice for minorities of the world when we have it [racial segregation] in our own back yard?"[48] In his remarks about the international dimension of Jim Crow, Waties conceived of racial oppression as a taint upon American democracy. It sullied the United States, both domestically and globally. Therefore, it needed to be cleaned up: "How are we going to plant the garden of democracy in the world until we clean up our own little dirty back yard?"[49]

The Soviet Union's propaganda campaigns exploited racial discrimination and violence in the United States.[50] Waties identified this problem when he told the Minneapolis Urban League that any progress in the South was too slow "in the face of national events and the international crisis, precipitated by the need for us to sell the democratic ideology to other peoples throughout the world."[51] In an interview with the Associated Press, Waties said that "American delegates in the United Nations are being asked by other nations, 'Where is democracy in South Carolina and Mississippi?'"[52] The persistent second-class status for Black citizens diminished the United States' standing on the global stage as it combated the Soviet Union. The Warings understood that abolishing Jim Crow laws would validate the United States as the leader of the free world and eliminate the Soviet Union's most potent propaganda tool. By connecting white supremacy in the South to America's international standing, the Warings cast Jim Crow as a national, not regional, issue.

At the same time, they acknowledged the barriers in the South for those who wished to change the situation. The Warings connected fear, silence, and courage to the ongoing battle to eliminate white supremacy's stranglehold on national politics and public conversation. As he did with the National Lawyers Guild members, Waties asked the Harlem Lawyers Association members to take the lead by carrying his message and making people face the issues because "That is the thing that is wrong with the South. They do not discuss, talk, or throw publicity on the race question, and as long as you keep it underground, the longer we will need relief."[53] Without any discussion, a problem did not exist. In order to turn public opinion against white supremacy, Elizabeth and Waties needed to activate a discussion about the Race Problem in the South. In her interview with Tom Poston, Elizabeth declared, "The really important thing is this: We've pierced the Iron Curtain. We've broken the conspiracy of silence on the mistreatment of Negroes in the Deep South. We've made them admit in South Carolina, for the first time, that it is an issue. Before, they wouldn't even talk about it, or let anyone else talk about."[54] The absence of a public conversation in the South fostered the illusion of consensus about segregation and discrimination. The Warings' propositions forced white supremacists to defend segregation. People were finally talking.

Based on the affirming letters that they received, the Warings knew that fear silenced white people who opposed racial inequality. In Washington, DC, Waties told the audience that people were afraid to speak out against segregation because they were afraid of losing their jobs and ostracism, "And maybe in some instances their lives are jeopardized if they step into the light and recognize the principle of anti-segregation."[55] Elizabeth characterized the people who were "still afraid to speak out yet" as an unorganized "small underground." Although small and unorganized, Elizabeth optimistically predicted that they would "help us rip down the Iron Curtain and carry on until liberation comes—as it must and will from outside the South."[56] Elizabeth insisted some white southerners agreed with her, but white supremacy censured any criticism so thoroughly that she implored those outside the South to lend their support.

To hasten liberation, Elizabeth and Waties had to transform attitudes about gradualism. Elizabeth and Waties condemned gradualism because if white southerners were left alone to remedy the situation, it would never right itself. Waties wrote of the impasse in his 1948 letter to President Truman: the white South would never voluntarily change race relations. To strengthen their central argument for federal interference in the South, they invoked medical imagery. The claim that white southerners were "sick, confused, and decadent" was attributed to Elizabeth. But Waties first said it in a 1948 interview with Lillian Scott.[57] The Warings called white supremacy a disease. As a disease, it required intervention. The Race Problem was not due to Black people's inferiority but white people's sickness. White southerners were sick and could not cure themselves. Therefore, outside help was necessary. The medical metaphor served to create a sense of urgency about a situation so that bold action was required.[58] It evacuated white southerners' agency, constituted gradualism as untenable, and offered federal law as the only possible curative.

Elizabeth and Waties proclaimed that the problem in the South was "not a Negro problem, but a white problem."[59] Waties first introduced this turn of phrase at the National Lawyers Guild Banquet in 1949. Instead of white supremacy's claim that segregation was due to "the characteristics of black people—if not their outright inferiority, something at least problematic about their attributes," Elizabeth and Waties attributed segregation to the diseased white supremacist.[60] Elizabeth clarified her characterization of white southerners in the Charleston YWCA speech: "There's no hope of reasoning with the Southern whites. They've all got the disease of supremacy."[61] Waties drew upon his ethos as a federal judge and native white southerner when he said, "The white people of my part of the country are sick mentally, obsessed with the false doctrine of white supremacy."[62] To support their assertion, the Warings circulated the condemnatory responses they received as evidence of white southerners' insanity. Waties acknowledged that they received "some crazy, crackpot, ignorant and unsigned" letters.[63] Elizabeth told Tom Poston, "Not that I need it but I said the white supremacists were suffering from insanity and obsession, and these letters prove it." Along with the letters, the Warings' detractors harassed them with phone calls. Elizabeth was undaunted: "I guess they got a surprise even in that. They expected me to slam down the receiver, but I didn't. I talked back." Waties "chucklingly recalled" to Tom Poston about the calls in the middle of the night, saying nothing and "just trying to keep us awake."[64] Reasonable people do not make harassing phone calls or send threatening letters.

Because racialism was a mental disease and insanity, it had to be handled as such.[65] It could not be cured with "sweet reason or psychoanalysis."[66] Elizabeth believed that "Brutal, cruel and insane people cannot be reasoned with and never have been cured that way."[67] Although they could not be reasoned with, they could be cured, but in a specific way. Elizabeth prescribed the "shock treatment" as the only treatment to penetrate the wall of silence in the South. Just as the mentally ill could not cure themselves, white southerners could not heal themselves or the region. Waties charged that the South, in order to cure its malady, needed "treatment just as does an alcoholic or mental patient."[68] The medical metaphor constituted white southerners as helpless. Therefore, the Warings claimed that "Only force from the outside will help."[69]

To substantiate the need for force, Elizabeth and Waties had to eliminate gradualism as a viable curative. Gradualism operated on the premise that "only through gradual change, acceptable to the white majority, could racial reform take place in the South."[70] Elizabeth and Waties condemned so-called southern liberals and the Good Southerners who balked at systemic transformation. For Elizabeth, "Parlor liberals are snakes in the grass."[71] Waties agreed. He said that the solution was to remove "all legal bars to equality" because "It will never cure itself by being let alone, by wishful thinking, by accession to the suggestions of the so-called southern liberal who goes only half-way, whose thinking is muddled, whose battle cry is 'Let us alone, we will reform ourselves.'"[72] At the Harlem Lawyers Association dinner, Waties assured the audience that they had no reason to fear white supremacists like Mississippi Congressman John E. Rankin or Georgia Governor Herman Talmadge because they would soon be wiped out. Waties warned the audience that they should be afraid of "our enemies, the people who call themselves liberals. . . . We must watch them, and be afraid of them."[73] Elizabeth considered parlor liberals as "the worst enemy to the cause of equality." They were immoral and "wolves in sheep's clothing."[74] The so-called liberals resisted any change to segregation. Their "courage and liberalism evaporated at the color line."[75] More dangerous than the loudmouth white supremacist demagogues, the gradualists and parlor liberals appeared reasonable and humane.

The gradualists' call for more time seemed to be a reasonable compromise to a persistent and complex problem. Gradualists insisted that white southerners needed time to become accustomed to Black people as full-fledged citizens before laws could change. Waties argued the opposite. People would adjust once laws were changed. In 1950, Waties knew, as Martin Luther King Jr. articulated in 1968, that laws cannot legislate morality. In "The Other America," King said, "And so while the law may not change the hearts of men, it can and it does change the habits of men. And when you begin to change the habits of men, pretty soon the attitudes will be changed; pretty soon the hearts will be changed."[76] Waties believed that the core issue in the South was "to change the feeling, the sentiment, the creed, of the great body of whites in the South that a Negro is not an American citizen."[77] He and Elizabeth knew from Waties's rulings that laws change behavior. Despite the dire predictions of bloodshed, Elizabeth and Waties repeatedly recounted white southerners' response to opening the all-white primary, "The whites have adapted themselves to the vote for Negroes quickly. They said blood would flow in the streets, if Negroes got the vote. It was the quietest election we ever had."[78] People's attitudes would change when the law forced them to behave differently.

The Warings insisted that "Gradualism is a false god." In his speech to the American Council on Human Rights, Waties admitted that he "once thought the South was working out its own problems in racial relations." But it would take five or six hundred years at the current glacial pace.[79] In Chicago, Waties conceded that wholesale change would not occur overnight. Even so, "as long as legal restraints are maintained, segregation, the dual school systems and underpaid teachers will remain."[80] The Warings reasoned that Black people should not have to wait any longer for white people to be willing to comply with the United States Constitution. They unmasked calls for time as unreasonable, un-American, and "an excuse to continue white supremacy."[81] Extending the medical metaphor, they claimed that to leave the South alone to solve its own problems was "comparable to the insane person who insists that he is normal or the alcoholic who insists that he is not drunk."[82] They created a sense of urgency and the need for action.

During their 1950 speaking tour, Elizabeth and Waties were based in New York at the iconic Essex House located across from Central Park. Elizabeth called the visits to New York her "soul refreshment," relief from white supremacy and social ostracism.[83] In New York, "prejudice does not have any legal respectability."[84] The Warings' stay in February and March enabled easier access for journalists. New York was also a convenient hub from which to travel to their speaking engagements. Fortunately, the Warings were not in Charleston on March 11. Around nine thirty that night, a cross went up in a tremendous blaze in front of the Warings' home at 61 Meeting Street. A telephone tip alerted two reporters for the *News and Courier*. The reporters turned over the charred cross to the local police. Three small finishing nails held the crossbar of about 30 inches to a piece of wood about four feet high. The initials "KKK" were scratched on the base of the cross that smelled of kerosene. The end was sharpened to shove into the two feet wide strip of grass between the Waring house and the sidewalk.[85]

Elizabeth anticipated local law enforcement's dismissal, saying that they "will probably try to white wash the cross burning as the work of pranksters."[86] She was correct. The Charleston police called it "the work of pranksters."[87] Elizabeth and Waties insisted that the burning cross was a legitimate threat from the Ku Klux Klan. Waties disclosed that he had knowledge from confidential sources of "at least 800 Klan members in Charleston alone."[88] He offered the Klan motorcades and parades throughout the Palmetto State as evidence of increasing Klan activity. Elizabeth clipped newspaper articles about the Klan and racial violence, so she was well-informed about the Klan's tactics. The Warings' concerns were not fanciful or feigned to publicize the incident. They viewed the cross burning "as a continuance of apparently organized attempts to intimidate the courageous couple who have slapped Southern racists as 'decadent and morally low.'"[89]

The organized attempts to intimidate the Warings included the petition to impeach Waties. Three days before the cross burning on Meeting Street, the Aiken men who organized the petition traveled to the District of Columbia to "confer" with South Carolina congressmen about the possibility of impeaching Waties. They presented petitions "bearing more than 21,000 signatures."[90] The South Carolina House had "tentatively approved a $10,000 appropriation to finance the proceedings against the Charleston jurist." The state was willing to pay the federal government to remove a federal judge so he could not undermine South Carolina laws that mandated segregation. In his customary fashion, Waties responded that he was "not aware that a judge could be impeached for enforcing, or advocating the enforcement of laws impartially without regard to race or color."[91]

The *Chicago Defender* printed Waties's statement in response to the petition and appropriation. He welcomed the "full light of publicity" on white supremacy's avoidance of the United States Constitution. Echoing his ruling in *Elmore v. Rice* that it was time for South Carolina to rejoin the Union, Waties pointed out that the attempts to remove him from the bench were reminiscent of South Carolina's course in the nineteenth century, namely "refusal to follow the laws of the nation resulting first in nullification and then in secession." Therefore, the present question was whether South Carolina was "part of the nation."[92] Waties repeatedly said, along with Elizabeth, that white supremacy contradicted the American ideal of equality for all. Never one to tolerate what he termed sophistry, Waties had no patience for white supremacists' subterfuges. He also clarified in the simplest terms that the attacks on him and Elizabeth were because they "had the decency to say" that white supremacy was un-American. Waties explained, "the resentment comes out in the open" because "those oppressors are getting scared."[93] He consistently juxtaposed white supremacy with the tenets of American democracy to highlight the contradictions between them and prod at white southerners' protestations of patriotism. The Associated Press carried the story of the cross burning, and numerous newspapers printed it. In his statement to the *Chicago Defender* that was also published in the *Afro-American*,

Waties declared that "This exhibition of the typical savagery of the Southern white supremacists proves it is time for the decent people of America to demand that their national government take steps to suppress these real enemies of the American way of life."[94] Waties made use of the cross burning to call for federal interference against white supremacists.

The week after the cross burning, Elizabeth and Waties traveled from New York to Washington, DC, to accept citations from the American Council on Human Rights. In his speech, Waties ridiculed the Ku Klux Klan and its supporters, then welcomed their outrage as an affirmative sign of their fear: "Oppressors are getting afraid when they have to go around with masks on their faces, sheets on their shoulders, speaking mumbo-jumbo. It's childish and insane." The cross burning and impeachment threat belied the consensus about white supremacy: "The fact that we are having outrages, Klan parades and cross burnings is one of the best signs that people are aroused and that the aggressors are worried."[95] The aggressors' worry manifested in threats and violence to quash opposition. Waties extended the medical analogy when he claimed that the Klan parades, cross burnings, and impeachment threat represented the "infection bursting to the surface where the problem can be dealt with openly and publicly."[96] Instead of acting fearful or even outraged, Waties hailed these efforts to intimidate him as a necessary step in the process to heal the South.

In their 1950 speeches, Elizabeth and Waties constituted white supremacy as a disease, then condemned gradualism as the possible antidote. They dismissed the South's panacea and offered the only remedy: federal law. In Harlem, Waties implored the audience, "We in the South need your help. We've got to have it." He said, "The cancer of segregation will never be cured by the sedative of gradualism. An operation is necessary, and you can send us the doctors."[97] By doctors, Waties meant the federal government. He cast the federal government as a beneficent and authoritative healer to displace the Lost Cause concept of the federal government as an unwanted and harmful interloper. Just as a parent must force a sick child to swallow bad-tasting medicine, the force of federal law would heal the South.

Elizabeth and Waties seemingly said in unison to the Richmond Committee on Civil Rights, "Force, not gradualism, is the only way to gain rights for the Negroes in the South."[98] The Warings did not invoke "force" in terms of bayonets, machine guns, or soldiers.[99] Instead, they meant "the force of public opinion, the force of the executive, legislative, and judicial branches of the government."[100] At no time did either Elizabeth or Waties call for violence. In fact, Waties clarified in multiple speeches that by "force," he meant the rule of law. Although Elizabeth was designated as the principal speaker at the Richmond Civil Rights Committee meeting, the Associated Press story attributed the phrase "force, not gradualism" to both Elizabeth and Waties. The *Asheville Citizen-Times* remarked that the Associated Press did not make clear "whether this was said in solo or in duet." The newspaper determined that Waties said it, "thus the very use of the word 'force' with all its ugly connotations is a pretty irresponsible bit of business coming from a Federal judge. We are afraid that is Judge Waring's ticket."[101]

Although Waties dismissed Congressman L. Mendel Rivers and others of his ilk, Rivers surveilled Waties throughout his tenure on the federal bench. A native of Charleston, Rivers seemed to perceive his role in Congress as defender of white supremacy in the Palmetto State. Waties threatened the racial status quo because of his power and authority as a federal judge. Rivers, like other white Charlestonians, attributed Waties's judicial rulings to the nefarious influence of his northern-born second wife. Rivers planted this seed of Elizabeth's influence over Waties three days after Elizabeth's YWCA speech in Charleston: "Her prophecy of things judicially to come is so deplorable and so charged with grave implications that I shall await with official interest the next judicial episode involving the race question in her husband's court, and I shall be prepared to take whatever action may be justified."[102] The report in white southern newspapers of Waties's advocating "force" afforded Rivers the excuse to take action. Rivers charged that Waties "had publicly advocated the use of force by a minority group to obtain its objectives."[103] He wasted no time in asking the House for articles of impeachment.

Rivers claimed that "the habit of J. Waties Waring, the United States judge, in speaking his mind off the bench and in an incendiary manner is a habit which can and will destroy the faith of the people in the integrity of the United States courts if it is allowed to continue unimpeded." Rivers referred to the faith of white supremacists, not Black people. Waties's rulings had preserved the integrity of the federal courts, not endangered it. Few of Waties's rulings had been reversed, which Rivers neglected to mention. Furthermore, Rivers argued—for the second time—that Waties would create a bloody revolution because "If the vast number of colored people in the South should follow his advice there would be bloodshed the like of which you have never seen since the War Between the States." While Rivers condemned Elizabeth and her speeches, he also recognized the continuities among the Warings' speeches and their united call for force: "That is her business because she is a private citizen but they make identical speeches on the same subject, and they speak on the war against 'gradualism.' And they talk about the Congress being too slow."[104] He purposefully construed force to mean armed revolution, not the force of law. As the *Afro-American* pointed out, Rivers and his allies defined "force" in its literal sense.¹⁰⁵ When he conferred the most negative connotation onto Waties's plea for federal legal intervention, Rivers furthered his goal of impeaching Waties. On April 7, 1950, the *New York Times* reported that South Carolina Representative Joseph R. Bryson, who sat on the House Judiciary Committee, said the matter was being studied. Nothing came of Rivers' charge against Waties, at least in terms of his impeachment. However, Rivers inadvertently generated media publicity about the Warings.

The Warings ended their rhetorical blitz in Philadelphia when Elizabeth delivered "Priorities at Home" on April 30 to mark the end of the National YWCA week. Sadie Alexander, the first Black woman to practice law in Pennsylvania, chaired the meeting at Tindley Temple Methodist Church. Although the speech did not generate the enormous publicity as Elizabeth's previous speeches, she did not soften her tone. The Philadelphia speech was bolder and more forceful than the Charleston speech—she was gaining momentum *and* publicity. She referred to "romantic sentimentality over those cruel and ruthless tyrants [master of slaves]" and accused white supremacists of sidetracking freedom's train (1, 5).¹⁰⁶ Elizabeth repeated the medical imagery from her previous speeches, "It is insanity that only the 'SHOCK TREATMENT' OF TELLING THEM THE TRUTH about themselves and their insanity, can shock them into facing facts" (emphasis in original, 9). She pleaded for force in the South because the issue was white southerners' insanity, not Black people, "It will take laws to be enforced . . . as this is not a Negro Problem but a White Problem in the South" (emphasis in original, 9). She condemned gradualism, saying, "Talk, talk, talk, whether a short or long time more should not be taken to enforce these rights of Negroes, ALREADY GIVEN THEM" (emphasis in original, 1). Elizabeth decried the need for interference necessary for Black people to be able to exercise their rights. She perceived those rights as already accorded to them by the Constitution.

Elizabeth turned her aim from white southerners to politicians across the country who refused to stand up for what was right and moral because they feared losing votes. Compared to the nation's founding fathers, she complained about "the terrifying difference in the quality and character of the men representing us today." Hubert Humphrey was the "lonely voice crying in the wilderness" among "cheap politicians" who did not stand for the good and decent thing because of "EXPEDIENCY, POLITICS, VOTES OF PRESSURE AND POWER INTERESTS, FEAR, FEAR, AND MORE FEAR, not even ashamed to express such weak and unmanly fear" (emphasis in original, 3–4). After blasting politicians for their fear, Elizabeth offered the solution—stand up and speak out: "But if a few of these politicians would stand up they would find they could amass many followers, for the Judge and

I know from our enormous mail and telephone calls, that are <u>NICE</u> CALLS and <u>NICE</u> LETTERS, that there are sufficient people to fall in behind if <u>one</u> leader would dare to stand up for his good convictions" (emphasis in original, 4). She had received the letters and phone calls, so Elizabeth knew that if elected representatives voted their conscience, their constituents would applaud their courage. Like earlier speeches, she linked silence with fear and implored the audience to pressure politicians to act courageously. She called the fear of social or political ostracism the curse of the South (4).

Elizabeth incorporated three letters into "Priorities at Home" as evidence of segregation's devastating effects on the daily lives of Black and white people. The first letter from a white man in Rochester relayed the story of a Black high school student who dreamed of going to medical school. Despite making the honor roll for three years and excelling as a football player, he could not secure a scholarship for medical school and ended up working in factories. The second letter came from a Black woman in Ohio who would soon receive a master's degree. The superintendent in her town pledged to never hire a Negro teacher. She relayed her disappointment and hopelessness: "The facts of Negro life is so ugly in most parts of the country." The last letter that Elizabeth read to the audience was from a white man living in exile. He and his family moved to Colorado after they were ostracized in their Arkansas hometown for trying to organize a church open to all people: "One day we were highly respected, the next—as soon as we made our intent known—we were 'out.'" The man explained that as schoolteachers, he and his wife did not have the protection of a federal judgeship like Waties. These letters evoked the outrage, guilt, and sympathy that Elizabeth felt at the Shull trial. Black people were discriminated against for no reason other than the color of their skin. White people were driven out of town for no reason other than trying to advocate for American democracy. The letters testified to the repressive rhetorical culture of Jim Crow for white people and the diminished opportunities for Black people.

In order to extinguish the looming threat of social or political ostracism, Elizabeth and Waties circulated the contents of the letters they received. Elizabeth and Waties likely hoped that Shaemas O'Sheel was right: "What has been lacking is the courage—for social approval is the one that most of silly mortals dread most. Mrs. Waring and you have given the example of courage—maybe it will spread."[107] The positive letters indicated, as Elizabeth revealed in her interview with Tom Poston, an "unorganized underground." To diminish the power of the threats for dissenting from white supremacy, Elizabeth and Waties revealed the existence of other like-minded white people. They constituted a collective of white people who opposed segregation through the circulation of responses to their speeches.

Elizabeth and Waties knew they were not alone because they had received confidential letters and whispered agreements of support. On *Meet the Press*, Elizabeth assured the audience, "However, there are plenty of Southerners who are with us. Some of our most encouraging letters have come from white Southerners."[108] Elizabeth repeated this claim in the Poston interview published in early March, "The most heartening thing has been the enormous mail received from the white people all over the Deep South, many right in South Carolina and Charleston itself, praising us for our courage, for saying things they don't yet have nerve to say."[109] The letters confirmed that those with the courage to enforce the constitutional rights of minorities would not stand alone. In Minneapolis, Waties told the Urban League audience that he and Elizabeth received hundreds of letters from across the United States. He lauded Lillian Smith, Aubrey Williams, Governor Luther Youngdahl, and Senator Hubert Humphrey for "the stand they have taken in the cause of civil rights" and "sounding the trumpet call for freedom and democracy."[110] Waties also acknowledged the letter writers' fear. Even though the writers were not ready to "step into the light," they wrote "God bless you" to Waties.[111] Once they circulated the responses, Elizabeth and Waties revealed that despite vocal and public assertions, not all white southerners subscribed to white supremacy. The circulated letters transformed the one-sided conversation about segregation.

Although "Priorities at Home" did not generate the national publicity of "Freedom Is Everybody's Job," it shined a light on the efforts to impeach Waties. At the mass meeting at Tindley Temple, the attendees adopted a resolution that cited Waties for his "righteous, fearless, courageous and completely American Democratic conduct." A group of attorneys pledged $1,000 for his defense against possible future impeachment proceedings.[112] Waties expressed his gratitude in a letter to Raymond Pace Alexander published in the *Philadelphia Tribune* and *Afro-American*. Waties called the threat of impeachment "idle gestures and mouthing" by Rivers, who was notorious for "extravagant and unsupported statements which never find fruition in actions." Even so, with his customary humility, Waties conceded that he was "not a man of strong financial resources" and that if the proceedings commenced, he would have to call upon others for assistance. He deeply appreciated their offer and the sincerity with which it was extended.[113] In Tennessee, delegates at the Southeastern Regional Conference of the NAACP passed a resolution "condemning the effort of certain white citizens to institute impeachment proceedings."[114] Fortunately, Waties's assessment of Rivers was correct. His blustery threats did not materialize into impeachment proceedings against Waties.

By the time Elizabeth arrived in Philadelphia to deliver "Priorities at Home," the *Collier's* issue featuring the Warings had hit newsstands. The "Lonesomest Man in Town" by Samuel Grafton did not focus on the Warings' stance on race relations. Instead, Grafton crafted an intimate look at Elizabeth and Waties's lives in Charleston, highlighting the degree to which the couple was isolated from white society in the city. A photograph of the Warings in their dining room, surrounded by smiling Black dinner guests, was the most provocative element of the article. For the most part, readers responded favorably to the *Collier's* article with a few exceptions. Mr. Foster from Inman, South Carolina, wrote, "You and your wife are making asses of yourselves, like children trying to show off. If you don't like Dixie 'as is,' why not move to some other section, where people are less inferior?"[115] Mrs. Kaltenbach from San Francisco had a similar opinion. She attributed the Warings' motives to "love of self, and an adolescent desire for notoriety."[116] Foster and Kaltenbach did not attempt to refute Elizabeth or Waties's propositions. They resorted to ad hominem attacks. Elizabeth and Waties anticipated such a response because they knew that those who attacked them had no legitimate defense for white supremacy.

The admiring letters praised Waties for his courage, often remarking on Elizabeth's role: "I admire your courage, and that of your wife, displayed in your fight for justice."[117] Chas and Ann Murphy from Pasadena wrote, "You Sir and Mrs. Waring have a very rare thing: the courage to <u>act</u> on your <u>convictions</u>. Its pioneers like you who finally break thru long held prejudice and customs" (emphasis in original).[118] Mrs. J. W. Curry from Florence thanked Waties and Elizabeth: "This note is an expression of sincere gratitude for two Christian people who subject themselves to all types of experiences by daring to live their convictions."[119] Mrs. Collins from Illinois appreciated Waties "not for what you do for Negroes, but what you do for humanity. Thank you for your example of courage and justice." Collins included Elizabeth in her letter, writing that Elizabeth deserved as much admiration as Waties.[120]

Before she returned to Charleston from her speaking engagements in the North, Elizabeth attended the Highlander Folk School's eighteenth-anniversary luncheon in New York.[121] Waties had agreed to be named as a sponsor of Highlander earlier in 1950. Myles Horton thanked Waties because Highlander would be identified in the public mind with the judge.[122] Highlander was the singular exception to the Warings' blanket refusal to officially affiliate with associations. In May, Waties refused the post of vice president of the National Lawyers Guild, reasoning that if the Guild had a case before him, he would have to disqualify himself.[123] In 1948, Waties declined James Dombrowski's invitation to serve on the Southern Conference for Human

Welfare's board. Waties wrote that he considered it a great honor to be associated with those already serving on the board, but he expected a number of segregation and discrimination cases to be brought before him. Waties did not wish any affiliation to interfere with those cases or force him to recuse himself.[124] While Waties ridiculed Mendel Rivers and scoffed at the impeachment attempts, he certainly realized that it would not be prudent to formally associate with groups that the House Un-American Activities Committee (HUAC) had in its crosshairs.

Instead of working within established organizations, Elizabeth and Waties constructed themselves as a two-person movement. They donated money to the Highlander Folk School, Southern Conference for Human Welfare, and Congress of Racial Equality, groups that figured prominently in the 1960s direct action campaigns. However, the Warings did not participate in these organizations as active members. Instead, Elizabeth developed and nurtured a far-reaching network of Black and white people. After each speech and meeting, she added contacts. Beyond their prolific and risky public advocacy, the Warings used their wealth, influence, and media access to assist activists at the grassroots and organizational levels. Their activism out of the public eye complicates questions about the Warings' motives.

J. Waties Waring was sworn in as federal judge in 1942. From Judge Julius Waties Waring Papers, Manuscript Division, Moorland-Spingarn Research Center, Howard University, Washington, DC.

Elizabeth and Waties Waring married in 1945. From Judge Julius Waties Waring Papers, Manuscript Division, Moorland-Spingarn Research Center, Howard University, Washington, DC.

Judge Waring addresses the Omega Psi Phi District Meeting on April 20, 1949, at Morris Street Baptist Church in Charleston. Courtesy of Avery Research Center for African American History and Culture, College of Charleston, Charleston, SC.

Elizabeth Waring faced a panel of journalists on NBC's *Meet the Press* on February 11, 1950. From Judge Julius Waties Waring Papers, Manuscript Division, Moorland-Spingarn Research Center, Howard University, Washington, DC.

Septima Clark invited Elizabeth Waring to speak at the Coming Street YWCA's annual meeting on January 16, 1950. Courtesy of Avery Research Center for African American History and Culture, College of Charleston, Charleston, SC.

At the Lincoln Memorial on June 29, 1947, President Harry Truman addressed the 38th Annual Conference of the National Association for the Advancement of Colored People. Credit: Abbie Rowe, National Park Service. Harry S. Truman Library & Museum.

African American voters waiting in line to cast their ballot in 1948 after Judge Waring opened the all-white primaries. From the John Henry McCray Papers, South Caroliniana Library, University of South Carolina, Columbia, SC.

John H. McCray was editor of the *Lighthouse and Informer* and a strong advocate for racial equality. From the John Henry McCray Papers, South Caroliniana Library, University of South Carolina, Columbia, SC.

The elementary school for white children in Summerton, Clarendon County District No. 22. Image Courtesy of the South Carolina Department of Archives and History.

One of the elementary schools for Black children in Clarendon County District No. 22. Image Courtesy of the South Carolina Department of Archives and History.

Reverend Joseph De Laine played a leading role in organizing parents to pursue legal action in federal court. From the Joseph A. De Laine Papers, South Caroliniana Library, University of South Carolina, Columbia, SC.

The parent-plaintiffs in *Briggs v. Elliott* at Liberty Hill AME Church on June 17, 1951. From the Joseph A. De Laine Papers, South Caroliniana Library, University of South Carolina, Columbia, SC.

Chapter 6

THE YEAR OF DECISION

In Waties's speech to the Harlem Lawyers Association on February 21, he proclaimed that "the spirit of the people, and the civil rights cases testing the theory of 'separate but equal' have made 1950 a year of decision." Waties was referring to three cases scheduled for oral argument before the Supreme Court on April 3–4, 1950: *Henderson v. United States*, *McLaurin v. Oklahoma*, and *Sweatt v. Painter*. He foresaw the upcoming Supreme Court decisions as the watershed that would propel the United States "back toward slavery, or we are going to wipe out the false doctrine of 'equal but separate.'"[1] Three cases from three different federal court districts arriving at the Supreme Court at approximately the same time were the fruits of Charles Hamilton Houston's plan. The appeals to the Supreme Court were part of a long-term strategy. Oliver Hill, a graduate of Howard University School of Law, pointed out, "Every time we went to court, we went to court determined to prepare a record that would compel the Supreme Court to rule in our favor. That was always our objective. We never expected to win any cases in the lower court." All three cases challenged "segregation at its weakest point, that is the inequality."[2] The trio of cases raised questions about the failure of universities and corporations to provide "equal" facilities and accommodations. Despite the expenditure of significant funds to maintain segregation, institutions were unable or unwilling to comply with the "equal" prong of *Plessy*.

On May 17, 1942, Elmer Henderson was a passenger on a train traveling from Washington, DC, to Atlanta, en route to Birmingham, Alabama. He was an employee of the Fair Employment Practices Committee (FEPC) and traveled across the United States to investigate claims of discriminatory practices. Southern Railway conditionally reserved two tables in the dining car for Black passengers. Because the seats were conditionally reserved, stewards could seat white people in them. Around five thirty that evening, when the train was in Virginia, Henderson went to the dining car when the first call to dinner was announced. The dining-car steward refused to seat Henderson because white people were at the tables reserved for Black diners.

Henderson returned to the dining car two more times before it was detached from the train at nine o'clock but was not served dinner on the trip. He filed a complaint with the Interstate Commerce Commission (ICC). Southern Railway changed its policies and increased the number of tables reserved for Black diners but still segregated them. ICC found that the modified rules did not violate the Interstate Commerce Act. On February 18, 1949, Henderson filed a direct appeal to the Supreme Court. On March 14, 1949, the Court agreed to review the case.[3]

The other two cases, *McLaurin v. Oklahoma* and *Sweatt v. Painter*, were similar. In Oklahoma, George W. McLaurin applied to the university's graduate school to pursue a doctorate in education. The university denied him admission because of his race. After legal action, the university admitted McLaurin but then required him "to sit apart at a designated desk in an anteroom adjoining the classroom; to sit at a designated desk on the mezzanine floor of the library, but not to use the desks in the regular reading room; and to sit at a designated table and to eat at a different time from the other students in the school cafeteria."[4] After the lower court upheld the university's restrictions, McLaurin appealed to the Supreme Court. The Court noted probable jurisdiction on November 7, 1949.

Heman Sweatt filed an application to the University of Texas Law School for the February 1946 term. The university denied his application solely on the basis of race. Much like the *Wrighten* case that Waties decided in 1947, the lower court gave Texas time to establish a law school for Black students. Sweatt refused the state's offer to enroll in the separate law school. The Texas courts decided that the separate law school for Black students provided comparable facilities and opportunities to study law as offered to white students. The Texas Supreme Court refused to hear Sweatt's appeal, so he appealed to the Supreme Court. On the same day as *McLaurin*, the Supreme Court granted certiorari "because of the manifest importance of the constitutional issues involved."[5]

In "Freedom Is Everybody's Job," Elizabeth had excitedly shared with the audience that a number of organizations had filed amicus or "friend of the court" briefs in the cases because they had a strong interest in the questions of law to be decided by the Court. In November 1949, Thurgood Marshall sent the Solicitor General's amicus brief filed in the *Henderson* case to Waties. Waties commended the Department of Justice for going to the heart of the whole question and advancing "the sound theory that segregation is un-American and in conflict with the principles of our form of government."[6] For the *Sweatt* case, James Dombrowski of the Southern Conference Educational Fund (SCEF) contacted Waties on December 13,

1949, and asked for the name of an outstanding lawyer, preferably a law professor, in South Carolina who would be willing to sign an amicus brief. Waties responded, "You have given me a very serious problem. It is hard to find anyone in this state who is sufficiently liberal minded enough to join in our views and practically impossible among those few to find one who has sufficient courage to say so openly." Waties suggested Stephen Nettles from the upstate region because he was a "very able and outstanding lawyer who is a fine liberal."[7] Dombrowski sent the first draft of SCEF's brief to Waties and asked him to review it: "If you feel free to criticize the document in an informal manner, we should be grateful to have the benefit of your wisdom and scholarship."[8] In addition to reviewing the brief, Waties also sent a contribution of twenty-five dollars to SCEF.[9] In early 1950, Robert Silberstein of the National Lawyers Guild (NLG) sent Waties a copy of NLG's brief in *Henderson*. Although Waties declined service positions in both SCEF and NLG, he contributed his expertise to their endeavors by reviewing their amicus briefs. Beyond his speeches and affirmed decisions from the bench, Waties worked behind the scenes to push the Supreme Court closer to reversing the separate-but-equal precedent of *Plessy v. Ferguson*.

The Supreme Court did not reverse *Plessy* in the three cases. While it inched closer, the justices confined their rulings to the specific case. In *Henderson*, the court ruled that the railroad's rules caused passengers to be subjected to undue or unreasonable prejudice or disadvantage in violation of the Interstate Commerce Act. As such, the Court did "not reach the other constitutional or other issues suggested."[10] The core issue in *Sweatt* was parity between the law schools provided to white and Black students. In a radical maneuver, the justices moved beyond tangible facilities to intangible factors, namely, "reputation of the faculty, experience of the administration, position and influence of alumni, standing in the community and prestige."[11] Citing the Fourteenth Amendment, the justices ordered the University of Texas Law School to admit Sweatt. The Court upheld McLaurin's right to equal protection under the Fourteenth Amendment, writing that once the university admitted McLaurin, he "must receive the same treatment at the hands of the state as students of other races," citing their ruling in *Sweatt*. In *Henderson*, *McLaurin*, and *Sweatt*, the Supreme Court applied the equal protection standard provided by the Fourteenth Amendment, focusing on the "equal" dimension of "separate but equal" without ruling on the constitutionality of segregated facilities or institutions. The NAACP had slowly and methodically chipped away at the unequal facilities for Black people. But the strategy to attack equalization was time-consuming and costly.

The NAACP had long struggled over the best strategy to gain equal rights for Black people and initiated numerous lawsuits attacking Jim Crow laws that disenfranchised Black citizens and discriminated against them in jobs, housing, and education. In addition, the Legal Defense Fund had stepped in when Black people were unjustly charged with crimes, such as the twenty-eight Black citizens charged with attempted murder in Columbia, Tennessee. The NAACP also intervened in cases of police brutality like the Isaac Woodard assault. However, legally sanctioned segregation in public schools remained a crucial issue. Robert Carter, one of the NAACP lawyers who argued *Brown*, said that the legal team "really had the feeling that segregation itself was the evil—and not a symptom of the deeper evil of racism.... The box we were in was segregation itself, and most of the nation saw it that way, too."[12] The debate within the NAACP concerned whether equalization or constitutional arguments would be most effective in dismantling Jim Crow.

Equalization cases or lawsuits that alleged that Black and white schools were unequal in facilities and opportunities were fairly clear-cut since Black schools rarely matched white schools. However, before the NAACP would institute legal action, suitable plaintiffs had to be found, and the community had to support the action. The NAACP carefully chose plaintiffs in supportive communities for several reasons. First, plaintiffs could be easily disqualified, as the *Pearson* bus case demonstrated. Second, plaintiffs could suffer severe repercussions for participating in a lawsuit. If jobless or homeless, they relied upon their neighbors to help them. Third, litigation is expensive. Even if attorneys worked *pro bono*, filing fees, expert witnesses, lodging, postage, clerical services, and transportation can quickly add up to thousands of dollars. Therefore, potential cases required support from the entire community. When the NAACP doubted support, they did not pursue legal action. In North Carolina, a significant accommodationist element stalled a university desegregation case. In Kansas, teachers in Wichita opposed a direct attack on segregation, so the NAACP went to Topeka, which is why *Brown* was filed against the Board of Education of Topeka, not Wichita.[13]

The other issue with equalization cases was that even if victorious, the ruling only applied to the local school district where the lawsuit was brought. In the end, Black schools in a specified locality may improve, but no substantial change took place, so separate-but-equal was affirmed. According to James Nabrit Jr., an NAACP attorney and former professor at Howard University School of Law, the equality approach was expensive, circuitous, and indecisive because in "each school or school district a separate case has to be tried to determine whether that particular school or school district provides equality."[14] Thurgood Marshall and other attorneys working with the Legal

Defense Fund questioned if equalization lawsuits were the most efficient use of their meager resources. In July 1950, a conference of NAACP lawyers recommended that the Association no longer handle education cases for the sole purpose of equalization. Their recommendation was approved by the national Board of Directors of the NAACP in October 1950.[15] With this resolution, the NAACP unequivocally stated its goal was to break up segregation, not equalize separate schools. Oliver Hill stated that the basic aim all along had been to challenge segregation, but "in the early stages we had to educate the public and educate judges and all that."[16] After success with Charles Hamilton Houston's strategy, the time had come for the NAACP to build on its foundation of equalization cases and challenge segregation outright.

On May 16, 1950, newspapers in South Carolina's major metropolitan areas, *Greenville News*, *The State* (Columbia), and *Evening Post* (Charleston), published an Associated Press (AP) report that Harold Boulware, Thurgood Marshall, and Robert Carter were preparing a complaint to file in federal court that alleged that the "Negro children of the Summerton (No. 22) district of Clarendon County are forced to use buildings and school facilities, inferior to those made available to white children."[17] The *Atlanta Daily World* published a similar story from the International News Service (INS).[18] The attorneys planned to file the complaint the next day, May 17, in Columbia, but the matter would be heard in Charleston.[19]

Reverend De Laine, Reverend Seals, and Black parents in Clarendon County had withstood the pressure and repercussions from the white power structure. They met Marshall's stipulations at the March 1949 meeting in Columbia. Through a series of meetings, the local NAACP had secured enough plaintiffs and identified a school district with both Black and white schools. Because of persistent groundwork in Clarendon County, NAACP attorneys could pursue the case against the school board. On May 17, 1950, the attorneys filed a lawsuit against the Board of Trustees for District 22, County Board of Education, and Superintendent of Education. The federal complaint requested that the court restrain and enjoin the defendants "from making a distinction on account of race and color in maintaining public schools for Negro children which are inferior to those maintained for white children."[20] Case #2505 *Harry Briggs, Jr., et al. v. The Board of Trustees for School District Number 22, Clarendon County, South Carolina, et al.* listed twenty Black parents on behalf of 102 children as plaintiffs. Because their names were arranged alphabetically, Harry Briggs was listed first.

When Elizabeth and Waties departed Charleston for the West Coast in late July 1950, they did so with the knowledge that Black parents in Clarendon County had filed a second complaint against the school board. In San

Francisco, Waties was assigned to preside over a high-profile case involving an attorney-defendant. The trip afforded the Warings an opportunity to continue their rhetorical campaign to shift public opinion against segregation. It was also a reprieve from the hostile environment in South Carolina. The Golden Gate city welcomed the Warings with favorable press coverage and social engagements. Waties and Elizabeth attended the morning service and coffee hour at the Church for the Fellowship of All Peoples, an interracial and interfaith church co-founded in 1944 by Alfred G. Fisk and Howard Thurman.

The Recorder published the full text of "Does White Supremacy Menace America?" that Waties delivered to the Council for Civic Unity on August 3, 1950.[21] The Council for Civic Unity promoted "equality of right and opportunity free from racial or religious discrimination."[22] Federal Judge Louis E. Goodman chaired the Council's luncheon at the Fairmont Hotel. He, like Waties, was confirmed to the federal bench in 1942 after Franklin Roosevelt appointed him. Judge Goodman's landmark rulings restored citizenship to thousands of Japanese Americans after World War II.[23] Waties's speech in San Francisco is significant because of the nine speeches that Waties delivered in 1950, "Does White Supremacy Menace America?" is the only one for which the full manuscript is available. Also, Waties delivered this speech knowing that Black parents in Clarendon County had filed a lawsuit in his jurisdiction that challenged the segregated school system. In San Francisco, he did not modify his call for the force of public opinion and federal law.

Waties adapted "Does White Supremacy Menace America?" for an interfaith and interracial audience on the West Coast. He retained the core elements of his earlier speeches that white southerners were diseased or contaminated, gradualism was an untenable curative, and the force of federal law was the only remedy. To support his call for force in the South, Waties incorporated the details of federal rulings that impacted jury selection, teachers' salaries, and primary voting as evidence that federal law could change the racial status quo in the South. Waties asked the audience to do its part by supporting litigation, executive orders, and legislation. He asked for the audience's help "through all the media of publicity, through news stories and editorials, magazine articles, and radio."[24]

Waties began by telling the audience that it was a rare pleasure to associate with "men and women measured entirely by their worth and their own attributes, and not because of their ancestry." In an adaptation for the audience and location, Waties explained that ancestry encompassed "people of all ancestries, races, and creeds," including people of Asian descent and Jewish people. Because "men and women are men and women," the American Creed was "built upon equality, freedom for all people, of all kinds and types." Although Waties's lived experience was as a white southerner, he included other groups who experienced discrimination because of their race, ethnicity, or religion. He recognized that white supremacy was not confined to Black people in the South but a pervasive ideology that tainted American democratic ideals. Then, Waties referred to the question that he would speak about informally, "Does White Supremacy Menace America?"[25] He said, "My response to that can be very brief—the answer is YES!" Waties called white supremacy "a great danger and menace to this country now and in the future." He offered two perspectives, international relations and American ideals, on how white supremacy menaced America.

The international ramifications of Jim Crow gained significance as tensions increased between the United States and the Soviet Union. Waties pointed out that "at least two-thirds of the inhabitants of this world are of darker skin." By continuing to appease the "ingrown prejudices" of a few "unthinking and unreasoning and uneducated people," the United States risked the enmity of "darker skin" regions. Waties connected Jim Crow's encroachment on American ideals to the United States' global reputation "to present a clean front to the rest of the world." Americans needed "to cleanse our own hearts and carry out those brave and fine ideals that our founding fathers enunciated." That was the "real reason why we must cleanse the situation." In San Francisco, Waties modified his characterization of racial prejudice from a disease to a contaminant. Instead of a cancer that needed to be cured or cut out, Waties affirmed to the audience that racial prejudice could be "cleaned out." He also called white supremacy an "evil." The modification was fitting for the Council audience because of the religious connotations associated with cleansing oneself of sins, the human body as a temple, and evil versus good.

Waties used the majority of "Does White Supremacy Menace America?" to persuade the audience that only people who lived in the Deep South understood the "complete pattern of white supremacy." He had to inform the West Coast audience about the far-reaching tentacles of white supremacy and impress upon his interlocutors how dire the situation was in the South. Waties drew upon his ethos as a native white southerner and federal judge by offering personal testimony that itemized the aspects of daily life dictated by Jim Crow. In his state, it was against the law for him to sit with a Black man in a restaurant or railroad station. If Black and white people worked in the same factory, they had to use separate entrances, exits, and washrooms. Waties recited the litany of Jim Crow practices so the audience would understand that the issue in the South was more than individual racial biases. Discrimination against Black people was systemic and sanctioned by law.

Waties outlined the long-time practice of school boards paying Black teachers much less than their white counterparts. While the practice stopped, it was not "because the school boards met and said 'Here is a great evil?'" The practice stopped because "a judge filed a decree." The teacher salaries cases demonstrated the efficacy of federal law, "And that's the way to cure it." When sharing the multiple attempts by South Carolina's white political machine to subvert the Supreme Court's ruling in *Smith v. Allwright*, Waties called it "an absurd situation" and acknowledged that some of the audience "don't believe me now when I tell you that that happened." As absurd as the situation was, it was righted by his threatening party officials with imprisonment, not fines. He pointed to his rulings as concrete examples of how federal law abolished second-class citizenship for Black people in the South. He cited those facts "to show you that 'force' does work and will work." By force, Waties meant the "strong arm of the law." The examples of the teacher salary and primary voting cases supported Waties's claim that federal law could extinguish Jim Crow.

Waties conceded that white southerners resisted his rulings at the time. But they bragged about them after they were forced to comply. Once Black and white teachers' salaries were equalized, "we're all quite proud of it and say we pay Negro teachers the same we do white." Mendel Rivers predicted bloodshed in the 1948 primary election if Black people voted. Two years later, in 1950, Rivers invoked Black people's voting in the primaries as evidence that the South had progressed and should be "left alone." Waties concluded that white southerners "liked it when they had to act decently under coercion." In San Francisco, as in other speeches, Waties relied upon his authority to persuade audiences that the issue in the South was the state laws that lent respectability to racism. His examples were evidence that federal law could eliminate Jim Crow.

Waties did not completely relinquish medical imagery in San Francisco. Later in the speech, he asked the audience's help to "cut out this cancer from the body politic of the South. We are a sick people—and only a few of us know it. We need help. You must send us physicians." He praised the work of the Council and progress in border states like Virginia. He raised these points in order to dismiss them as viable methods in the Deep South: "In my country we have to be cured by the other good people of the United States of America." By referring to South Carolina as "my country," Waties cast the state as a foreign entity within the United States. As such, it required more extreme measures. In the closing paragraphs, Waties implored the audience to help "eradicate the great menace of white supremacy" so that the South could recover its health. Waties constituted white supremacy as a national ill. Just as segregation harmed white people, white supremacy in the South harmed the rest of the United States. He reasoned that with the South healthy, the health of the entire nation would improve. But the cure for the South would not come from within the region. Therefore, others needed to intervene.

They could intervene by supporting "essential litigation for human rights, of executive orders, and legislation." Waties made the same appeal to the audience at the 1949 National Lawyers Guild Convention. Truman's civil rights initiatives continued to lie dormant due to what Elizabeth called the "unholy alliance of Dixiecrats and Republicans" in conjunction with Truman's "appeasement methods."[26] Because of the filibuster, southern Democrats had blocked legislation from being considered for debate. Far removed from the Solid South, the West Coast audience had the means to pressure its elected representatives to push through civil rights legislation. Waties reminded the audience that "our servants"—elected representatives—needed to "support the American way of life in all things!" If their constituents pushed them, then senators and congressmen had incentive to support federal civil rights legislation.

The Warings left the West Coast at the end of August and journeyed to New York for Waties to preside over a term of court. After settling into Essex House, Elizabeth traveled to Providence to address the Rhode Island Citizens' Committee on Civil Rights at Hope High School auditorium on September 15. Her "talk on 'Civil Rights'" did not gain the national attention as her shock treatments. The *Providence Journal* reported on the event, as did the *Afro-American*. The *Philadelphia Tribune* carried the Associated Negro Press (ANP) story. To a hospitable audience of four hundred, Elizabeth shared that her white southern friend's resignation after "a Negro had his eyes plucked from his head by a white constable" triggered her crusade. When Elizabeth moved to Charleston, she had no previous knowledge or experience with Jim Crow or Black people. The social circles in which she moved insulated her from the everyday lived experience of Black people, so she had no preconceived notions about race relations in the South. Her experience at the trial of Lynwood Shull was Elizabeth's shock treatment. Beyond the jury's acquittal of Shull, Elizabeth could not fathom the resignation from her white acquaintances about the violence against Black people. She was unwilling to accept the report from her white friends "that police abuse of colored persons was a routine thing in this community."[27] White people's silent acceptance of immoral and undemocratic practices prompted Elizabeth to educate herself. Armed with knowledge about race relations in the South, she set out to break the silence and provide a plan of action to others.

Her remarks in Rhode Island were not without a political element. Elizabeth repeated Waties's appeal in San Francisco for the audience to voice their opinions to their senators and congressmen. She urged the audience to vote for representatives "who would make filibusters impossible and would not enter into 'deals' with southern white supremacists." To infuse her message with hope and give the audience concrete action to take, Elizabeth recommended that the audience "mix more racially, not patronizingly, but on a friendly, helpful basis." Although the newspaper coverage did not include Elizabeth saying "only force will work," she expressed the same idea when she said, "once laws establishing FEPC and outlawing lynching and poll taxes are passed, the 'South will like it,' just as many of the democratic leaders in the deep south 'accept' the idea of Negroes voting now."[28] As in her previous speeches and interviews, Elizabeth cited Black citizens voting without incident in the all-white primaries as evidence that federal law could effect change in the South.

She shared with the Rhode Island audience that her home in Charleston had become a small island because "she had been cut off completely from the social life of her adopted city for espousing the Negro cause." The audience learned of the anonymous phone calls and obscene insults on the streets from "drug store cowboys" that Elizabeth endured in Charleston. Elizabeth also warned the audience that 1950 was a dangerous time for liberals because they were vulnerable to the communist label simply "because they embrace the plight of the Negro in America." Elizabeth minimized her and Waties's actions, stating that they had "done nothing more than their share to better the lot of the Negro in the South."[29] By adopting an attitude of humility, Elizabeth constituted the audience as capable of performing the same deeds.

While Elizabeth and Waties were in San Francisco and New York, violence erupted in South Carolina. On August 26, 1950, a Klan motorcade of about twenty-five cars paraded through Happy Hill, a segregated neighborhood in Myrtle Beach. The Klan targeted Charlie's Place, a popular dance hall owned by Charlie Fitzgerald. When Fitzgerald defended his business and did not back down from the Klan's intimidation tactics, the hooded and robed men beat him. The Klansmen left but then returned about three hours later. Shots were fired—three hundred—and a Klansman died. He wore his police uniform under his Klan robe.[30] The Horry County sheriff rigorously pursued an investigation just as Strom Thurmond activated law enforcement to arrest the taxi drivers who lynched Willie Earle. The Sheriff arrested the Grand Dragon and four other Klansmen on charges of conspiracy to commit mob violence. The grand jury failed to indict the five men. With possible remedies at the state level exhausted, Walter White, on behalf of the NAACP, requested that the US Department of Justice investigate the matter.³¹ The Happy Hill shooting made national headlines, partly because of the location and partly because of the dead Klansman/police officer. From New York, Elizabeth wrote to Ruby Cornwell that "the KKK outrages are coming out in the open at last. Wholesome to have the volcano erupt for all to realize the truth." Elizabeth was gratified that the incident occurred in Myrtle Beach because "the news gets out better than Charleston with our censored newspaper."³² She stuffed the scrapbooks in August and September 1950 with articles about the Happy Hill shooting and other Klan activity.

In Summerville, about twenty-five miles from Charleston, Officer James Adams shot and killed Mose Winn. He had a pending civil rights lawsuit arising from police wounding him seven months before he was killed. In the earlier incident, a Summerville police officer shot Winn twice in the legs after an argument over a bill that Winn allegedly owed another Black man. Winn sued the city, and his attorney contacted federal authorities because Winn's civil rights had been violated. At three in the morning on September 30, Officer Adams supposedly tried to serve a warrant on Winn at his home. The officer said he was forced to shoot Winn four times because Winn resisted arrest.³³ The officer was arrested, released on $2,000 bond, and tried. Much like the Shull case, the jury deliberated less than thirty minutes before rendering its not guilty verdict.³⁴

The violence spread throughout the South Carolina lowcountry. Reverend De Laine wrote to Elizabeth in September 1950 and described a "sly reign of terror and fear" against those responsible for getting signatures for the petition against the school board. Parents were fired from their jobs. Debts and mortgages were called in that were not expected to be paid until much later. De Laine's two sisters and niece were fired from their jobs at Liberty Hill School after teaching there for ten years. De Laine asked Elizabeth for the opportunity to "relate the general story to you and your dear husband." He contacted her again on November 1, 1950, outlining more of the situation in Clarendon County.³⁵ Due to Reverend De Laine's correspondence with Elizabeth and the Warings socializing with prominent NAACP leaders, the Warings knew much more about the situation in Clarendon County.

The intimidation and violence reached Charleston on October 9, 1950, when the animosity towards the Warings escalated from phone calls and letters to an attack on their home. In the days leading up to the attack, they had received a number of mysterious phone calls.³⁶ Over the course of the year, the couple had received ominous letters alluding to the Ku Klux Klan. The same writer from Charleston who accused Elizabeth of using a "n-word trick" to steal the judge warned her, "The KKK will not put up with you much longer."³⁷ James Laring of Miami, Florida, included a postscript in his letter, "Viva La K.K.K."³⁸ The Ku Klux Klan threatened Elizabeth with a letter: "We don't agree with what you say about southern states. You know what this means when you get to Charleston."³⁹

Elizabeth and Waties were playing canasta in the living room of their Meeting Street home when a missile crashed through the window. Waties said, "Whatever it was that smashed the window sounded like an explosive. . . . The front window was broken, glass scattered all over the room and back into the adjoining room."⁴⁰ He also believed that shots were fired, either bullets or blanks, but investigators did not find any bullet holes in the house.⁴¹ Like the burning cross a few months earlier, the Charleston police and *News and Courier* characterized the attack as a prank. Waties called the FBI, but the Savannah office would not probe the incident since no federal laws were broken. From there, the situation deteriorated into a political tug of war. J. Edgar Hoover upheld the Savannah office's decision, but the US attorney general pressured him, so the FBI began an investigation.⁴² Whether the attack was the work of the Klan or not, Waties pointed out the lawlessness in South Carolina: "You can expect this sort of thing in South Carolina. It's a State dominated by the Klan—a crime committing Klan that goes unpunished."⁴³ He issued a press release and said the attack was

> evidence of the stubborn savage sentiment of this state and particularly of this community in fighting the American creed and the creed of true religion. It is an attack upon the union which I represent. It is well that the eyes of the nation be turned upon this great evil and that the people of America awake to the necessity to STAMP IT OUT, by taking active measures to make these people recognize and obey the tenets of the Constitution of the United States (emphasis in original).⁴⁴

Along with the FBI's investigation, several US deputy marshals were assigned to guard Waties.⁴⁵ Mendel Rivers intruded upon the situation and, at the end of October, filed a complaint with Attorney General J. Howard McGrath about the guards.⁴⁶ McGrath ordered the guards removed, but less than an hour later, they were back.⁴⁷ News of the attack, FBI investigation, and Rivers's maneuvers hit the headlines. The Warings received letters of support from their friends and family. They also received letters like George Smith's: "What you deserve is not your window broken, but a brick bounced off your idiotic head, you are a disgrace to the white race, if you are white, we have many negroes in the South that are a better gentleman than you are."⁴⁸ Smith's insult was not unique. White supremacists frequently labeled Elizabeth and Waties race traitors because they called for citizenship rights for Black people.

As a visible sign of support for the Warings' courage, James Dombrowski and Aubrey Williams of SCEF organized a pilgrimage to the Warings' home in Charleston. Black and white supporters held a mass meeting at Morris Street Baptist Church on November 26, the Sunday after Thanksgiving. At the church, the group approved a citation that commended Waties for his primary rulings.[49] Approximately one hundred Black and twenty-five white persons marched from the church to the Waring home on Meeting Street. When Waties accepted the citation, he said, "We do not live in darkest Africa but in darkest South Carolina. This day will live long in my memory."[50] No local white people attended, but a large number of Black people from Charleston came to the meeting and marched to the Warings' home. Waties and Elizabeth were deeply grateful "to the very fine persons who went to this great trouble and expense to come to see us."[51] Subject to harassing phone calls, vile letters, attack on their home, and then dismissed by the local police, the SCEF pilgrimage was a wave of support in the midst of the hate bombarding the Warings.

In his letter to Judge Hubert Delaney, Waties connected the attack on his home to the violence in Happy Hill and the murder of Mose Winn. He told Judge Delaney that the Horry County grand jury's failure to indict the Klansmen "shows the futility of leaving the South to cure its own ills."[52] White South Carolinians publicly decried the violence. Yet, they consistently failed to impose any legal or social consequences against the perpetrators. And they refused to trace the violence to its roots. Viewed as less than full-fledged citizens, Black people were subject to violence and discrimination without any recourse. Jim Crow reinforced the image of Black people as inferior, which, in turn, was used as a defense of segregation and second-class treatment of Black citizens. The federal lawsuit from Clarendon County had the potential to strike at the root.

Waties scheduled a pretrial conference in *Briggs v. Board of Trustees* for November 17, 1950. The initial complaint only mentioned equalization. As such, it could be tried before a single judge. Because of the jurisdiction, that judge would be J. Waties Waring. If the lawsuit directly challenged South Carolina's constitution that mandated segregation in public schools, then a three-judge panel would need to be convened to decide the matter. Needless to say, Thurgood Marshall preferred to keep the case in front of Waties. Despite Marshall's insistence at the pretrial conference that the complaint did attack the state's segregation laws, Waties was not convinced. In his *Reminiscences*, Waties recalled, "At the hearings, mention was made of the segregation issue, and I mentioned that it didn't seem very clear-cut, but I would allow them to dismiss without prejudice and bring the whole case over." He told Marshall, "I'll expect you to file a suit bringing that issue clearly before the court."[53] With that proclamation, the case would have to be heard before a three-judge panel, the situation Marshall tried to avoid.

In a letter to Franklin Williams, Marshall wrote, "We had drafted the pleadings to make an attack on segregation without raising the issue of constitutionality of the segregation statute in order to escape the necessity of having a three-judge court." Marshall added that he was sure Williams knew "why we preferred a one-judge proceeding instead of the three-judge proceeding in this particular case."[54] Marshall was keenly aware that other federal judges were likely to be much less sympathetic than Waties.[55] Jack Greenberg, the only white attorney at the NAACP, explained that the case could have been framed two ways: "It could have asked for an injunction to prohibit enforcement of the South Carolina school segregation *statutes* as unconstitutional or merely could have claimed that segregation and inequality were unconstitutional—with no mention of the statutes" (emphasis in original). The former charge would require a three-judge panel because it named the statutes, while the latter could be heard by a single judge. Marshall chose the latter route. The complaint claimed that the plaintiffs were denied equal protection by the "*policy, custom, usage, and practice* of the defendants in maintaining public schools for Negro children because of their race and color which are in every respect inferior to those maintained for white children" (emphasis added).[56] Marshall did not claim the South Carolina statutes were unconstitutional. Instead, he mentioned "policy, custom, usage, and practice." Marshall's attempt to keep the matter before only Waties failed. Waties was determined that the case would clearly challenge South Carolina's constitution that mandated segregation in public schools.

Waties wanted the three-judge panel because if he ruled on the constitutionality of segregation as the case was initially crafted, Clarendon County school officials were certain to appeal. But with the three-judge panel ruling on the constitutionality of segregation, win or lose, the case would be appealed to the Supreme Court. If the NAACP won, the County officials would appeal. If the County won, the NAACP would appeal. As a federal judge, Waties knew that rulings from the three-judge panel could be appealed directly to the Supreme Court without going through the Court of Appeals.[57] Greenberg outlined this possibility: "Even if Waring agreed to try the case alone, an appellate court might overrule him and order a three-judge hearing."[58] If Waties was the solitary presiding judge, then the case would go back and forth between the Court of Appeals and local district court with affirmations, remands, and more appeals, possibly taking years before reaching the Supreme Court.

Marshall may not have been aware that Waties communicated with Franklin Williams and Walter White before the pretrial conference. Williams became acquainted with Waties when Williams accompanied Isaac Woodard to Columbia for police chief Lynwood Shull's trial. Williams told Walter White about his impatience with Marshall's wariness in bringing a segregation suit, and "White was not hesitant about confiding to the judge that he feared Marshall was indecisive about taking the plunge."[59] Greenberg claimed that Waties was also in contact with Hubert Delaney and John Hammond of the NAACP. They were concerned that Marshall was not militant enough in litigating the school cases.[60] According to John McCray, "the decision to change to a lawsuit challenging segregation was actually a secret agreement between Walter White of the National Office of NAACP and Judge J. Waties Waring." McCray also noted that the two powerful men with their wives worked over the best courses to take to establish equal rights, especially in South Carolina. It was commonly known that Waties wanted all the cases possible on the subject and he hammered on the futility of pursuing separate-but-equal any longer.[61] With the Clarendon County case, Waties finally got the case he later admitted he wanted all along: "a straight constitutional segregation issue."[62]

Waties allowed Marshall to withdraw Case #2505 *Briggs et al. v. Board of Trustees et al.*, without prejudice. The NAACP filed its third case from Clarendon County, *Briggs et al. v. Elliott et al.*, on December 22, 1950. Civil Case 2657 questioned whether the South Carolina State Constitution statute that forced the plaintiffs to attend segregated public schools was constitutional. Because the case raised a constitutional issue, it would have to be heard by a three-judge panel. In early January, Waties wrote to Chief Judge John J. Parker to coordinate the date and time.[63] On January 31, 1951, Judge Parker signed the order designating himself and George Timmerman Sr. to preside over the matter with Waties in Charleston on May 28, 1951.[64]

A few weeks after Thurgood Marshall filed the third lawsuit from Clarendon County, the Palmetto State inaugurated James F. Byrnes as its governor on January 16, 1951. A native of Charleston and of the same generation as Waties, Byrnes had served as a US senator, Supreme Court justice, and US secretary of state. South Carolina's Democratic Party strongly supported Byrnes, and he handily defeated his opponents in the primary. Still a one-party state in 1950, Byrnes ran unopposed in the general election. In his gubernatorial inaugural address, Byrnes did not rely on the demagoguery or overtly racist language of his predecessors like Ben Tillman and Olin

Johnston. Nevertheless, firmly entrenched white supremacist beliefs about Black people were embedded within his vision for South Carolina. In his address, Byrnes invoked South Carolina's rights as a state, but those rights encompassed certain responsibilities: "If we demand respect for state rights, we must discharge state responsibilities. A primary responsibility of a State is the education of its children. While we have done much, we must do more. It must be our goal to provide for every child in this State, white or colored, at least a graded school education." By graded school, Byrnes meant elementary school education. In response to the lawsuit from Clarendon County, Byrnes affirmed his support for separate-but-equal: "It is our duty to provide for the races substantial equality in school facilities."[65] Byrnes did not relinquish South Carolina's so-called right as a state to circumvent federal law. After perpetually underfunding Black schools, the pending federal lawsuit from Clarendon County forced a reckoning for white South Carolinians.

Less than two weeks after his inauguration, Byrnes presented an equalization plan to the South Carolina General Assembly on January 24, 1951. Byrnes proposed a 3 percent sales tax "to secure the revenue necessary to give the children of South Carolina the educational opportunities to which they are entitled." After ignoring Black children's rights, Byrnes called upon all citizens to bear the expense of equalizing Black schools because "Some districts never could provide adequate buildings without state assistance." Byrnes offered a legitimate reason for those school districts who had routinely denied funding to Black schools. His plan ensured that South Carolina educated all of the state's children while "at the same time providing separate schools for the races." He invoked the Good Southerner persona and asserted that "The overwhelming majority of colored people in this State do not want to force their children into white schools." The claim that Black parents did not want their children in white schools reinforced Jim Crow storytelling that race relations were fine in the South. An elected official claimed that Black people in South Carolina were satisfied with segregation. He echoed those who wrote to Elizabeth and enthusiastically supported better schools as long as the schools remained segregated. Byrnes deployed Lost Cause mythology when he characterized those who called for the elimination of segregation as "selfish politicians and misguided agitators" whose resistance denied "innocent colored children" an education.[66] By shifting blame for unrest onto outsiders, Byrnes and other white southerners disguised the oppressive nature of segregation and abdicated responsibility for their role in the continued dehumanization of Black people.

Byrnes's paternalistic call for "the humane white people of the State" to see that "innocent Black children" received an education reinforced the belief that Black people needed the benevolence and guidance of white people. However, his *noblesse largesse* tone evaporated when Byrnes threatened to close the public schools in South Carolina to avoid desegregation. The threat emphasized the racial hierarchy in South Carolina. Byrnes pointed out that white people would adjust without a public school system, but "Our Negro citizens will suffer." He deflected blame for any future school closures from the white supremacist state government onto the NAACP. When Black children are out of school and Black teachers are out of jobs, Byrnes predicted that the NAACP was certain to desert them. For his audience of white voters, Byrnes crafted a comfortable tale of cause-and-effect that named those outside of South Carolina as the origin of the current unrest. In doing so, he offered equalization as the solution: segregation would be maintained, and the state would fulfill its responsibilities to Black students. Byrnes's sales tax plan was not without controversy. Even so, white South Carolinians were willing to pay if it meant maintaining segregation.

Revenue to equalize the Black schools was one prong of Byrnes's "preparedness plans." He was not preparing white South Carolinians to desegregate schools. The preparedness plan was developed to resist desegregation. He was preparing the state for the pending lawsuit from Clarendon County and the Supreme Court possibly reversing *Plessy*. Byrnes knew that no matter the outcome in federal district court, "the case will go to the Supreme Court of the United States." Byrnes shared with the South Carolina Education Association, the white teachers group, that he hoped that "regardless of how we may have failed in the past to provide substantially equal facilities," the Supreme Court would look favorably upon a "courageous and forward looking Legislature" that enacted an equalization plan.

On the one hand, Byrnes expressed skepticism that three judges in federal district court could reverse *Plessy*, "a law of the land for more than a half century."[67] On the other, he expected the Supreme Court to overlook a state's failure for more than a half century to comply with the law and provide equal but separate facilities. The other element of the "preparedness plan" was a committee of fifteen chaired by L. Marion Gressette, a state senator from Calhoun County. Governor Byrnes charged the committee "to seek legal means to avoid forced integration of the state's public schools."[68] The South Carolina political machine exerted considerable time and money to withstand the Black parent-plaintiffs' complaint. However, the efforts were just as much to combat any future Supreme Court decision. The plan was forward-looking but without progress or transformation.

A white supremacist clipped a newspaper article, "House Endorses Byrnes' Stand for White Schools," and mailed it to the Warings. Enthusiastic about Byrnes's plans to maintain segregation, the letter writer proclaimed, "Regardless of what you or any other NEGRO-COMMUNITY agitator says, our Honorable Governor WILL KEEP THE STATE OF SOUTH CAROLINA WHITE. You should be in Russia where you belong, not here trying to wreck this good state. The people of Charleston can't be much to allow you to continue to live there among their wives and children" (emphasis in original).[69] Even with control of the state's political machine, white people in South Carolina felt compelled to insult Elizabeth. Fortunately, she was headed to New York for more "soul refreshment" at the end of January 1951 while Waties presided in the southern district.[70]

Bolstered by the Supreme Court decisions and public support for their cause, Elizabeth and Waties resurrected their rhetorical campaign in the New Year to ignite the spirit of the people so that freedom would prevail. They delivered a consistent message that white supremacists were mentally ill, then circulated the negative responses to their speeches as evidence of their claim. Elizabeth and Waties unmasked calls for "more time" as disguises for continued segregation. Deploying an extended medical metaphor, they constituted white southerners as incapable of healing themselves. Therefore, doctors in the form of the federal government were needed to cure the South's ailment.

From New York, they traveled to Philadelphia for Lincoln University's annual Founders' Day celebration, where Waties received the University's Abraham Lincoln Award on February 7.[71] In his remarks, Waties returned to America's standing on the world stage. The nation's credibility was at stake: "The United States can sell democracy to the world if it shows the world it practices what it preaches." Jim Crow created two brands of citizenship. As long as white Americans tolerated racial violence and discrimination, the United States was hypocritical in its battle with the Soviet Union. Therefore, the nation had to clean its own house "before we have something to give to the world." Waties never wavered in his stance that "The false doctrine of white supremacy must be stamped out with direct, unflinching means."[72] Gradualism would not fulfill the promise of American democracy. In his speech, Waties emphasized the contradiction between the ideal of American democracy and the reality as practiced in South Carolina. He underscored the point that state laws usurped federal laws and that only federal intervention would end the travesty.

On February 16, Elizabeth spoke before three hundred National Freedom Day delegates at a luncheon at the Ritz Carlton in Philadelphia. Elizabeth insisted that "freedom is a dream unfulfilled in South Carolina, not wanted or understood by that state's political or business leaders." When she cited injustices in government, politics, labor, and other phases of life in South Carolina, Elizabeth received "ovation after ovation." Based on her evidence, she concluded that democracy was better at work in Africa than in South Carolina.[73] Elizabeth appropriated Waties's language from the SCEF pilgrimage and said that South Carolina was darker than darkest Africa.[74] The barb stabbed at white supremacists' belief that Black people were less than white people. White supremacists likened people of African descent to apes, they accused Black people of cannibalism, and they refused to countenance any suggestion that Black people contributed to western "civilization."[75] Elizabeth turned the claim back onto the white supremacists and charged that they were less than people of African descent, just as she did at the Black Charleston YWCA. Furthermore, the Palmetto State was "laced down with white supremacy ideas and fogisms; with endless witch-hunting and with everything which belies the full spirit of freedom."[76] Less than four months before *Briggs* was scheduled to be heard in Waties's courtroom, Elizabeth delivered another shock treatment to provoke white southerners.

In New York City, Waties spoke at a meeting sponsored by the Committee on Racial Equality (predecessor to Congress of Racial Equality—CORE). At CORE's Brotherhood Month meeting on February 23, 1951, Waties delivered "Jimcrow Convicted" to over four hundred people.[77] Before its well-publicized involvement in the Freedom Rides of the early 1960s, CORE engaged in direct action campaigns as early as 1947. The organization's founders, James Farmer and George Houser, were greatly influenced by Gandhi's teaching of nonviolent resistance. Elizabeth and Waties first met Houser in the spring of 1950. After the attack on their house, Houser wrote to the Warings to express his dismay and admiration: "I don't know of anyone who has stood his ground more firmly in the face of bitter opposition than you have."[78]

After corresponding during the winter of 1950-1951, Houser and Waties agreed on the date, location, and topic for Waties to address CORE. Along with the CORE meeting at Salem Methodist Church, Waties and Elizabeth met informally with a small group at Essex House on March 5. Houser thanked Waties and relayed the "many heart-felt comments" from people impressed with Waties's speech, "Jimcrow Convicted." Houser did not neglect Elizabeth. He had received "every so many comments about her graciousness and the fine way in which she stands with you." Houser knew that Waties spoke extemporaneously but asked Waties, since a number of people had asked Houser, if the speech was available in writing. Houser regretted, "I just wish we had had someone there to take it down."[79] If a transcript had been available, Houser could have circulated it and reached more people than those who were physically present at the meeting.

Waties's speech, "Jimcrow Convicted," repeated the primary themes and appeals from the 1950 rhetorical campaign. He touched upon the social ostracism due to his rulings, then acknowledged that he did not have any white friends in Charleston, "but I've got some pretty good friends." Waties summoned medical imagery to create the need for intervention. He described racial prejudice as a vile cancer and said, "If you cure these prejudiced people, they'll like it in the long run." Just as the ill may not welcome treatment at first, once cured, they praise the doctors. He denounced gradualism and repeated his desire to see Jim Crow eliminated in his lifetime, not "500 years from now." A consistent theme was the idea of rights that Black people already had. Their rights were established in the constitution and now needed to be legally enforced. Elizabeth and Waties transformed "rights" from something white people bestowed upon Black people as a matter of favor to something Black people already possessed and upon which white people infringed. Waties reframed his decisions in the primary cases: "I didn't give anyone the right to vote. All I did was to stop the thieves from depriving them of the right to vote." The judge assigned to preside over a school segregation case in three months concluded his speech to CORE with "Let us wipe out, kill and bury jimcrow."[80] Waties did not back down.

Throughout 1950, Elizabeth and Waties worked tirelessly to fulfill Waties's prophecy in Harlem that 1950 was the year for decision. They assumed an active and public role to ensure that the scales tipped in favor of freedom. With no progress in the executive or legislative branches, they delivered eighteen speeches across the United States in approximately two years. In their speeches and media interviews, they constituted white supremacy as a disease that could not be cured on its own. They called for "doctors"—the American public and federal law—to perform an operation to rid the South of white supremacy. The festering infection burst forth in the form of Klan violence and impeachment threats that supported the Warings' claim that the South was sick. The heinous nature of the violence demonstrated that the South could not heal itself. From the bench, Waties pressured Thurgood Marshall to challenge South Carolina's segregation statutes before Marshall felt it prudent to do so. Although the question of legally mandated segregation in public schools would not be decided in 1950, the lawsuit was filed and scheduled to be heard the following year. Waties would preside over the matter with two other judges.

Chapter 7

THE DAY DREAMED AND PRAYED WOULD ARRIVE HAS COME

At the pretrial conference on November 17, 1950, Waties upset Thurgood Marshall's carefully orchestrated legal strategy, but the judge also most certainly ensured that Black parents' challenge would end up in the highest court in the country. The NAACP filed the third case from Clarendon County, *Briggs et al. v. Elliott et al.*, on December 22, 1950. Instead of a straightforward equalization case, the lawsuit challenged South Carolina's constitution and, therefore, had to be decided by a three-judge panel. Chief Judge John J. Parker and Judge George Bell Timmerman Sr. joined Waties to hear Case #2657 on May 28, 1951, in Charleston at the federal courthouse.

Timmerman was an outspoken segregationist, and his family, including his son George Jr., were leaders in the battle to preserve Jim Crow in South Carolina.[1] Judge Timmerman was the very antithesis of Judge Waring.[2] There was little doubt that he would refuse to rule that school segregation in South Carolina was unconstitutional. Parker was chief judge of the Fourth Circuit Court of Appeals. He was fairly progressive and favored change, but only if it was gradual. Marshall had won two appeals before Parker, but his opinions did not break new ground in redefining civil rights. He was probably too cautious to overturn *Plessy*.[3] With a segregationist, gradualist, and advocate presiding over the case, the situation did not bode well for Marshall. He could be certain of Waties's vote, but it would be canceled out by Timmerman, and Parker did not have the temerity to set new precedent. With these judges, the best outcome for Marshall and the plaintiffs was a spirited dissent from Waties.[4]

Briggs v. Elliott was the first case in the United States to directly attack the constitutionality of segregation supported by the separate-but-equal precedent set in *Plessy*. If the plaintiffs won, the state would be enjoined from ever requiring school children to attend racially segregated schools.[5] The case attracted national attention and major newspapers like the *New York Times* sent reporters to cover the trial. The Black plaintiff-families met at St. Mark AME Church in Summerton to make the trek to Charleston. Hundreds of Black people filled the courthouse steps and corridors in what Waties called a "press of humanity." In his *Reminiscences*, Waties described the scene as heartening: "They had never known before that anybody'd stand up for them, and they came there because they believed the United States district court was a free court, and believed in freedom and liberty."[6] Elizabeth was also cognizant of the day's significance. She wrote in a diary that she kept during the trial, "The day dreamed and prayed would arrive has come. . . . How hard I have manoevoured and pressed the NAACP into this militant course." Despite her jubilance, Elizabeth did not go to the courthouse because she and Waties thought her presence might cause a riot: "I am so hated here for my OUTSPOKEN SPEECHES FOR NEGRO RIGHTS AND DIGNITY (IN PARTICULAR) and criticism of the decadence and low morality of the South" (emphasis in original). She took no risk to upset the trial and stayed home close to the phone. Waties's secretary called with frequent reports from the courthouse.[7]

The trial did not get off to a good start for Marshall. Robert Figg Jr., a close associate of Strom Thurmond, served as opposing counsel. Elizabeth referred to Figg as "the brilliant Mephistopheles lawyer for the State Defense of segregation in the schools of South Carolina."[8] Before testimony began, Figg conceded that Black schools in Clarendon County were not equal to white schools. He gained more with the concession than he lost. Marshall had carefully choreographed his trial strategy to begin with the discrepancies between white and Black schools. Figg upset Marshall's plan. Marshall charged that Figg tried "to keep from the record any testimony that would graphically portray the extreme differences in the quality of the school facilities in the county."[9] The morning witnesses' testimony was not needed, and afternoon witnesses had not yet arrived in Charleston. Marshall appeared incompetent and unprepared.

It did not take an expert to determine that the County underfunded and understaffed Black schools. Hired by the NAACP, Matthew J. Whitehead thoroughly assessed the Black and white schools in District 22.[10] Whitehead visited the schools in Summerton, South Carolina, on November 16 and 17, 1950, and again on April 18 and 19, 1951. According to his report, Summerton (District 22) had two schools for white students and three for Black students. The Black schools served 808 students in the 1950–51 school year; the white schools 276. The average student-to-teacher ratio in the white schools was 28:1. The ratio was 47:1 in Black schools. While the white elementary school had a teacher for each grade, the Black elementary school had only two teachers teaching seven grades. The Black schools were wood, while the white schools were stucco or brick. The Black schools had no running water, indoor drinking fountains, or flush toilets. The students used open galvanized buckets with dippers for drinking water and outhouses for toilets. One of the Black elementary schools had no electric lights. Whitehead's report documented the conditions in the Black schools, including no surfacing or fences in the outdoor spaces, deficient number and quality of blackboards, absence of desks, no auditorium or lunchroom, janitorial services performed by teachers and students, so-called library used for class instruction, shortage of books and periodicals, no visual aids, and no transportation. In his account of buildings, grounds, furniture, and fixtures, the inspector calculated a $41,950 differential between the Black and white schools in the district.[11]

After Figg's concession, he informed the court that the State had appropriated $75 million to equalize the school facilities. The equalization program would be financed by a 3 percent sales tax proposed by Governor Byrnes. With the sales tax enacted and the equalization program approved, South Carolina was finally complying with the "equal" prong of *Plessy*—fifty-five years after the decision. Figg argued that a racial conflict heritage in the South warranted certain segregation practices: "There was an 'emotional' feeling about race in most communities that would make it 'dangerous' to mix the children in public schools at this time."[12] The equalization plan and community defense offered Judges Parker and Timmerman an escape route so they would not have to address the constitutionality of segregation.

More than one observer noted that Marshall made a poor showing on the first day. Elizabeth wrote: "The surprise move of that diabolically clever demon Figg left Thurgood Marshall flat."[13] To climb out of the separate-but-equal trap, Marshall produced several witnesses. Dr. Kenneth Clark presented social scientific evidence that separate schools were more than a matter of buildings, teachers, and books. Instead, "Segregation was said to be building into the Negro 'the very characteristics' which were then used to justify prejudice."[14] Separate schools were inevitably unequal because "Whites had social opportunities unavailable to blacks in separate schools no matter how new or well-staffed the black schools were; separate schools induced a sense of superiority in whites and a sense of inferiority in blacks, which in turn influenced what each race could make of the education they received in materially equal facilities."[15] Separation of the races inflicted such psychological damage that it always produced unequal status in society. Myrdal argued that segregation worked to institutionalize Black people's alienation and widen the gap between the races. The so-called inferiority was not so much a fact of nature as it was the result of willful public and private policy.¹⁶ With his doll tests, Clark argued that for Black children, segregation "resulted in a lowering of self-esteem, a strengthening of resentment and hostility and a personality development that emphasized a desire to escape or withdraw from social participation." Segregation did not only affect Black children. It also had harmful effects for white students because the practice "developed a guilty-feeling that stemmed from having the same people teach them the doctrine of brotherly love and also to support discriminatory practices between the races."¹⁷ Clark's testimony validated Elizabeth and Waties's belief that segregation was harmful to white people.

As an experienced litigator in race-related cases, Marshall deduced the inevitable outcome when Judge Parker asked Figg during the trial what sort of decree the attorney would suggest. Figg suggested a decree that outlined an equalization plan. After the trial ended early on the second day, due to Figg's concession that Black and white schools were unequal negating the need for testimony on the issue, the three judges met in chambers. Waties said it was "a long talk, but hardly much discussion." He was a rigid antisegregationist, Timmerman was a rigid segregationist, and Parker was an able judge who unwillingly followed federal law in the Jim Crow South. The judges' conference at the courthouse came to a stand-still. Judge Parker fixated on *Plessy*. Waties insisted that *Plessy* was about trains, not schools. He said that *Sweatt* and *McLaurin* pointed the way and that they could no longer avoid the issue that segregation in education was unconstitutional.¹⁸ Judge Parker tried to get Waties and Timmerman to agree to a unanimous decision. Parker was furious when Waties "told him firmly he was going to write a strong DISSENTING OPINION." Elizabeth wrote,

> He had been in conference with the other two Judges for an hour and a half. With complete disillusionment and utter contempt he told me of Judge Parker's throwing aside all the testimony and issue of segregation just reasoning on the basis of 'Jim Byrnes will equalize the schools.' . . . Judge Timmerman just a dummy throughout. . . . The die was cast for of course the two Judges decision finishes the case in this court but no doubt to be appealed to the Supreme Court.¹⁹

Waties stood firm on his decision to dissent.

Parker wrote in the majority opinion that the plaintiff-parents were entitled to "a declaration to the effect that the school facilities now afforded Negro children in District No. 22 are not equal to the facilities afforded white children." But he would not outline a plan because that was "a matter for the school authorities and not for the court." Instead, Parker retained the matter on the docket and required the school board to report in six months of its actions to equalize the Black and white schools. As far as South Carolina's constitutional requirement that public schools be segregated, Parker avoided the issue. School segregation was "a matter of legislative policy for the several states, with which the federal courts are powerless to interfere." He cited states' rights, declaring that education was a "local problem" and resolving it on a local level was essential to preserving peace and happiness.[20] By accepting the county's ploy, Parker and Timmerman avoided the real issue in the case.[21]

Waties's dissent offered the NAACP the grounds for its appeal. He used judicial rhetoric in the form of his *Briggs* dissent to create a different legal atmosphere. Daniel M. Berman wrote that the aim of a dissenting opinion is to preserve the views of the judge for the record in the hope that someday, "with new Justices on the Court or with a different atmosphere prevailing, these views may be translated into law."[22] In his strongly worded dissent, Waties argued that the Court had refused to rule on the issue at law and thereby avoided the primary purpose of the plaintiffs' suit: "This was brought for the express and declared purpose of determining the right of the State of South Carolina, in its public schools, to practice segregation according to race."[23] J. Louis Campbell argues that dissents function analogously to acts of civil disobedience because "They locate wrong in the majority, inform the audience of such wrong, and persuade the audience to reconsider."[24] The other judges decreed that the schools were unequal and gave the school authorities six months to remedy the situation. Waties proclaimed the majority decision erroneous, then outlined the reasons why segregation was unconstitutional, unreasonable, and illogical.

Waties denounced the other judges for relying on separate-but-equal: "And so we must and do face, without evasion or equivocation, the question as to whether segregation in education in our schools is legal or whether it cannot exist under our American system as particularly enunciated in the Fourteenth Amendment to the Constitution of the United States." He was convinced that segregation was rooted in irrational biases, and that these prejudices were acquired in early childhood, "There is absolutely no reasonable explanation for racial prejudice. It is all caused by unreasoning emotional reactions, and these are gained in early childhood . . . the system of segregation in education adopted and practiced in the State of South Carolina must go and must go now."[25] At the bottom of page nineteen of the twenty-page dissent, centered and underlined, Waties wrote, "Segregation is *per se* inequality." Waties separated that sentence "in the hopes that it might catch the eye of the readers and particularly that it might put squarely before our highest court an issue that must and should be decided."²⁶ The question was not whether the facilities were equal. Separation in and of itself was unequal. There could be no equality when the law mandated separate facilities.

Warren Earl Wright explained that dissents are often colorful and fiery, characterized by gladiatorial fire and vigor.²⁷ Waties did not temper his utterances. His *Briggs* dissent brimmed with contempt for white people in South Carolina, including Judges Parker and Timmerman. Aware that the *Briggs* dissent would reach an audience far beyond the immediate litigants, Waties preached a sermon. The dissent was his rhetorical opportunity to expose the incompatibility of segregation with the American Creed. Furthermore, Waties raised the question of whether equality was possible with segregation. Benjamin Mays, president of Morehouse College, summarized the stakes: "Let us not confuse the issue. The question is not mixed schools. The question is, can there be equality in segregation?"²⁸ Regardless of facilities, segregation was institutional affirmation of Black inferiority.

Elizabeth praised Waties's dissent: "This striking at the root of the whole evil starting with children to develop both White and Negro child without warping their whole fabric with hypocrisy and cruelties made respectable by State Law in the Southern section of the country. To have this case in Charleston the heart and core of the disease should cut the cancerous infection at the basis of the infection." While Elizabeth was proud of her husband and his stand in the case, most white South Carolinians were not. In the diary she kept during the trial, Elizabeth wrote on June 19, 1951, that they kept getting phone calls with "the same deep gruff man's voice," saying, "Get yourself a body-guard." While the Warings were not unused to harassing phone calls, something in the man's tone concerned Elizabeth. She was apprehensive about the consequences for them. She urged Waties to place his dissent in a sealed envelope in the clerk's office instead of the normal practice of mailing it to Judge Parker. Securing it in the clerk's office guaranteed that the contents of the dissent would not be known until Parker's majority opinion was publicly filed. On June 23, 1951, the day the opinion was released to the press, she wrote, "The die is cast and the repercussions will be violent against Waties in the South and in the Reactionary North." Four days later, she ominously wrote, "There is in the air INTANGIBLES of Fear, Confusion, and Worry for the future."²⁹ She could have been referring to the couple's future in South Carolina or the future of civil rights. The future was uncertain.

After the loss in federal district court, the next step for Civil Case 2657 was an appeal to the United States Supreme Court. In a letter to Thurgood Marshall thanking him for his "very kind remarks in regard to my dissenting views," Waties pointed out several cases to consider in the appeal.³⁰ In July, Marshall sent the jurisdictional statement for Waties to review. Waties commented that it was somewhat lengthy and showed signs of hurry, but, on the whole, it was adequate because "I do not see how the Court can possibly fail to realize the importance of the questions involved and that this is at last a frontal attack on Segregation." Waties was incensed that the lower court had avoided the core issue in question. Marshall had amended the pleadings to explicitly address the constitutional issue of segregation at Waties's behest. For Waties, the basic question was the constitutionality of segregation. To emphasize this, Waties wrote, "May I suggest the use of the phrase 'Segregation is per se inequality.'" Waties recommended that Marshall begin work on the brief: "The really important thing is to start in now in the preparation of the brief that will cover the case adequately and block all efforts by the opposition to induce the Supreme Court to evade this basic question." Waties instructed Marshall that "it is easier to write arguments when the matters are fresh and that they grow stale when delayed. And also you may find that another emergency or rushed job will arise. We do not want this Brief to be a rush job."³¹ Waties's concerns were well-founded. Black people across the United States called upon the NAACP for help because law enforcement and the court system did not protect them. Too often, the NAACP was the only institution to help African American citizens.

In October, Waties wrote to Walter White and suggested that he solicit amicus briefs like those in the *Sweatt*, *McLaurin*, and *Henderson* cases.³² Waties was anxious that the appeal be handled in a militant manner. He wanted to see real enthusiasm, fire, and imagination put into the appeal.³³ Jack Greenberg recalled:

> But Waring's efforts to push Thurgood to measures he didn't want to take, his backdoor dealings with Walter White and NAACP board members (he urged Walter to enlist other organizations to file amicus briefs in the school cases), and efforts to instruct Thurgood about strategy and argument irritated Thurgood and made him a bit uncomfortable about the propriety of being in that court. If Waring's extrajudicial communications became public, it could cause trouble nobody needed.³⁴

When *Briggs* went to the Supreme Court, Waties could not do anything about it, either one way or the other.³⁵ Just as Waties had to wait for cases to be filed, he had to wait and see if the Supreme Court would hear *Briggs*. In the meantime, he pushed the NAACP to maximize the chance that the

Justices would agree with him that the Court had to definitively address the question of legally mandated school segregation.

Thurgood Marshall filed an appeal in *Briggs v. Elliott* on July 23, 1951. Parker had given the county school officials six months to report on the improvements in Black schools. The defendants filed their report on December 20, 1951. The report created a procedural dilemma because the case was on appeal. Which court should review and rule on it? The Supreme Court had not acted on the plaintiffs' appeal when the school board submitted its report.[36] When the report had been on file for ten days with no objection from the plaintiffs, Judge Parker suggested that the three-judge panel issue an order indicating it had been received and that the defendants were to file further reports at later dates. Waties refused to join in such an order because it continued the present system of separate schools in South Carolina. Parker then proposed that the panel merely permit formal filing of the report, send a copy to the Supreme Court, and withhold action while the appeal was pending. Waties said no once again—the report had no place in the case. Finally, on January 8, 1952, the district court announced that it would send the report to the Supreme Court, where the case had been appealed.[37]

On January 28, 1952, the Supreme Court vacated the district court's original decision and remanded the case for further proceedings in South Carolina. In its majority opinion, the Supreme Court decided that before hearing the case on appeal, it should have the benefit of the views of the district court on the additional facts contained in the school authorities' report. Just as importantly, this action allowed the district court to "take whatever action it may deem appropriate in light of that report."[38] Justices Black and Douglas dissented because they agreed with Waties that the school board's equalization report was wholly irrelevant to the constitutional challenge to segregation. The Supreme Court's remand meant that the NAACP's appeal was dismissed. It could appeal again depending on the district court's final disposition of the case.[39]

The district court scheduled a hearing in *Briggs* for March 3, 1952, to review the report and the defendants' progress in equalizing schools in Clarendon County. Waties refused to participate because the matters to be considered at the hearing were entirely under the separate-but-equal theory and irrelevant to the constitutionality of segregation. Judge Parker designated Armistead M. Dobie to replace Waties on the panel.[40] Based on the school officials' report that the equalization plan would be completed within a reasonable time, the district court decided unanimously in favor of the county. The three-judge panel ruled that the Black schools would be equalized and did not ask for further progress reports. Instead, the judges relied on the state and county's "good-faith fulfillment of the equalization program."[41] This decision affirmed the earlier opinion and did not address the constitutional issue. On May 10, 1952, the NAACP appealed *Briggs* for the second time to the Supreme Court.[42]

While the district and Supreme Courts wrangled with how to proceed in light of an appeal and subsequent school board's report, Waties sent a letter to President Truman and Judge Parker announcing his retirement, effective February 15, 1952, and that he would no longer serve on the *Briggs* judicial panel. The extent of Waties's judicial influence in *Briggs* was exhausted as he expressed to Judge Hubert Delaney,

> My work here is through. I have done all that can be done and disposed of all matters that were brought before me. . . . There is nothing more to be done here. . . . I am convinced that I have done everything in Charleston that could be done. . . . I may be of greater use in other parts of the country. The evil here and throughout the deep South has got to be cured by the militant sentiments of Americans and not by self-dosing of the Dixiecrats.[43]

Waties had done all he could in *Briggs*. The likelihood of another precedent-setting case coming before him was negligible. Instead, he would be hearing separate-but-equal cases.[44] Firmly convinced of the futility of this type of case, Waties retired.

Elizabeth and Waties boarded a train to New York City on February 18, 1952, just three days after his official retirement. Elizabeth wrote in her diary that "I feel now that IT IS DONE that this is our last act, that we have driven the last nail in the coffin of SEGREGATION at its roots in the elementary schools. Our period of usefulness is over in the South at least."[45] Waties and Elizabeth talked about their situation in Charleston "far, far into the night" and reached the conclusion that he was really of no further use in South Carolina. Waties said that the feeling against them was so strong and pervasive, "almost anything I did would be colored by the ill-will of these people. They would feel that I'd done it from wrong motives."[46] Elizabeth and Waties's speeches triggered insults and harassment from white supremacists for years. The primary rulings could be managed because voting was a "civil" right, but his dissent in *Briggs* violated the taboo against interracial sex. As Neil McMillen wrote, for segregationists, the way to the bedroom was through the schoolhouse door.[47] First, Elizabeth on *Meet the Press*, and now her husband, a federal judge, violated the taboo against interracial sex. Because he was a federal judge, Waties had the power and authority to force white children to sit next to Black children in classrooms. White South Carolinians would neither forgive nor forget his transgression.

Charleston had become a war zone for Elizabeth and Waties. While they were very happy together, just the two of them, Charleston felt like a foreign land where they were hated all the time.[48] In 1948, Elizabeth repeatedly said that Waties loved Charleston with a passion but for her, "You feel living in South Carolina, honestly, you are living in another country."[49] Waties said, "But life down there [Charleston] became very uncomfortable.... We lived with practically no contact while there or when we went off to courts in other places in the state." Not only were they isolated, but Elizabeth, especially, was subject to verbal and physical attacks on the streets of Charleston. Waties said people would not get out of her way. They would jostle her as she walked down the street. Boys called her names. The situation was intolerable, as Waties described: "Life was getting more and more burdensome down South. If one is very unhappy in his own home, where, he goes through all the insults—because there were insults that occurred day and night, night and day—and the complete ostracism, it hurts, it pains, and it runs you rather miserable."[50] Elizabeth and Waties were socially isolated in Charleston and endured a barrage of hate mail, phone calls, and insults. Their trips away from South Carolina offered a respite from being insulted for speaking out against white supremacy. The trips gave the Warings a glimpse of what their lives could be without the constant harassment they experienced in Charleston.

Even their acquaintances recognized that the Warings' situation in Charleston was unbearable. On January 22, 1952, Sadie T. M. Alexander wrote, "I now realize that it is impossible for you to longer live in your present surroundings, in an atmosphere controlled by Hitler tactics."[51] Elizabeth and Waties decided to move to New York City "where the Judge can be more effective outside the Iron Curtain of White Supremacy."[52] New York City offered the couple an escape from the confining culture of Charleston: "I retired and moved to New York where I can breathe the air of freedom and help a little here to urge national action to eradicate the national (and international) cancer."[53] Retiring from the bench released any prohibitions against Waties accepting office in an organization or speaking publicly on any topic at any venue.

A few months after the Warings moved to New York, Palmer Weber invited Waties to address the annual NAACP convention in Oklahoma City.[54] Initially, Waties accepted the invitation and the NAACP prepared a press release announcing his attendance at the convention.[55] On June 17,

Waties received by special messenger two train tickets to Oklahoma City. The next day, he wrote to Louis Wright, Chairman of the NAACP Board, and explained that, after carefully considering the matter, he would not be able to attend the convention. In the letter, Waties referred to Walter White's attempts earlier that year to organize a dinner to honor the judge upon his retirement. After weeks of being unable to secure a suitable chairman for the event, Waties asked that the matter be dropped. It was embarrassing to have so many people decline the invitation. Also, earlier that year, an invitation was extended to Waties to speak at the convention. However, no one followed up until Weber's overture two weeks before the convention

Waties questioned if he was the second, third, or even fourth choice as speaker since Weber's invitation came so close before the convention. Then, for the train tickets to appear nine days after Weber's phone call and a mere week before the convention, indicated poor organization and disarray. Waties explained to Wright that he was concerned that the convention would be as unorganized and chaotic as the retirement dinner since White would be handling the arrangements, not the Board. Waties pointed out that on numerous occasions, NAACP staff failed to perform its duties and fulfill its responsibilities in carrying out the resolutions and policies of the Board. Because of his feelings, Waties did not feel he could speak at the convention without airing his grievances. He then mentioned the Legal Defense Fund and its handling of the Clarendon County school case.[56]

Waties had not been silent about his displeasure with the NAACP legal team's handling of the case. According to Modjeska Simkins, Waties thought the NAACP "dragged its feet a long time" and "didn't push this federal case as it should for finishing off the Clarendon picture."[57] The first point of contention was that the NAACP brought very few cases before Waties, and, if not for the intervention of John Hammond and Walter White, the Clarendon case may never have been a constitutional attack on segregation. Furthermore, Waties complained that it took three attempts before *Briggs* was adequately prepared: "after three tries gave me a chance to write an opinion although without the benefit of briefs or serious preparation or presentation by the NAACP legal department."[58] When the case was still in the lower court in Charleston, the plaintiffs' attorneys did not file any briefs in *Briggs* until the court requested them, and the one that was filed was "one of those colorless routine affairs reciting the various decisions which we all know."[59] Waties felt the national Board should oversee the *Briggs* appeal with "eternal vigilance and downright methods" without delays for conferences, consultation advice, or reconsideration. He had real doubts about the NAACP attorneys working on the case: "I do not know if the present staff is sufficiently equipped to carry forward this matter or whether some particular Association counsel should be employed." Waties correctly assessed that the NAACP and the fight to end segregation was at a crucial juncture: "This is the opportunity to achieve a great victory."[60]

Although Waties retired from the bench, he did not retire from public life. No longer constrained by his judge's robe, Waties took advantage—again—of the publicity surrounding his dissent and retirement to ensure the "great victory" that he so desperately sought. While the NAACP attempted to secure a chair for a dinner to honor Waties, other organizations showered him with awards and citations. The National Newspaper Publishers Association named Waties as one of ten recipients of the 1952 Russwurm Award for "taking [a] forthright stand constantly in behalf of equal rights."[61] The American Civil Liberties Union gave a luncheon in Waties's honor on April 16, 1952, in the Town Hall Club in New York. Forest Neighborhood House presented citations to Waties and the United Nations Secretariat at a grand affair at the Waldorf Astoria Hotel.[62] In May, the Warings traveled to Chicago for two events. For the sixth time, the *Chicago Defender* conferred the Robert S. Abbott Memorial Award upon Waties.[63] While in Chicago to receive the Abbott Award, Waties addressed an audience of ten thousand at the General Conference of the AME Church.[64] Waties also addressed Watermargin (the interracial fraternity at Cornell University), the Congress of Racial Equality, the Yale Moot Court of Appeals, and the Queens Women's division of the American Jewish Congress.[65] He ended 1952 at the Irvine Auditorium of the University of Pennsylvania, where Omega Psi Phi Fraternity presented its Distinguished Service Award to him.[66]

With the Clarendon County school segregation case on appeal to the Supreme Court, the Warings' rhetorical campaign entered a new phase. Their speeches in 1950 and 1951 focused on the need for federal interference in the South through medical imagery. As South Carolina poured money into equalizing schools, the Warings feared that Black people would retreat from pursuing the appeal because they would be satisfied with modern, yet still separate, schools. Waties's rhetoric in 1952 focused primarily on Black people and politicians. He strove to impart a sense among Black people that they were American citizens and entitled to the rights enumerated in the constitution. Waties warned politicians that American voters cared about racial equality.

Throughout 1952, the news media relegated Elizabeth to the same role she had filled before the 1950 Coming Street YWCA speech. Although nearly always mentioned as "wife of the judge who . . . ," reporters omitted her rhetorical efforts in 1950 and 1951, before *Briggs* was heard. Photographs included Elizabeth smiling by Waties's side as he received an award or citation. In photographs of Elizabeth without Waties, she received corsages or engaged in "informal" conversations with other women. She nearly always sat on the dais, but never had a speaking role. Associations awarded and cited Waties for his public judicial acts. News media featured Elizabeth in more interpersonal exchanges. Elizabeth's role as supportive wife aligned with gender standards in the 1950s, as Clifford Durr and Thurgood Marshall remarked in 1949 at the National Lawyers Guild banquet.

A few weeks after they moved to New York City, Elizabeth and Waties traveled to Philadelphia. Mourners and activists filled the auditorium at First Baptist Church to pay tribute to Harry and Harriette Moore. The NAACP, Catholic Interracial Council, and Jewish Community Relations Council sponsored the memorial for the Moores. On Christmas night, 1951, a bomb decimated their home in Mims, Florida. Relatives transported Harry and Harriette thirty miles to the hospital. Harry died shortly after arriving at the hospital; Harriette died nine days later. The bombing was in response to Moore's resistance to white supremacy through voter registration drives, letters to elected representatives, and NAACP organizing in Brevard County. In Philadelphia, Waties called the Moores' death "a good old-fashioned white supremacy lynching." Relying upon a 1950s definition of lynching, Waties explained that although not technically lynchings, the motives behind the murders were in the traditional style of southern terrorism. Waties did not name Isaac Woodard or Mose Winn, "But everytime some fellow begins to stand up for his rights, a policeman finds him troublesome and ends up shooting him. This teaches the poor devils that the threat of lynching is always there."[67] The violence perpetuated against individuals was calculated to intimidate and silence entire communities.

Waties connected the Moores' death and police murders to segregation. The law established two separate classes of citizens; therefore, "You can't have two classes without one feeling better than the other." Waties witnessed the impact of second-class citizenship for Black people in his courtroom with teacher salaries, police brutality, voting, higher education, peonage, and schools. He conceded that "you can't legislate decency" and "you cannot make people good by law." At the same time, "we must wipe off the books laws that make us indecent."[68] Waties implicitly pointed out that legally mandated segregation was not a symptom but the source of racial violence. Segregation perpetuated the image of African American people as second-class citizens who were not entitled to the protection of the law.

Waties closed his tribute to the Moores by saying that he would not shed tears for them: "Instead I glory in them. Brave, valiant souls, they laid down their lives for a cause." Then he charged the audience, "But what are we going to do? Let it not be said that they have died in vain." To give meaning to the senseless loss of the Moores' lives, the audience must carry on Harry and Harriette's work. Waties's message was that it was not enough to pay tribute or mourn the Moores. Their deaths could fulfill a higher purpose if the audience took action in their names. Waties asked the audience to use their right to vote in the upcoming national election and let candidates know that any appeasement of the Dixiecrats would not be tolerated. Voters would no longer stand by while politicians "sell out the rights of thousands of others."[69] Votes and pressure from the audience in Philadelphia could shut down the southern Democrats.

In the four speeches that Waties delivered from March to May 1952, he revived the core elements of the Warings' 1950 rhetorical campaign: white supremacists were sick, gradualism could not cure them, and only outside force would work. Waties denigrated white southern politicians and invoked "Uncle Tom" in reference to some Black leaders. The speeches were remarkably similar with slight modifications. The most marked difference occurred in the Chicago speeches for the Abbott Award and AME Conference. Waties took advantage of the venue to present a proposed civil rights plan for the Republican and Democratic parties, whose conventions were scheduled for the following summer in the Windy City. No longer a federal judge, Waties's speeches in the weeks after his retirement were his most stringent and most political.

In Chicago, Waties solidified the impression of the South as a foreign land when he announced that he had come from behind the iron curtain of white supremacy.[70] By invoking "iron curtain," Waties set the South apart from the rest of the United States and likened the region to the communism of the Soviet Union. The South kept an iron curtain between their prejudices and plain facts. The comparison to the Soviet Union's iron curtain emphasized the absolute nature of white supremacy. It affirmed his declaration in *Elmore v. Rice*: "It is time for South Carolina to rejoin the Union. It is time to fall in step with the other states and to adopt the American way of conducting elections."[71] In San Francisco, Waties had expressed the same sentiment that the South should become part of the United States "not only in a technical sense but in spirit as well as law and letter."[72] Laws in the South granted respectability to segregation and impunity for racial violence, so Black citizens' constitutional rights were violated. The region subverted American principles.

Waties landed a preemptive strike when he applied "iron curtain" to the South. To diminish the potency of the "communist" label on civil rights activists, Waties appropriated the fear of communism and turned it upon white supremacists. Elizabeth likened white supremacists to communists and Nazis in the Black Charleston YWCA speech and media interviews in 1950. The South adopted the Soviet Union's practice of erecting an iron curtain to shield itself from criticism, hide its deficiencies, and foster its propaganda. Those who spoke out against white supremacy practiced the American Creed. Those who adhered to white supremacy practiced communist principles. The Warings referred to the South's iron curtain as a shield between facts and delusion, a barrier to dissent, and a haven for injustice. No matter the function, Waties declared that the only way to settle the issue of segregation "that had been defended behind an iron curtain" was "by constitutional measures instituted from outside the barrier."[73]

Behind the iron curtain, racial prejudice festered like a cancer. At the Forest House event, Waties said, "Racial discrimination is the cancer and sore that is likely to eat out our body. We have to kill the disease that is eating within us or it will eat our vitals."[74] In Chicago, he called prejudice "a figment of imagination from warped, contorted and confused minds."[75] Just as he and Elizabeth argued in 1950, Waties declared that "a cancer cannot be cured by a palliative." Instead, it must be cut out "by the very roots or the disease will spread and affect every part of our national body."[76] In 1952, Waties engaged medical imagery again to affirm his conviction that the South could not resolve its racial problems. Just as humans required medical expertise when diseased, so did the South require assistance from beyond its iron curtain. He considered gradualism to be a ruse to continue segregation. The laws that mandated segregation were the root of the disease because they sustained white people's beliefs about the inferiority of Black people.

While Waties acknowledged that racial discrimination occurred in other regions of the country, the issue in the South was that such discrimination was fastened by law.[77] Waties determined that the laws that prohibited Americans from acting decently and in a Christian manner were the source of the South's disease.[78] The law required little children to go to separate schools. The children did not have racial prejudice or hatred, but were taught it because they were not allowed to mingle together in elementary schools.[79] The law required separate theatres, separate schools, separate waiting rooms, and even separate churches. Waties declared to the AME Conference attendees in Chicago, "It is our job to smash those laws so people, both white and colored, can again enjoy the freedoms guaranteed by our Constitution." In order to effect a cure, one must determine and treat the cause. Therefore, "No improvement can be made until these laws are uprooted and changed."[80]

Waties perceived any path other than the total elimination of segregation laws as unacceptable and appeasement. He called gradualism "the most dangerous attitude" because the gradualist "is denying to American citizens their rights."[81] He cautioned audiences that calls from the Byrnes, Russells, and Talmadges for states' rights were a "continuation of the Negro in the category of second class citizenship." And just as masters never willingly gave up their slaves, "neither will white supremacists give up their prejudices."[82] The white supremacists would never give up any of the things from which they have made financial and political gains. He explained that spending money to equalize schools was a desperate attempt to postpone the inevitable final decision that segregation was a violation of the constitution.[83] Waties expressed an "abiding faith in the judiciary of the United States" and predicted a complete breakdown in segregation laws in education.[84]

Based on this conviction, any surrender by the Black community would stall the pending appeal. Just as Waties believed that white southerners had to change their image of Black people, he demonstrated a similar belief that Black people needed to envision themselves as citizens entitled to rights. Elizabeth expressed the same belief at the Black Charleston YWCA when she said, "ATTAIN THE RIGHTS YOU ALREADY LEGALLY HAVE, TO ENFORCE THESE RIGHTS" (9). As testimony, Waties shared that when Black people in South Carolina thanked him for the vote, he responded, "I did not give you the vote; I did not let white supremacists steal any more of your rights." Voting was not a gift but a right. Even so, Waties exhorted the audience, "There are some things that you must do for yourselves, don't think that somebody else is going to do it for you."[85] Waties attempted to instill a sense of citizenship in Black members of the audience. Because they were entitled to rights under the United States Constitution, they could and should seek enforcement of those rights in the federal courts. His perspective belied the reality for those Black citizens who asserted their rights like Isaac Woodard, Charlie Fitzgerald, and Black parent-plaintiffs in *Briggs*.

Waties warned the audience that white supremacists would try to compromise and appease, "We want no Chamberlain." In 1938, Neville Chamberlain, as Prime Minister of the United Kingdom, attempted to forestall another war by appeasing Hitler. Chamberlain's strategy failed. If Black people accepted "equal" schools that remained segregated, they would not be able to exercise their rights. To those Black leaders who pointed with pride to the modern schools built under separate-but-equal, Waties asked the audience to renounce them as Uncle Tomism. Waties knew white supremacists' methods. He knew the white power structure would try to appease Black people's demands for their rights. In 1950, 1951, and again in 1952, Waties tried to instill a sense of entitlement so that his audience would not be satisfied with anything less than full citizenship rights.

At the *Chicago Defender* event, the "audience rose and gave him an enthusiastic ovation" in response to Waties's declaration that "we are not satisfied with the pouring out of gold. We do not want the chains of slavery to be gold-plated. We want them stricken off."[86] The audience at the General Conference of the AME Church responded in like fashion when he said, "we do not want chains even when they come gold-plated. We do not want gifts, we want rights."[87] Waties must have realized how tempting it was for the plaintiff-parents to accept the modern schools after years of repercussions, lawsuits, and their children attending school in shacks. If the parents withdrew their appeal, then their children would go to modern schools. But the badge of slavery would remain. His concern was the long-term ramifications. South Carolina's school equalization plan presented a danger to reversing *Plessy*.

Waties said the same thing three years earlier when the Omega Psi Phi fraternity honored him in Charleston: "Negroes should not want charity, but first class citizenship and all that citizens are entitled to receive."[88] Charity was not one of the pillars of American democracy. He did not foresee Black people being able to exercise their rights without the total elimination of segregation laws. When he delivered these 1952 speeches, he was waiting for the Supreme Court to announce whether it would review *Briggs*. He was confident that the Court's decision would remove the stigma of segregation.[89] But he needed audiences to support the plaintiffs until the case reached the Supreme Court so his vision could be realized.

Although Waties spoke of the Supreme Court's decision eradicating segregation in schools as an inevitability, he did not relinquish the need for federal law to interfere in the South. Waties called for help from beyond the South to cure the region. He reasoned that "you can't teach people of South Carolina and Mississippi to act decently because the law says you can't."[90] White southerners were not going to cure themselves, so the help must come from the outside. As he did before the *Briggs* trial, Waties offered personal testimony to affirm his call for force. He recalled again that politicians predicted blood would flow in the streets if Black people voted in the primaries, but 1948 was one of the quietest primary elections that South Carolina had ever had. By 1952, Waties had more examples of force. The Supreme Court's decisions in *Henderson*, *McLaurin*, and *Sweatt*: "This is the kind of force which has to be used to make the South observe the simple tenets of human decency."[91] The force of federal law, not armies, changed state laws. Waties ended the speeches in Chicago with a proposed civil rights platform for the Democratic and Republican Parties. In presenting the plan, Waties asked, irrespective of party affiliation, "are they Americans?

Do they stand for civil rights?" He insisted that political candidates should stand for the right to vote, equal opportunity to work, and security in person and property. Waties ended dramatically by questioning whether the parties "mean to restore a lost America." For people who asked what they could do to help, Elizabeth suggested in her 1950 interview with Tom Poston that they vote against race baiters "and let them know how you intend to vote."[92] Waties put the political parties on notice that voters intended to question their stances on civil rights.

After a whirlwind schedule of speaking engagements in the spring of 1952, Elizabeth and Waties traveled to Washington, DC, for Howard University's commencement on June 13. Before the ceremony, Waties wrote to President Truman and enclosed his proposed civil rights plank for the president's consideration: "I have no pride of authorship in this but give it to you for such use as you may think it merits." Waties belittled the Dixiecrats for destroying the Democratic Party and warned Truman that "no successful compromise or alliance can be made with the Dixiecrat leaders." The Dixiecrats' supposed support for "our party" was "merely a desire to retain their own selfish power through the un-American doctrine of 'white supremacy.'" In his letter, Waties admonished the president of the United States. The liberal-thinking people—the ones who voted for Truman in 1948—looked to him to uphold the principles of the Democratic Party: "We adhere to our promises and march forward again to victory as the Party which stands for true Americanism by eliminating this cancer of racial persecution which infects parts of our body politic." Waties tried to impress upon Truman the danger and urgency even as he flattered the president, "You, and only you, can definitely save the day."[93] At times arrogant and other times humble, the letter to Truman reflects Waties's increasing anxiety and impatience surrounding race relations in the United States as well as the pending *Briggs* appeal.

At Howard University's commencement, President Harry Truman delivered the keynote speech, and Waties received the honorary degree of Doctor of Laws.[94] Waties addressed four hundred guests at the University Annual Trustees' Dinner for honorary degree recipients. Waties said that the new schools sprouting up all over the South were to appease Black people and "buy them off." He repeated his comparison of the new modern schools to gold-plated "chains of slavery." Waties did not waver from his concept of segregation as a form of slavery. In his speeches, he barely contained his frustration that Black people accept the so-called "equal" schools because "it is just plain cowardice to try to appease and compromise with someone who is denying you your rights."[95] Now retired from the bench, Waties insisted on

Black citizens' rights and repudiated attempts to compromise because he believed that the Supreme Court was on the brink of declaring segregation unconstitutional. If Black people were content with new but still segregated schools, then Elizabeth and Waties's carefully laid plans would be for naught.

When the Warings arrived in Washington, DC, for Howard University's commencement, they knew that their carefully calculated attack upon what Waties called "the citadel of 'white supremacy'" had borne fruit.[96] On June 9, 1952, the last day of the 1951–52 term before the summer recess, the Supreme Court noted probable jurisdiction in *Briggs* and scheduled oral argument for October 1952.[97] Clarendon County was not the only location where Black parents were pursuing lawsuits to improve educational opportunities for their children. In Topeka, Kansas, the Black and white schools were comparable, but Black students rode long distances on buses to the Black schools when white schools were closer to their homes. The initial complaint was filed in March 1951, heard in June, decided in August, and appealed in October. The Supreme Court scheduled *Brown* and *Briggs* to be heard at the same time.

When the Supreme Court reconvened in October 1952, *Davis v. County School Board*, which originated in Prince Edward County, Virginia, had been appealed from the lower district court. Similar to Clarendon County, the Black high school was inferior to the white high school because the local school board did not want to spend money. *Davis* was different than *Briggs* in that it was student-led. The stalemate between the local white power structure and Black students resulted in a two-week student strike.[98] Argued before the US District Court for the Eastern District of Virginia in February 1952, the lower court found the schools substantially unequal and ordered the defendants to equalize forthwith. As in South Carolina, the court sustained the validity of legally mandated segregation. The district court entered its decision on March 7, 1952, concluding that "the separation provision rests neither upon prejudice, nor caprice, nor upon any other measureless foundation. Rather the proof is that it declares one of the ways of life in Virginia. Separation of white and colored 'children' in the public schools of Virginia has for generations been a part of the mores of her people. To have separate schools has been their use and wont."[99] The plaintiffs appealed to the United States Supreme Court on July 12, 1952. At its first conference in October, the Justices agreed to hear *Davis* with *Briggs* and *Brown* so postponed oral argument until December 8, 1952.[100]

Cases from Delaware and the District of Columbia were also argued before the Supreme Court along with *Brown*, *Briggs*, and *Davis*. In the Delaware case, *Gebhart v. Belton*, the lower court ruled on April 1, 1952, that substantial inequality existed between the Black and white schools and ordered immediate admission of Black children to schools previously attended only by white children. On appeal filed by the school authorities, the Supreme Court of Delaware affirmed the lower court's decision on August 28, 1952.[101] On November 13, the United States Supreme Court contacted the Delaware attorney general and informed him that the case was set for argument in December, following the District of Columbia case.[102]

The case from the District of Columbia, *Bolling v. Sharpe*, was filed on different grounds because of its jurisdiction. Segregation resulted from congressional statutes, not state constitutions. Therefore, the Fourteenth Amendment was not applicable. Instead, the plaintiffs argued that the Fifth Amendment's due process clause imposed equality obligations on Congress.[103] In April 1951, the United States District Court denied the relief requested in the parents' petition. James Nabrit Jr., counsel for the plaintiffs, immediately filed an appeal with the United States Court of Appeals. While the appeal was pending, the Supreme Court contacted him and requested that he petition the Court to have the case brought up with the other three cases (*Brown* of Kansas, *Briggs* of South Carolina, and *Davis* of Virginia) scheduled for oral argument in December. On November 10, 1952, the Court set *Bolling* for argument after the Virginia case.[104]

Oral arguments before the Supreme Court in *Briggs* took place on December 9, 1952, in conjunction with the other school segregation cases: *Brown*, *Davis*, *Bolling*, and *Belton*.[105] In a rebuke to Judges Parker and Timmerman and echoing Waties, Marshall began his opening argument in *Briggs* with "there can be no question that from the beginning of this case, the filing of the initial complaint, up until the present time, the appellants have raised and have preserved their attack on the validity of the provision of the South Carolina Constitution and the South Carolina statute."[106] After hours of argument spread across three days, the Justices were unable to come to a decision by the end of the Court's 1952–53 term in June 1953. The Court scheduled the cases for further oral argument in October 1953. For the second hearing, the Court requested briefs from all parties that addressed the following issues: "the historical origins of the Fourteenth Amendment, its original purpose with regard to schools, the power of the Court to adjudicate the constitutionality of segregated schools, and the procedure the Court should follow in the event that segregation was found unconstitutional."[107] Oral argument in the five cases was postponed from October to December 7–9, 1953, due to the unexpected death of Chief Justice Fred Vinson Jr. in September. Under a recess appointment, President Eisenhower nominated California Governor Earl Warren to replace Vinson. The Senate confirmed Warren as Chief Justice in March 1954.

Much like the 1951 *Briggs* trial in Charleston, spectators began lining up outside the Supreme Court at dawn on December 7, even though argument was not scheduled to begin until one o'clock in the afternoon. For its case before the Supreme Court, South Carolina hired John W. Davis to defend segregation in its public schools. A former ambassador under Woodrow Wilson, Davis was confident that the Supreme Court would validate Judge Parker's majority opinion, especially since South Carolina had complied with the "equal" prong of separate-but-equal.[108] Spottswood Robinson, Robert L. Carter, George E. C. Hayes, and James M. Nabrit Jr. joined Thurgood Marshall for the allotted eleven hours for oral argument.[109] All four men were connected to Howard University Law School and Charles Hamilton Houston. The Court reserved one hour for US Assistant Attorney General J. Lee Rankin. The United States Department of Justice had submitted an amicus brief on behalf of the parent-plaintiffs, as did the American Jewish Congress, American Civil Liberties Union, American Federation of Teachers, Congress of Industrial Organizations, and American Veterans Committee.[110] Oral argument in December 1953 occurred four years after Black parents sent their petition to the Clarendon County School Board on November 11, 1949. They would have to wait a bit longer for the Supreme Court's decision.

Chapter 8

DEMOCRACY AND DECENCY PREVAIL

The Supreme Court finally rendered its landmark unanimous decision in *Brown v. Board of Education* on May 17, 1954, five months after the Justices heard oral argument and six years after the *Pearson* bus transportation case was dismissed. The ruling consolidated all five school segregation cases: *Briggs* from South Carolina, *Davis* from Virginia, *Brown* from Kansas, *Belton* from Delaware, and *Bolling* from the District of Columbia. In their decision, the Justices found that segregation of Black children generated feelings of inferiority. The Court ruled that "Separate educational facilities were inherently unequal," which was remarkably similar to Waties's dissent, "Segregation is *per se* inequality." However, Chief Justice Warren did not credit Waties. After decades of legal battles fought by the NAACP and supported by Black communities, the Supreme Court finally reversed *Plessy v. Ferguson*, the separate-but-equal precedent that legalized segregation. The end of legally mandated segregation reasserted the basic American principle that "all men are created equal."[1]

In New York, on the evening of May 17, the Warings had an impromptu celebration at their Fifth Avenue apartment. At the party, Walter White praised Waties, recalling the pounding that Waties took when he wrote the dissenting opinion in *Briggs*. Poppy Cannon, Walter's wife, remembered Waties saying that "Eventually the Supreme Court, if not in this generation in some future generation, is going to come to the position that I have taken here. I'm not saying this out of pride of authorship but because it is the only position which the Court can eventually take."[2] Condemned for his *Briggs'* dissent in 1951, the *Brown* decision vindicated Waties: "Therefore, with considerable gratification, I sometimes laughingly say that nine Supreme Court justices were just as big damn fools as I was, apparently, because they happened to decide my way."[3] In response to the Court's decision, Waties prepared a statement for the press:

> I am delighted to learn that the Supreme Court has now spoken. This decision will make history and will erase the shame of the Dred

Scott and Plessy against Ferguson cases. The Court has re-affirmed our belief in the Declaration of Independence and the Constitution and has finally killed the hypocrisy of those who practised a vicious form of racial bias under the sophistry of the so called Separate but Equal doctrine. For a long time we have suffered under the taunts of foreign enemies who have proclaimed that we did not live up to our protestations of true democracy. We are now freed from that charge; and democracy and decency prevail.[4]

In November 1954, the Warings returned to South Carolina, their first visit since they moved to New York when Waties retired in 1952. They had not veered from their declaration that they would not return to South Carolina as long as segregation was the law of the land. Cheering citizens met the Warings when they arrived at the train station, then formed a motorcade for the seven-mile trek into downtown Charleston.[5] The local television station broadcast the Warings' arrival.[6] During the three-day visit, the couple stayed with Ruby Cornwell and her family.[7] The South Carolina NAACP sponsored a dinner honoring Waties on November 6, 1954, at Biust Elementary School, a Black school in Charleston. Over three hundred people attended, paying ten dollars per plate.[8] A. J. Clement, president of the Charleston NAACP branch, James Hinton, president of the state NAACP conference, and Robert Carter from the NAACP's New York headquarters made remarks. Hinton said that the *Briggs* dissent made Waties "the No. 1 American for human rights." Carter praised Waties for cutting "through the legal sophistry" in his rulings that equalized Black and white teachers' salaries, prohibited the state's Democratic Party from disenfranchising Black voters, and denounced separate-but-equal. Marion Wright, president of the Southern Regional Council, delivered the principal address at the testimonial. Wright said that Waties's decisions "have helped to break the shackles which have bound the twentieth century to nineteenth or even the eighteenth."[9] Wright's assessment aligned with what Waties and Elizabeth had learned about the legacy of slavery in South Carolina. The speakers' remarks reflected appreciation for the ground-breaking nature of Waties's rulings and his courage in rendering them. Without Waties's rulings, the legal battles in South Carolina would most assuredly have stretched out for many more years, exposing the plaintiffs to retaliation and prolonging second-class citizenship for Black residents.

As was his habit, Waties did not prepare a manuscript but scribbled notes from which he spoke. Visibly moved by the outpouring at the testimonial, he said, "I don't deserve the honor you so graciously bestow upon me and Mrs. Waring tonight." He declared that on May 17, 1954, *Plessy v. Ferguson* "went where it had belonged for many decades—into the garbage pail." Waties closed by telling those who gathered to pay tribute to him, "Tonight, I have seen my dream come true." His dream was upsetting the laws that impaled a group of American citizens into physical and mental slavery. Elizabeth and Waties returned to New York carrying with them "the good will of hundreds" from South Carolina.[10] Upon their return to New York, Elizabeth and Waties individually sent letters to Ruby Cornwell and her husband, thanking them for their kind hospitality. Elizabeth wrote of the "comfortable realization of the love we have received from all of you and which we feel so deeply" generated by the visit to Charleston.[11] In his letter, Waties assured the Cornwells that the Warings had a comfortable trip back to New York, Elizabeth seemed to be in fine physical shape, and "of course we are mentally and spiritually uplifted and very very happy."[12] The testimonial dinner organized by the Charleston and South Carolina NAACP soothed Elizabeth and Waties's sense of betrayal and abandonment.

Based on their conviction that federal interference was the only way to end segregation, the NAACP was the Warings' best ally because the NAACP pursued the legal course of action. Elizabeth and Waties cultivated relationships with higher-ups in the NAACP National Office like Walter White, John Hammond, Palmer Weber, and Thurgood Marshall. Not content to patiently wait, Waties actively campaigned to get the NAACP to file a school segregation suit and to bring it in his courtroom. Once the initial lawsuit was filed, Waties exploited his position and power as a federal judge. He went behind Thurgood Marshall's back and colluded with Walter White and John Hammond. But even those relationships deteriorated because of slights, real or imagined by the Warings. As much as he praised Marshall in the late 1940s, Waties criticized him for not filing briefs in *Briggs*. Then when the briefs were filed, Waties called them lackluster.

The NAACP's unforgivable sin was not objecting when the school board filed its report in December 1951. If they had objected, the initial appeal of *Briggs* would have been the first school segregation case appealed to the Supreme Court. Because the NAACP did not object in the Supreme Court or lower court, another hearing was scheduled for *Briggs* in March 1952. Once that hearing was scheduled, the pending appeal before the Supreme Court was dismissed. Before the NAACP could appeal the lower court's decision a second time, the appeal in *Brown* was filed. The delay in the *Briggs* appeal resulted in the Supreme Court decision ending legal school segregation being known as *Brown v. Board of Education*, not *Briggs v. Elliott*. Instead of his dissent being *the* basis for *the* Supreme Court decision, it was lost as one of the *Brown* companion cases. Therefore, Waties's opportunity for a legacy and immortality as a federal judge and civil rights advocate was extinguished.

Based on his correspondence, Waties believed he had single-handedly offered the Supreme Court the means, through his *Briggs* dissent, by which to overturn *Plessy v. Ferguson*: "I have great hopes that the Briggs case may shove them [Supreme Court] across and I believe they certainly have an opportunity (and God knows I have done my best to give it to them) to finally declare that segregation is per se inequality."[13] He also believed that his retirement focused the eyes of the country on the Supreme Court's sidestepping the issue : "But my retirement and refusal to go with the futility of a separate-but-equal situation points up clearly and distinctly that there is no further issue in the lower court. . . . I hope that my refusal to sit may have some influence upon the Supreme Court and the mind of the country."[14] In addition to his speeches, Waties acted through his dissent and retirement to shift the nation's perspective on segregation and push it to the forefront of the public conversation.

Beyond the school segregation case, Elizabeth and Waties encountered conflict with prominent NAACP leaders. John Hammond was on the NAACP's board and one of the few white people officially associated with the organization. During the *Briggs* trial in Charleston, Elizabeth wrote about Hammond with enthusiasm and admiration in her diary. She commended his devotion to his stepdaughter and his militant stance against segregation. She loaned her typewriter to Hammond and David Anderson, a reporter for the *Chicago Sun-Times*. The men dined with the Warings on May 29, 1951, the last day of the *Briggs* trial.[15] The relationship between Hammond and the Warings deteriorated in 1954. At some point, Hammond and his wife had invited the Warings to the Hammond home but did not receive a response from the Warings. Waties extended an invitation to Hammond to attend the testimonial dinner in Charleston. The invitation did not include Hammond's wife. Hammond decided not to attend the testimonial because he thought the tribute was for Black South Carolinians who brought the suit and stood up in the face of terror and abuse.[16] Although Hammond did not attend the testimonial in Charleston, he delivered remarks at the Alpha Kappa Alpha Sorority's tribute to Waties in 1959.[17]

The conflict with John Hammond was not an isolated incident. Elizabeth butted heads with "friends for the National Association for the Advancement of Colored People" when they organized a tea in Elizabeth's honor. Mrs. Roy Wilkins helped plan the tea in March 1950.[18] Elizabeth objected to the guest list because it included Walter White's first wife but did not include

Poppy Cannon, his second wife. White obtained a divorce from his first wife of twenty-seven years in Mexico. Less than a week later, on July 6, 1949, he married Cannon, a white woman.[19] Much like Elizabeth and Waties's divorces and marriage, White's divorce and marriage to Cannon created a scandal, and he faced calls to resign. Initially, Elizabeth agreed to attend the tea. When she discovered that Cannon was excluded, Elizabeth rescinded her acceptance. In a telegram, Elizabeth stated that she and Waties considered the omission of Cannon on the guest list as "an insult to our friends the Walter Whites and hence I refuse to attend."[20] No one in Charleston had stood up for Elizabeth when she was excluded from the downtown group's invitations. Elizabeth's loyalty to Cannon prevented a rift in the Warings' relationship with the Whites. But it was also a not-too-subtle declaration of support for White's continued leadership of the NAACP in the midst of the scandal surrounding his marriage to Cannon.

Alongside their rhetorical campaign to end legally mandated segregation, the Warings turned to the Black community in Charleston for friendship and support. Even in that, people questioned their motives. Elizabeth blamed white supremacists for turning Black people against the Warings. In July 1951, she wrote to Ruby Cornwell:

> The idea was implanted in the Negro suspicious mind that the WARINGS WERE LONELY AND HAD TURNED TO THE NEGROES AS A SUBSTITUTE FOR THE OSTRACIZM BY THE WHITE PEOPLE SINCE THE JUDGE'S PRIMARY DECISION GIVING THE NEGRO THE RIGHT TO VOTE. EVEN WORSE THEIR MACHINE OF PROPAGANDA WENT TO WORK ON THE ATTACK THAT THE JUDGE AND I WERE GETTING REVENGE ON THE WHITE PEOPLE (emphasis in original).[21]

As Elizabeth tried to refute claims that her actions were motivated by revenge, she invoked a racial stereotype with "Negro suspicious mind." Ruby Cornwell explained that Elizabeth and Waties refused to contemplate that "a lot of black people viewed him as a friendless man who suddenly wanted to be friends with them."[22] Elizabeth's righteous indignation flared at any criticism of Waties. She turned her wrath upon Black people if she perceived any hint of disapproval. Her umbrage was similar to white supremacists' responses to her speeches. Overly sensitive and defensive, Elizabeth often assumed a martyr-like attitude.

Elizabeth failed to account for the reasonable fear within the Black community after a cross was burned at the Warings' home in March 1950, and their home was attacked with pellets in October 1950. McCray reported that the score or more of Black Charlestonians who had visited the Waring home dwindled to two or three families. Then at Christmas, Black teachers took their students to serenade white families below Broad Street. The group passed by the Warings and sang at the homes of people who the Warings considered enemies.[23] The Warings stood up for Black Americans despite the danger. They did not believe that those for whom they had risked so much would desert them. White supremacy reached far beyond voting and segregation. The Klan threatened Waties, a cross was burned at their home, Elizabeth was jostled on the street, not to mention the phone calls and letters. If a white federal judge and his wife were not immune from white supremacy's tactics, then who was? The attacks on the Warings were intended to scare other white and Black people from speaking out against white supremacy.

While living in Charleston became more and more unpleasant for Elizabeth and Waties because of white southerners' harassment, the Black community's desertion wounded the Warings more. On March 16, 1952, a month after Elizabeth and Waties left South Carolina, John McCray delivered a speech in Greenville and shared that the Warings might not have decided to move elsewhere if "Negroes in this state stood with them in their fight to break down discriminations based on race and color." In response to Black people who said that the Judge "was going too far," McCray shamed them by saying that never in their lifetimes would a federal judge in South Carolina "use the power of his office to help us, who will stick his neck out to help us."[24] McCray's remarks exemplified the widely held admiration for the couple, but the African American community was not monolithic. Despite his rulings from the bench in favor of African American plaintiffs and against white supremacists, Waties and Elizabeth's sharp words were not confined exclusively to white people. Although not as often, they also criticized Black people for accepting too little or not doing enough. The Warings' radical stance left little space for compromise. Elizabeth and Waties knew what was best for everyone, and if people would do what they said, then segregation would end.

A couple of weeks after the ruling and dissent in *Briggs* were publicly released, Waties met with Albert J. Dunmore of the *Pittsburgh Courier* in Charleston. Dunmore's article, "Judge Waring Fears Weak Negro Leaders," appeared on July 7, 1951, while Waties was pressuring Thurgood Marshall about the *Briggs* appeal.[25] Waties's anxiety surrounding a potential loss on the appeal clouded his judgment. He told Dunmore, "No, we can not be left alone to wage this battle. The white citizens of South Carolina must be shamed into cleaning up their dirty, filthy house . . . and it only can be done by folks outside the house." Waties adopted Elizabeth's antagonistic tone but strayed from the Warings' extended argument that the South was sick, gradualism could not cure it, and only force would work. After denigrating the NAACP, Black South Carolinians, and northern philanthropic organizations, Waties "flayed those Negro leaders who profit through the system of segregation." He praised James Hinton, John McCray, and the "poorer people of your group" who fought fearlessly but needed "stronger and surer support." The people who should lead, like ministers, school teachers, and professionals, "benefit directly from this system of discrimination." Although he qualified his remark by saying many of them were terrified, he said that "The only people I fear in this fight are the weak-kneed colored people of our state."[26] His remark was unwarranted and uninformed. It also supported Governor Byrnes's claim that Black people in South Carolina did not want desegregated schools because people would lose their jobs.

Echoing Elizabeth's exhortation that "Freedom Is Everybody's Job," Waties said that repealing the laws that upheld segregation was everybody's job: "It isn't a fight that must be fought by a few brave people here in the South. It must have the support of everyone throughout this land." He criticized newspapers, northern organizations, churches, unions, and the United States government for not doing enough and prescribed measures each could take to support the "Negroes of South Carolina [who] stand their ground in this fight for human dignity."[27] Overall, Waties's tone in the interview was sanctimonious. His off-hand qualifications about the danger and repercussions facing those who opposed white supremacy reflected his privilege. When he retired, Waties hoped it "puts them on their mettle and says to them that it is time they showed courage and come out on their own fighting basis."[28] Waties criticized Black people for not being more courageous and standing up for themselves. Yet, he refused to countenance any route to eliminate segregation other than the one he formulated. He would have approved if they had risked their lives to further the cause as Waties thought it should be fought.

In a rare rebuke, the *Pittsburgh Courier* published an editorial shortly after Waties's 1952 speeches in Chicago. The editorial pointed out that Black leaders were in difficult positions and "the situations with which they are faced day-to-day are delicate." The *Courier* commended Waties for his rulings because "they were landmarks on the road to freedom." Even so, it was unfair and unrealistic for Waties and, by extension Elizabeth, to expect Black people "to sacrifice themselves and their families in order to avoid the 'smear' of gradualism when they have no alternative."[29] Elizabeth and Waties simultaneously reproached Black people for bowing to white supremacy even as they, two white people, tried to dictate how Black people should resist. They routinely criticized people and groups that did not agree with their ideas about the best way to end segregation.

Many African American people called for more time so white southerners would accept white and Black children side by side in schools. Although she was in high school, Miriam DeCosta questioned the wisdom of immediate desegregation: "However, I beg to differ with you on the steps which must be taken against segregation. I think that there must be a gradual change, say over 20 years.... I'm for bringing it out in the open but I'm wondering if it will have the affect upon people that we so earnestly desire."[30] Miriam had personally experienced the reaction to forced integration at Westbury, the private boarding school she attended due to Elizabeth's sponsorship. None of her schoolmates' parents were willing to let their white daughters share a room with Miriam, a middle-class Black girl from Orangeburg, South Carolina, even at an exclusive northern school for wealthy white girls. Miriam wrote: "Can you imagine how I would feel if I knew that a girl was forced to room with me against her parents' wishes? There would be nothing but resentment on the part of her parents and there might be serious repercussions through the alum. It is a problem which must be handled very delicately."[31]

Miriam's letter about the roommate situation was in response to Elizabeth's urging her to push the matter with the school. Elizabeth's shortsightedness in this instance was related to her single-minded focus on her goal. However, the result was the same—pushing people into actions they were wary of and then cutting them off for their hesitation and refusal to abide by the Warings' suggestions. While they courageously spoke out against white supremacy, Elizabeth and Waties were merciless if crossed. In her correspondence with Ruby Cornwell during the summer of 1951, Elizabeth told Cornwell, "There is no half-way." She warned Cornwell not to trust anyone and expressed her disappointment in Black South Carolinians: "The election behavior and many other tragic revelations have slowly and thoughtfully made us come to this grave decision that our work in Charleston is done. It is finished" (emphasis in original). In this letter to Cornwell, Elizabeth enclosed a copy of her letter declining an invitation to speak at Emanuel AME Church because "Judge Waring and I have given you advice which few of you have chosen to follow."[32] The condescension and anger in Elizabeth's letters reflect her either/or mentality. People were either with her or against her. She was unaware of the contradiction in her attitude and how it replicated white supremacy in certain aspects. Neither Elizabeth nor Waties collaborated with

Black people on the means to end Jim Crow. If Black people hesitated when the Warings pushed them, then the Warings, usually Elizabeth, unleashed their fury. Elizabeth's insistence on Black people complying with the Warings' plan reproduced white paternalism. Despite Waties's acknowledging people's fear in his speeches, he and Elizabeth dismissed the genuine threats that people faced.

The *Brown* decision redeemed Waties's professional reputation. In 1951, he appeared spiteful and vindictive. Although it took three years, his *Briggs'* dissent eventually became law. Shunned and mocked across the South for their efforts to end segregation, the Warings finally achieved their goal of a Supreme Court decision reversing *Plessy v. Ferguson*. Instead of vengeful and mentally unstable outsiders, the Warings were heralded as visionaries. Elizabeth's friend from Detroit wrote, "And except for Waties, it might have been delayed for years. When I think how dearly the two of you have had to pay for your prophetic position I rejoice that you had had this deserved recognition and honor in your own time."[33] The Warings believed segregation was the source of racism as did the NAACP legal team starting with Charles Hamilton Houston. Because racial prejudice was irrational and a result of ignorance, social contact between Black and white people, especially for school children, would eradicate bias and bigotry. Waties believed that "if you can have this integration starting with the little children in the first grades, you will get rid of racial prejudice."[34] Knowledge of and appreciation for each other could never take place if the races never came in contact. Just as importantly, continued segregation reproduced white southerners' erroneous belief that Black people were inferior.

In 1949, Waties said that the greatest problem in the South was changing the white southerner's state of mind, so they would recognize the rights of their fellow citizens, regardless of race. White people negatively judged Black people for the characteristics that were actually a consequence of segregation and not an inherent biological defect. Hodding Carter wrote in 1948: "Thus, the white Southerner remains largely convinced that when the Southern Negro is functionally illiterate, unskilled, unkempt, diseased, lawless and recalcitrant, it is because he is a Negro and not because of the handicaps that come from being a Negro."[35] Waties expressed the opinion that any so-called inferiority was the result of living conditions and lack of opportunity: "If you put him in a poor school, bad housing, sorry living conditions, then he's going to be dirty, diseased and ignorant."[36] Although some white southerners were willing to concede that Black people deserved "better schools, churches, and better living conditions," they questioned Black students attending white schools because of Black students' supposed lower intelligence, hygiene, and moral standards.[37] White southerners were unwilling to relinquish the image of Black people as inferior or different. With such an indelible image, they did not perceive Black people as entitled to citizenship. The Warings were convinced that eliminating segregation would change white people's image of Black people. Little did the Warings know to what lengths white southerners would go to preserve segregation. For them, there was no "American dilemma."[38]

When the Supreme Court decreed in its initial decision in 1954 that segregation was unconstitutional, it failed to state how and when its constitutional proposition was to be enforced: "The question of 'how' and 'when' was set down for further argument."[39] The Justices feared immediate desegregation would cause violence and school closures. Also, they wanted to reduce resistance from white southerners. Klarman writes that several justices had insisted on gradualism in desegregating public schools in exchange for their voting to overturn *Plessy*.[40] Another round of oral argument in the school segregation cases was scheduled for April 1955. The issue at hand was how best to implement the court's ruling taking into consideration local sentiment and school systems. Justice Warren's quest for a unanimous decision in *Brown* and the justices' determination to avoid school closures, violence, and animosity resulted in the infamous "with all deliberate speed" in its *Brown II* decision issued on May 31, 1955: "the cases are remanded to the District Courts to take such proceedings and enter such orders and decrees consistent with this opinion as are necessary and proper to admit the parties to these cases to public schools on a racially nondiscriminatory basis with all deliberate speed."[41] The Supreme Court relinquished implementation to localities.

A continuing theme in Waties and Elizabeth's rhetorical campaign was "If you tell them what to do and if you make them do it, it's going to come out all right."[42] Elizabeth and Waties often used the example of the 1948 Democratic Primary to demonstrate that despite the predictions of bloodshed and violence, the election took place without incident, even with Black people voting. They insisted that white people would comply with federal law. Waties believed that "however much a fellow might object to having his face forcibly washed, when it is washed he's pretty proud of the fact that he's got a clean face." Waties explained, "In other words, I'm a great believer that if people are forced to do the right thing, it won't take long before they'll be very glad. They won't acclaim the person that forces them, but they will pretty soon point with pride to what they have accomplished. And it doesn't matter who gets the credit or how it comes about, if the result is there."[43] However, Elizabeth and Waties underestimated the depth of white sentiment against Black and white children sitting side by side in elementary schools. Charles M. Payne explains that "part of the miscalculation involved a widespread tendency to overestimate the power of the law to make change and to underestimate the degree of racial intransigence outside the South."[44] Elizabeth, Waties, and Supreme Court justices expected the region that had seceded from the Union and fought a war to preserve slavery would comply with *Brown*.

In response to *Brown II*, South Carolina prohibited white schools from admitting Black students, closed schools that were under court order to admit Black children, and denied funds to schools that used student assignments or busing to further integration.[45] When a federal court ordered desegregation in Summerton, white parents opened Clarendon Hall, a private school. County officials closed the public schools in September 1970, the court's deadline for integration.[46] The 2013 documentary *Corridor of Shame* illuminates the condition of schools in rural counties along Interstate 95, including Clarendon County. The *Post and Courier's* multi-part series in 2018, "Minimally Adequate," exposed *de facto* segregation, underfunding, and lagging standardized scores in South Carolina's public school system.[47] The persistent deficiencies in public schools across South Carolina demonstrate the historical neglect by the state's elected representatives. White students still attend the private schools established in the 1950s, and Black students compose the majority of students in public schools. The current governor in South Carolina, Henry McMaster, along with the state's United States senators, tout "school choice" as the remedy for what ails public schools. Although *Brown* eliminated legal sanction for segregation, the public schools in South Carolina remain racially segregated due to decades of underfunding fueled by veiled white supremacist beliefs.

Throughout the Warings' rhetorical campaign to end segregation, Black and white people questioned the couple's motives. Did they champion the cause of school segregation because they genuinely believed in racial equality? Or did they seek revenge against white southerners for spurning Elizabeth? I argue that they were not motivated by revenge. However, they must have laughed a little inside at how white people reacted. For the *Collier's* article, Elizabeth staged the interracial meal in her dining room, which could be perceived as symbolic, but was also provocative because "breaking bread across the color line was heresy, perhaps as much a threat to Jim Crow as interracial consensual sex."[48] Septima Clark recalled that Elizabeth was good at things like that.[49] Ann Hyde, Elizabeth's daughter, agreed that her mother enjoyed the role of shocking people.[50] Elizabeth confounded her family and friends in Detroit when she divorced her first husband and married a man twenty years her senior whom she barely knew. By the time she arrived in

Charleston, she had already experienced social ostracism. On some levels, she had nothing to lose by speaking out so frankly and vehemently against white supremacy.

Waties, on the other hand, had more to lose. Granted, his social standing in Charleston diminished significantly when he divorced his first wife, Miss Annie, to marry Elizabeth, especially with rumors flying that he and Elizabeth were having an affair while still married to their respective spouses. He may have recovered, at least socially, were it not for his strong public stand against the Southern way of life. The way that he spoke of civil rights and white supremacy crossed the acceptable line of white southern liberalism. White people in Charleston and eventually across the South believed that the Warings' activism to end segregation was calculated to exact revenge for being ostracized from white society.

Reducing Elizabeth and Waties's activism to an agenda like petty revenge removes the possibility that they genuinely cared about racial equality. From this perspective, two privileged white people (and one a native southerner) could not possibly care for equality unless they stood to personally gain from the effort. If this were the case, then the Warings' argument was easily dismissed because it was not genuine. Furthermore, those whom the Warings attacked did not have to examine their personal beliefs about race because what the Warings said came from a position of self-promotion or pettiness. Attributing the Warings' stance on segregation to anything other than genuine means that they were the problem, not white supremacy and Jim Crow.

Along with their public address, the Warings maintained friendships with Black people that were not so public. For example, Elizabeth gave gifts to Septima Clark.[51] Also, Elizabeth invited Clark to her house on Meeting Street and visited Clark's home, despite Clark's mother's refusal to receive Elizabeth.[52] Ruby Cornwell always sent gifts to Waties and Elizabeth for their birthdays.[53] Some declared that the Warings only socialized with Black people because the couple had no white friends. Therefore, they socialized with Black people to either outrage Charleston society or because white people would not enter the Waring home. Elizabeth choreographed public performances of interracial socializing to refute the claims that she and Waties co-opted segregation as a means to exact revenge on white people. These interactions indicate that along with their explosive rhetoric, the Warings lived the principles they advocated for in their speeches.

The Warings were friends with Frank and Beautine DeCosta, faculty members at South Carolina State College for Negroes in Orangeburg. The DeCostas had two children, Miriam and Frank Jr. Elizabeth and Waties took interest in the children's education and sponsored Miriam's admission to Westover School in Connecticut in 1950. She was the first Black student to attend the school and graduated in 1952.[54] Elizabeth and Waties also attempted to get Frank Jr. into Phillips Academy, a prestigious boarding school in Andover, Massachusetts. The Warings did more than get Miriam into Westover. Elizabeth corresponded with her regularly, sent her gifts, and visited her. Miriam wrote to Elizabeth regularly, even after graduating from Westover.

Miriam, the recipient of the Warings' generosity, questioned their motives. Shortly after her arrival at Westover in September 1950, Miriam wrote to Elizabeth:

> You know, when I first met you I was wondering what alterior motive you had behind what you were doing. I just couldn't believe, being a Southerner, that you were really being completely honest. But the more I listened to you talking, that day in Charleston, the more I liked you. . . . I know that you are really a person who could without regard for herself, try to do so much for my race.[55]

Her parents may have questioned the Warings' motives also but the opportunity for Miriam to attend Westover could not be rejected. The Warings may have been genuinely interested in Miriam receiving an excellent education at an exclusive finishing school. But a Black girl attending an all-white school furthered their argument that segregation was based on irrational biases. The apocalypse predicted by the segregationists did not occur when the races mingled in schools.

The Warings did not limit their influence to the DeCosta children. They were also acquainted with Reverend De Laine, one of the local leaders in Clarendon County who facilitated the *Briggs* lawsuit. He was instrumental in gathering the necessary signatures and commitment from parents in Clarendon County to pursue the lawsuit. Reverend De Laine's son speculates that his father and Waties met in the late 1940s through a mutual acquaintance, Roscoe Wilson, a Black dentist living in Florence, South Carolina.[56] The relationship between the Warings and De Laine was such that Reverend De Laine wrote Elizabeth about the situation in Clarendon County after the lawsuit was filed. In late 1951, Waties suggested to Walter White that De Laine be nominated for the Spingarn Medal. Waties could not officially nominate De Laine because the *Briggs* case was pending before the Supreme Court. In his letter to White, Waties wrote that De Laine was "one who is not so well known but who has been a real martyr to the cause and should be recognized as a great figure in the fight for opportunities for Negroes."[57]

The Warings invited the De Laine family to dinner during the holidays in 1951. During dinner, Waties asked Jay, Reverend De Laine's son, about his attending Johnson C. Smith University in Charlotte. Jay replied that JCS was his parents' choice. He wanted to attend Lincoln University in Philadelphia. Waties proposed that he could easily get Jay into Howard University, but Jay had his heart set on Lincoln. Waties indicated he would see what he could do, and within three weeks, Jay received a letter that Lincoln was awaiting his application and he would receive a partial scholarship.[58] From the correspondence, Waties contacted Septima Clark, who then put him in touch with Sadie Alexander, a prominent attorney in Philadelphia who had also served on the President's Committee on Civil Rights.[59]

The situation in Clarendon County became increasingly dangerous for Reverend De Laine as the school segregation cases progressed. His bishop transferred him to a church in Lake City, South Carolina. Lake City was a known hub for Klan activity. By 1955, after *Brown* and *Brown II*, the Citizens' Council was active and vigilant in the town. On October 1, 1955, De Laine received a letter warning him that he had ten days to leave town or else he would end up like Frazier Baker, a Black postmaster in 1898 who refused to resign his post and leave town. A white mob set the post office on fire where Baker and his family lived. Then, the mob started shooting into the house, killing Baker and his two-year-old daughter. His wife and four other children fled to safety despite gunshot wounds.[60] On the seventh day after receiving the letter, Reverend De Laine's church, St. James AME, was destroyed by fire. On the tenth day, October 10, 1955, motorcades drove by the De Laine home, shooting at the house. De Laine returned fire when the cars came by the third time. Supposedly, De Laine's shots injured two people, and he was charged with intent to kill. He fled Lake City that night and headed to Florence on his way out of South Carolina. En route to New York City, De Laine contacted the FBI. He informed law enforcement authorities of his whereabouts and foiled South Carolina's attempts to issue a federal fugitive warrant against him. In New York, the courts refused to extradite De Laine back to his home state.[61] South Carolina Governor George Timmerman Jr. did not press the matter because he did not want to give the NAACP another martyr who could be used for fundraising.[62] The De Laine family ended up in Buffalo, New York, where Elizabeth and Waties used their influence to help find a job for Mrs. De Laine and housing for the family. Reverend De Laine founded an AME church that was dedicated as De Laine-Waring AME Church. When the family left Buffalo for Queens in 1957, the Warings helped out again, with Waties securing a teaching position for Mrs. De Laine and a church for Reverend De Laine.[63]

The Warings' altruism beyond the public eye points to their public position on race and segregation as more than an elaborate ruse to exact revenge. Their stance on race relations was not confined to publicly condemning white supremacy. At the same time, their socializing with Black people in their home contained shock value that served the Warings' purpose. Beyond that, the couple worked behind the scenes and used their influence and contacts to assist the DeCosta and De Laine families. Granted, they could use Miriam attending an elite white boarding school to further their cause. Yet, their assistance to the De Laine family appears selfless. What did they have to gain by Joseph Jr. attending Lincoln University, a historically Black college? Furthermore, Waties's nominating Reverend De Laine for the Spingarn Medal indicates his respect for De Laine. The Warings' continued association with De Laine, well after *Brown*, demonstrates a depth of good will and respect that contradicts or at least complicates the widely held opinion that the Warings acted purely out of spite. The Warings' detractors alleged that the couple coopted race relations as their cause in order to infuriate and humiliate the white society that shunned them. Probing beneath the obvious motivation, the Warings' private actions construct a more complex account of the impetus for their controversial stance.

Waties and Elizabeth remained in New York City until his death in January 1968. Elizabeth corresponded with her network, and Waties served as director of the National Committee Against Discrimination in Housing, trustee of the National Urban League, president of the National Committee for Rural Schools, and vice-chair of the Board of Directors of the American Civil Liberties Union.[64] On the radio show, *Report to the People*, Waties discussed the acquittal of the men who lynched Emmett Till. In 1956, a young Black minister from Alabama delivered "Desegregation and the Future" at the National Committee for Rural School's annual luncheon. The Committee promoted "adequate unsegregated public school facilities."[65] The following month, Martin Luther King Jr. invited Elizabeth and Waties to attend the Montgomery Improvement Association's Institute on Nonviolence and Social Change. Waties declined, citing Elizabeth's failing health, but he commended King and MIA on their "great fight for freedom and the American Creed."[66] Waties also appeared on the television show, *The Open Mind*, with King. The men discussed the "New Negro" in 1957. Waties lent his name to Eleanor Roosevelt's Committee of Inquiry into the Administration of Justice in the Freedom Struggle. Roosevelt founded the committee in response to the violent images of the 1961 Freedom Rides.[67] Through *Brown II*, Massive Resistance, and 1960s direct action campaigns, the Warings remained informed and involved.

By 1959, Elizabeth's health was deteriorating. When Alpha Kappa Alpha organized a testimonial luncheon honoring her and Waties in November, only Waties attended. Elizabeth asked Mrs. Maude Veal, a friend from South Carolina whom Elizabeth considered her little sister, to stand beside Waties at the ceremony.[68] According to Yarbrough, Elizabeth suffered from a hiatus hernia that required her to sleep sitting on a sofa. She rarely left the couple's New York apartment but continued to collect newspaper articles and correspond regularly with her friends across the country. She and Waties traveled to Massachusetts, where Ann, Elizabeth's daughter, and her family lived. Ann's children often visited the Warings in New York. The visits filled Waties and Elizabeth with joy.[69]

In a 1963 interview published in the *Detroit Free Press*, Waties, with Elizabeth by his side, delighted in his life in New York, where he enjoyed "complete independence of movement and thought." Although he and Elizabeth rarely left their apartment, they watched television and subscribed to four newspapers to stay up-to-date on current events. The elderly Waties still lacked patience. He lambasted the argument that the South needed time to adjust and, overall, exhibited intolerance about the slow progress in the region, especially after federal law intervened.[70]

Fifteen years Elizabeth's senior, Waties's sight and hearing diminished, so she read aloud to him. By 1967, he was suffering from indigestion due to an intestinal blockage. Waties's physician recommended surgery to remove the obstruction, but Waties declined.[71] He died on January 11, 1968. The *New York Times* reported that Black and white mourners sang "We Shall Overcome" and "O Freedom, No More Weeping Over Me" at a memorial service held at Community Church in New York.[72] At the funeral in Charleston, only eleven white people attended among more than two hundred Black people who paid their respects to the judge. Waties's daughter, Anne, planted a magnolia tree at the gravesite at Magnolia Cemetery, but vandals uprooted it. The harsh sentiment towards Waties had not diminished, even sixteen years after he left Charleston.[73] Along with the memorial service in New York and funeral in Charleston, the South Carolina Conference of Branches, NAACP held a memorial service for the Judge at Allen University on January 28, 1968.[74] Elizabeth died less than a year after Waties in October 1968. She is buried next to the Judge at Magnolia Cemetery. Only nine people attended her funeral.

CONCLUSION

On May 18, 1954, the *New York Times* printed excerpts from newspaper editorials published in response to the Supreme Court's decision in *Brown v. Board of Education*. The *Amsterdam News* emphasized the historical significance of *Brown*: "The Supreme Court decision is the greatest victory for the Negro people since the Emancipation Proclamation." Amongst the declaration of the historic significance of the *Brown* decision, other editors pointed out its inevitability. The *Louisville Courier Journal* wrote, "For some time, every sign pointed to the decision which the Supreme Court finally came to." The *Pittsburgh Post-Gazette* ventured, "This ruling could hardly have come as a surprise to even the most determined advocate of segregation." Other editorials lauded the *Brown* decision as the end of racial inequality. The *Boston Herald* concluded that the *Brown* decision "recognizes the growing feeling that the separation of Negro (or other minority) children from the majority race at school age is an abuse of a democratic process and the democratic principle." The *Washington Post and Times-Herald* stated that the decision "will bring to an end a painful disparity between American principles and American practices."[1]

The pronouncements of *Brown*'s historic significance connote an onerous struggle towards a potentially unachievable end. The comments about the decision as an inevitable outcome suggest *Brown* was an episode within a larger narrative of American progress and exceptionalism. The dual and contradictory emphases raise critical questions about the public conversation and rhetorical culture of Jim Crow in the years leading up to *Brown*. James D. Anderson notes that the struggle for equality of opportunity at the local level is one of the overlooked themes in the historical scholarship on *Brown*.[2] In the midst of the legal battles, local communities sustained the plaintiffs as the cases meandered through the appeals process to the highest court in the United States. As African American communities supported the plaintiffs, white allies with access to platforms publicly denounced segregation. Those rhetorical efforts evoked a response, both positive and negative.

With a rhetorical lens, we see that *Brown* was more than a legal battle, more than Black activists versus white racists, and more than normative white morality. This account of the Warings' rhetorical campaign and networking alongside Black parents' resistance shows that *Brown* was the culmination of decades of activism. The Black parents' resilience and perseverance shifts them from rescued survivors to radical objectors. The themes, appeals, and arguments in the Warings' speeches reveal the rhetorical culture of the Jim Crow South. Their strategy of circulation indicates their conviction that the culture repressed dissent. Beyond hooded night-riders, the responses to the Warings' speeches verify that "polite racism" was as potent as violence. Any assertion that *Brown* was expected or inevitable abstracts that ruling from the social and rhetorical contexts of the grassroots struggles that made *Brown* possible.[3]

Charles M. Payne points out that *Brown v. Board of Education* was more than a legal battle. Instead, "It was one element in a decades-long struggle for equity in education, a struggle that required Blacks in local communities across the South to expose themselves to physical violence and economic repression."[4] The struggle culminated in a legal decision after Black parents persisted.[5] *Briggs* as a legal challenge initially began with the *Pearson* bus transportation case in 1947. Even before *Pearson* was filed, Black parents in Clarendon County organized to purchase and maintain a school bus for their children. Neither the Warings nor the Supreme Court rescued Black parents. Their organizing, resistance, and persistence—despite repercussions—point to the "depth and breadth of Black oppositional spirit and activity."[6] While the NAACP legal team crafted arguments, pleadings, and strategy, the parent-plaintiffs had to sustain themselves. While the Warings delivered speeches and corresponded with other activists, the parent-plaintiffs lived in Clarendon County. They still had to go to work, send their children to school, buy groceries, go to the post office, and walk down Main Street. They persevered for decades while they lived side by side with white supremacists who levied consequences.

Too often, social movements are reduced to two opposing factions, an either/or proposition that lacks nuance and dimension. The Warings' lives and rhetoric dispel that notion. Elizabeth developed a wide network of other white activists like James Dombrowski, Aubrey Williams, and Myles Horton. The white allies in her network sought to eliminate segregation without the equivocating of what Elizabeth called "parlor liberals." While associations existed that advocated more humane treatment of Black people, the members typically stopped short of speaking out against segregation, especially in elementary schools. The Warings cultivated relationships with white people who believed that white southerners would not voluntarily change the racial status quo. These white people were not consumed with misplaced loyalty to the Lost Cause or the South. The Warings and other white allies likely had biases and paternal tendencies, but nevertheless, worked to eliminate segregation at a time when most white people were silent.

Elizabeth and Waties launched their rhetorical campaign in response to their experience at the trial of Lynwood Shull. They believed that segregation perpetrated second-class citizenship for Black Americans and removed their protections under the law. To activate their rights and protections, segregation had to end. Myrdal argued that the "inadequate function of justice in the region" is "tolerated and upheld by the same *public opinion*" (emphasis added).[7] Waties wrote to James Dombrowski, "I believe that we have got to break the back of the present legal sanction of segregation before we can accomplish any good by talking or conferences in the South; this must come from the people of the whole nation awaking [sic] to the necessity of action through national legislation and court action."[8] The belief in the power of public opinion was not exclusive to the Warings. In his stance against *Brown* and desegregation, Strom Thurmond said, "public sentiment controls the actions of people. . . . If the sentiment of the people is strong enough then I am sure that the representatives of the people will carry out their wishes."[9] Of course, Thurmond was referring to resisting *Brown*, but the strategy of rallying public support was just as applicable to those opposing segregation. Elizabeth and Waties's public address supported the lawsuit from Clarendon County. The Warings sought to inject the cure for the racial malady in the South, the ministrations of federal law, by exciting public opinion.

In a little over three years, Elizabeth and Waties addressed thirty-five audiences but rarely delivered their speeches from full manuscripts. Through innovative research methods, I retrieved and curated digital surrogates culminating in a collection. The recovered and reconstructed texts reveal that the Warings developed a methodical campaign to rouse public opinion against white supremacy. Their rhetoric in the tradition of the agitator was a "persistent and uncompromising statement and restatement of grievances through all available communication channels, with the aim of creating public opinion favorable to a change in some condition."[10] They developed an extended medical analogy during the spring, 1950 campaign to discredit white southerners' calls for gradualism because "postponement and appeasement and soft talk are not ever going to get you any place."[11] The medical imagery evacuated white southerners' agency and rendered them helpless to cure their ailment. In their joint effort to end segregation, Elizabeth and Waties did not believe that white southerners would voluntarily change the racial status quo. They took steps to ensure that their appeals reached a national audience because only help from outside could heal the sick South. A transformed rhetorical culture opened a space for American voters to pressure their elected representatives.

A year after Elizabeth delivered "Freedom Is Everybody's Job" to the Black Charleston YWCA, she wrote to Bicknell Eubanks, editor of the *Christian Science Monitor*, and told him that she and Waties "had come to the definite conclusion that extreme methods were needed for this feeble and fast dying Negro Cause." She deliberately wrote her shock treatment because:

I INTENDED TO MAKE THE WHITE SOUTHERNER SO ANGRY THAT THE STONE WALL OF SILENCE WOULD BE BROKEN DOWN BECAUSE OF THEIR FURY AGAINST ME. IT WORKED, AND THEY TALKED AND TALKED AT LONG LAST AND HAVE NOT STOPPED SINCE (emphasis in original).[12]

When Elizabeth called white southerners "sick, confused, and decadent," she purposefully set herself on a collision course with white supremacists. The crash exposed the mythical defenses for segregation. The collision uncovered the racism ingrained within the responses from white people who likely considered themselves morally superior to the Ku Klux Klan. Misogyny and white supremacy embedded their civil and polite letters. Their letters appeared nonthreatening when compared to Klan violence. Nevertheless, even as they condemned violence and discrimination against Black people, they upheld and maintained white supremacy.

Elizabeth along with Waties determined the best and only way to end segregation was federal law because the *Elmore* and *Baskin* primary cases demonstrated that change would occur if the federal courts intervened. Once change was initiated in the form of federal law, white southerners would comply. In his oral history, Waties explained that "reform can come about by something that may be unpopular at the time. . . . I think there is a great timidity in regard to enforcement of law because it's unpopular in the community."[13] Time would not change white southerners' attitudes and beliefs about African American people. Such change would come about only when white southerners were forced to acknowledge African American people as full-fledged American citizens under the law. Such an acknowledgment would never come about as long as separate facilities for white and Black people were required by state and local laws. Segregation laws reinforced the inaccurate belief that Black people were inferior.

Elizabeth's speech to the Coming Street YWCA in Charleston is often partitioned from the other speeches and actions that she and Waties took prior to *Brown*. Waties's remarks off the bench are most often ignored. As a result, Elizabeth is constituted as a vengeful woman and Waties is reduced to the dissent in *Briggs*. However, as I have demonstrated throughout this book, Elizabeth and Waties's lives were more nuanced and multifaceted when grounded in their *full* historical circumstances, not just the social ostracism that they faced. They used their privilege and access to promote their conviction that Jim Crow was incompatible with American democracy. Although arrogant and even condescending at times, Elizabeth and Waties pursued a course of action that other white people lacked the courage to embark upon. While nearly impossible to determine the direct effect of Elizabeth and Waties's rhetorical campaign, its contributory influence cannot be denied.

Elizabeth Waring's speech to the Charleston Black YWCA on January 16, 1950, was neither an isolated rhetorical event nor her revenge on elite white Charleston society. Instead, the speech was the first public step in a rhetorical campaign that she and Waties launched in order to influence public opinion and the outcome of the Clarendon County school segregation case, *Briggs v. Elliott*. Whatever their private motives, Elizabeth and Waties used uncompromising and condemnatory language to oppose white supremacy. With their public address, they presented themselves as powerful white allies with national connections. They firmly shut the door on their white neighbors, subjecting themselves to ridicule. Waties jeopardized his position on the bench. Elizabeth and Waties achieved their goal of opening up a discussion about race relations. Their speeches and media interviews generated a response including harassing phone calls, mail, and media coverage.

The negative letters from across the nation confirm Jeanne Theoharis's argument that "polite racism" functioned to uphold white supremacy. While Elizabeth and Waties received threats and overtly racist missives, the majority of the negative letters veiled racism in coded language. The Good Southerner defended segregation with paternalism that precluded a concept of Black people as full-fledged American citizens. The paternalism manifested as superficial good will as it invoked Black people's inferiority to rationalize segregation without acknowledging that any so-called inferiority was due to segregation. The outsider label affixed by politicians echoed the sentiment of their constituents. As white southerners, they were uniquely qualified to speak for and about Black people's abilities, needs, and wants. Faced with these deeply embedded and pervasive beliefs, the Warings crafted their speeches to constitute African American people as American citizens entitled to rights.

Under cover of anonymity, letter writers spewed misogynistic and racist bile. The Warings received harassing phone calls from anonymous callers.

The unadulterated racism and threats conform with stereotypes of twentieth-century white supremacists. Elizabeth and Waties welcomed the outrage, as unpleasant as it was for them, because it supported their claim that white southerners were sick. At the same time, the attacks against the Warings—verbally and otherwise—served as a warning to others. Those who harassed the Warings with letters and phone calls could do so without fear of consequence. People were not punished for defending white supremacy. The polite racists might condemn violence, but when the Warings condemned the culture that fostered it, Good Southerners criticized the Warings, not Jim Crow.

Waties and Elizabeth circulated the positive responses to their speeches to loosen the grip of fear that effectively quashed dissent. The responses primarily remarked upon the Warings' courage in publicly saying what other people were too afraid to say publicly. In a repressive rhetorical culture, the consequences did not have to be imposed for each infraction. Knowledge of those consequences was sufficient to silence people. Retribution against one transformed a vague threat into potential reality. The lesson was for the entire community, not just one person. To inspire others to speak out, Elizabeth and Waties revealed to a national audience that others felt like them. Although white people who opposed segregation felt isolated, they were not. Elizabeth and Waties knew other white people agreed with them and opposed segregation. They courageously said what white people wrote privately in letters, but would not say publicly.

In response to Waties's efforts to remove the cancer of segregation in his native state, white South Carolinians tried to impeach him, allocated funds to support impeachment proceedings, and passed a resolution to buy Elizabeth and him one-way tickets out of town. Elected officials called him insane. For her efforts, Elizabeth was subject to vile sexual insults. White men jostled her on the street. The same men who would lynch a Black man for looking at a white woman had no qualms about assaulting a white woman because she opposed white supremacy. Through the insults and attacks, white people continuously accused Elizabeth and Waties of seeking revenge against white society. In their speeches, Elizabeth and Waties made no effort to accommodate white sensibilities. Instead, they blamed white people. White people's unreasonable and irrational biases were the cause of the South's subversion of American democracy. White people reacted by insulting the Warings, questioning their motives, and debasing them.

During their lifetimes, white people pointed at Elizabeth as the reason for Waties's transformation. In his *Reminiscences*, Waties remarked that he and Elizabeth were in thorough accord about race relations. Marguerite Cartwright wrote:

Seeing them together, it is clear that there is complete agreement and understanding between them. Nor is Elizabeth Waring any less convinced of the evils of racial discrimination than is her husband. When they are interviewed, it is hard to determine precisely where his philosophy ends and hers begins, — yet one has the feeling that they arrived at their views independently. Perhaps it is most accurate to say that they complement each other.[14]

White supremacists rejected Cartwright's assessment. Most declared that Elizabeth determined Waties's philosophy. They accused her of turning Waties into a radical "n-word lover." Yet, Elizabeth's friend from Michigan, Isabella Finnie, wrote that "Waties was the head of the firm of Waring, and I knew you had not taken a single step without consultation and agreement with him; second, that the firm of Waring felt that gradualism had had its chance and lost it."[15] Waties was not a feeble old man manipulated by a younger wife.

When white southerners tried to reconcile their native son rejecting white supremacy, Elizabeth underpinned their explanations. Waties sought revenge on white society because they shunned his second wife or the liberal Yankee wife unduly influenced him. In the House, Mendel Rivers questioned Waties's sincerity, "To begin with, I charge that J. Waties Waring is a hypocrite. I charge that he is insincere in his present campaign. I make that charge for this reason—at no time during his political life, and he was very active in this field, did he ever raise his hand in behalf of the Negro. . . . He has always been part and parcel of the organization he now claims to be un-American."[16] There could be no other explanation, and most definitely, it could not be that Waties, as an individual and a federal judge, began to see the injustice of race relations in the South. Gedney Howe concluded, "I think that his second wife did, yes, convert him . . . she opened up a new window of concern to him. . . . But, I don't think he would have ever considered it otherwise."[17] Pointing the finger at Elizabeth as the reason for Waties's controversial rulings rendered them a product of an outsider interloper, his Yankee wife.

By placing the responsibility on Elizabeth for Waties's transformation, white southerners could absolve themselves of any culpability in the racial power structure and maintain their insular culture. Samuel Grafton wrote in the 1950 *Collier's* article, "To shrink this down into a story of a cold man and a divorce is, in an odd way, to make it more socially acceptable. For if Charlestonians were to concede that the judge suffered a sincere revulsion of feeling, they would imply that portents of impending social change have popped up in the heart of their society. By comparison, when they try to reduce it to a mere social scandal, it is more acceptable."[18] White southerners absolved themselves of guilt or wrong-doing when they attributed the cause of Waties's racial conversion to the machinations of a northern liberal wife.

Based on the Warings' correspondence and behind-the-scenes activity with people and organizations that sympathized with their ideas, I conclude that their stance on race relations was genuine and not an elaborate masquerade to humiliate white South Carolinians. Their experience at the trial of Lynwood Shull pushed them onto a journey. They learned about the historical roots of white supremacy and race relations in the South. Based on the knowledge they gained through their reading and interactions with other activists, the Warings determined that the power of public opinion could eliminate Jim Crow and relied upon rhetoric to transform the public's perception of Black people and segregation.

Furthermore, the Warings' activism demonstrates that the roots of *Brown* were planted years before *Briggs* was appealed in 1952 and the *Brown* decision in 1954. The *Brown* decision is a significant landmark in the Black Freedom Struggle, but it is not a bookend. As Charles W. Eagles points out, the events and people of the 1930s, 1940s, and early 1950s are too often viewed as precursors rather than parts of the actual movement and the relationship between the earlier work and conventional 1954–1968 period needs to be clarified.[19] Tracing *Brown* to its source in Clarendon County with James Pearson's petition for a school bus connects the pre-1954 people and events as integral elements of the movement. The Warings participated in the movement with their incendiary rhetoric. Therefore, an understanding of the Warings' public address transforms our understanding of *Brown* and also disrupts the traditional narrative of the civil rights movement.

The Supreme Court's decision in *Brown v. Board of Education* is often proffered as evidence that the struggle for racial equality is distant, individual, and now resolved. Such is not the case. President Joseph Biden acknowledged the issue in his inaugural address on January 21, 2021, "Our history has been a constant struggle between the American ideal that we are all created equal and the harsh, ugly reality that racism, nativism, fear, and demonization have long torn us apart. The battle is perennial."[20] Examples abound of continuing racial injustice and police brutality across America including the murders of George Floyd, Breonna Taylor, and countless others, just in 2020. Five years after the massacre at Emanuel AME Church in Charleston, South Carolina remains one of only two states with no hate crime legislation. That searing gap infiltrated headlines in the summer of 2019 when a South Carolina high school student posted videos of himself shooting a rifle at shoe boxes that he said represented Black people. In the videos, he hurled racist slurs. Leon Lott, sheriff of Richland County, told the press that without a hate crime law, he could only charge the minor with making student threats. The South Carolina legislature's refusal to pass a hate crime law mirrors the abiding belief that racism occurs at an individual level—like the high school student—and does not reflect society. This perspective erases the systemic racism embedded within the state's legislature, businesses, law enforcement, and schools.

The Warings' rhetorical campaign and Black parents' activism transform "how we imagine what a movement looks like, sounds like, and pushes for, and understand how it is received and often reviled."[21] The movement that culminated in *Brown* was a collective struggle among Black parents and their neighbors in Clarendon County. The NAACP's role in *Brown* can be traced to the graduate and law school cases initiated before the five school segregation cases. The NAACP attorneys expended effort and funds to slowly chip away at *Plessy* and set up a constitutional challenge to separate-but-equal. White and interracial associations supported the challenge with amicus briefs. White radicals attempted to reach other white people to dispel stereotypes about Black people. The Warings took advantage of their status and access to the media to publicly denounce white supremacy. They pushed for outside help in the form of federal interference to repeal Jim Crow laws as South Carolina's governor and white voters responded with a multimillion-dollar campaign to equalize schools to avoid the Supreme Court's reversing *Plessy*.

To attract media publicity and heighten public awareness, the Warings embarked on a rhetorical campaign to expose the incongruity between the American Creed and second-class citizenship for African American people. In sum, Waties's position as a federal judge, the Warings' privileged status as well-to-do white people, and their relationships with the media and NAACP allowed them to speak before both Black and white audiences, then circulate their message across the United States to even more people. Yet, despite their perseverance, their efforts are little known or if acknowledged, attributed to the Warings' quest for revenge against white southerners. If mentioned, scholars have failed to consider a motive beyond revenge, failed to consider the audiences that the Warings addressed, and failed to understand the "distinctively rhetorical features" of their speeches. As a result, their rhetoric is relegated to footnote status.[22] As part of the rhetorical history of *Brown*, the Warings' public address in conjunction with Black parents' resistance to white supremacy transform our understanding of the landmark

Supreme Court decision. Elizabeth and Waties's speeches and the responses to them rewrite the historical record of the case. With this historical revisionism, *Brown* becomes more than the sole result of the NAACP's legal pursuit of desegregation or the Supreme Court justices' moral awakening. Rather, our understanding of activists and activism is disrupted. Gains during the Black Freedom Struggle were the result of Black and white people working collectively and individually even as they withstood opposition to their efforts.

NOTES

INTRODUCTION

1. Brook Thomas, ed., Plessy v. Ferguson: *A Brief History with Documents* (Boston & New York: Bedford Books, 1979), 3. For more on the Comité des Citoyens and its strategy to challenge the law with Plessy's arrest, see Steve Luxenberg, *Separate: The Story of* Plessy v. Ferguson*, and America's Journey from Slavery to Segregation* (New York: W. W. Norton, 2019).

2. Plessy v. Ferguson, 163 U.S. 537 (1896).

3. Benjamin P. Bowser, "Racism: Origin and Theory," *Journal of Black Studies* 48, no. 6 (September 2017): 580, https://doi.org/10.1177/0021934717702135.

4. Milton R. Konvitz, "The Extent and Character of Legally-Enforced Segregation," *Journal of Negro Education* 20, no. 3 (Summer 1951): 430–31, https://doi.org/10.2307/2966015.

5. Constance Baker Motley, "The Historical Setting of *Brown* and Its Impact on the Supreme Court's Decisions," *Fordham Law Review* 61, no. 1 (October 1992): 15, https://ir.lawnet.fordham.edu/flr/.

6. *Plessy*, 163 U.S. 537 (1896).

7. Thurgood Marshall, "The Supreme Court as Protector of Civil Rights: Equal Protection of the Laws," *Annals of the American Academy of Political and Social Science* 275, no. 1 (May 1951): 107n45, https://doi.org/10.1177/000271625127500113.

8. Memorandum from Charles H. Houston to Miss Brady, Miss Brown and Mr. Lindsay, June 16, 1952, Papers of the NAACP, Part 1, Meetings of the Board of Directors, Records of Annual Conferences, Major Speeches, and Special Reports, Special Correspondence, 1910–1939, Charles H. Houston, May/June 1935, ProQuest History Vault.

9. Leland B. Ware, "Setting the Stage for *Brown*: The Development and Implementation of the NAACP's School Desegregation Campaign, 1930–1950," *Mercer Law Review* 52, no. 2 (March 2001): 642, https://digitalcommons.law.mercer.edu/jour_mlr.

10. Richard Kluger, *Simple Justice: The History of* Brown v. Board of Education *and Black America's Struggle for Equality* (New York: Vintage Books, 2004), 136.

11. Oliver Hill, interview by George Gilliam, *The Ground Beneath Our Feet Project*, Virginia Center for Digital History, University of Virginia, accessed January 17, 2021, http://www2.vcdh.virginia.edu/saxon/servlet/SaxonServlet?source=/xml_docs/modernva/modernva_transcripts.xml&style=/xml_docs/modernva/interview_modernva.xsl&level=single&id=Oliver_Hill.

12. James M. Nabrit Jr., "Resort to the Courts as a Means of Eliminating 'Legalized' Segregation," *Journal of Negro Education* 20, no. 3 (Summer 1951): 469, https://doi.org/10.2307/2966018.

13. Brown v. Board of Education, 347 U.S. 483 (1954).

14. Robert A. Prentice, "Supreme Court Rhetoric," *Arizona Law Review* 25, no. 1 (1983–84): 88, HeinOnline.

15. Celeste Michelle Condit, "Democracy and Civil Rights: The Universalizing Influence of Public Argumentation," *Communication Monographs* 54, no. 1 (March 1987): 1, https://doi.org/10.1080/03637758709390213.

16. Elmer W. Henderson, "The Elimination of Segregation through Protest, Propaganda and Education," *Journal of Negro Education* 20, no. 3 (Summer 1951): 475, https://doi.org/10.2307/2966019.

17. Konvitz, "The Extent and Character of Legally-Enforced Segregation," 430.

18. Thurgood Marshall, "The Supreme Court as Protector of Civil Rights," 109.

19. Michael Leff, "Textual Criticism: The Legacy of G. P. Mohrmann," *Quarterly Journal of Speech* 72, no. 4 (November 1986): 384, https://doi.org/10.1080/00335638609383783.

20. Marouf Hasian Jr., Celeste Michelle Condit, and John Louis Lucaites, "The Rhetorical Boundaries of 'The Law': A Consideration of the Rhetorical Culture of Legal Practice and the Case of the 'Separate But Equal' Doctrine," *Quarterly Journal of Speech* 82, no. 4 (November 1996): 326–27, https://doi.org/10.1080/00335639609384161. See also Celeste Michelle Condit and John Louis Lucaites, *Crafting Equality: America's Anglo-African Word* (Chicago: University of Chicago Press, 1993), xii.

21. Nira Yuval-Davis, *The Politics of Belonging: Intersectional Contestations* (Los Angeles & London: Sage, 2011), 93.

22. "Southern way of life" is a euphemism for white supremacy. Tony Badger, "Fatalism, Not Gradualism: The Crisis of Southern Liberalism, 1945–1965," in *The Making of Martin Luther King and the Civil Rights Movement*, ed. Brian Ward and Tony Badger (New York: New York University Press, 1996), 88.

23. Lillian Smith, "Addressed to White Liberals," *New Republic* 111 (September 18, 1944): 333.

24. Theodore G. Bilbo, "World War II: Increasing Racial Tensions," in *The Development of Segregationist Thought*, ed. I. A. Newby (Homewood, IL: The Dorsey Press, 1968), 145. Reprinted from US *Congressional Record*, Vol. XC, Part 9, 78th Cong. 2d sess. (Washington, DC: Government Printing Office, 1944), pp. A1795–A1802. Delivered to joint session of Mississippi legislature on March 22, 1944.

25. Jeanne Theoharis, *A More Beautiful and Terrible History: The Uses and Misuses of Civil Rights History* (Boston: Beacon Press, 2018), 85.

26. W. J. Cash, *The Mind of the South* (New York: Alfred A. Knopf, 1941), 139.

27. Letter to George F. Zook, December 22, 1947, quoted in Tinsley E. Yarbrough, *A Passion for Justice: J. Waties Waring and Civil Rights* (New York: Oxford University Press, 1987), 66.

28. "Warings Through with S. Carolina," *Afro-American*, March 8, 1952, 14.

29. Martin J. Medhurst, "Thirty Years Later: A Critic's Tale," *Rhetoric Review* 25, no. 4 (2006): 381, http://www.jstor.org/stable/20176743.

30. Tinsley E. Yarbrough, *A Passion for Justice: J. Waties Waring and Civil Rights* (New York: Oxford University Press, 1987).

31. Richard Gergel, *Unexampled Courage: The Blinding of Sgt. Isaac Woodard and the Awakening of President Harry S. Truman and Judge J. Waties Waring* (New York: Sarah Crichton Books/Farrar, Straus & Giroux, 2019), 238.

32. David Zarefsky, "Four Senses of Rhetorical History," in *Doing Rhetorical History: Concepts and Cases*, ed. Kathleen J. Turner (Tuscaloosa: University of Alabama Press, 1998), 26–31.

33. Martin J. Medhurst, "Public Address and Significant Scholarship: Four Challenges to the Rhetorical Renaissance," in *Texts in Context: Critical Dialogues on Significant Episodes in American Political Rhetoric*, ed. Michael C. Leff and Fred J. Kauffeld (Davis, CA: Hermagoras Press, 1989), 36.

34. Medhurst, "Thirty Years Later," 381.

35. Amos Kiewe and Davis W. Houck, "Introduction," in *The Effects of Rhetoric and the Rhetoric of Effects: Past, Present, Future*, ed. Amos Kiewe and Davis W. Houck (Columbia: University of South Carolina Press, 2015), 6, 17.

36. Robert Hariman, "Relocating the Art of Public Address," in *Rhetoric and Political Culture in Nineteenth-Century America*, ed. Thomas W. Benson (East Lansing: Michigan State University Press, 1997), 164.

37. Kathleen J. Turner, "Introduction: Rhetorical History as Social Construction," in *Doing Rhetorical History: Concepts and Cases*, ed. Kathleen J. Turner (Tuscaloosa: University of Alabama Press, 1998), 4.

38. Herbert W. Simons, "From Post-9/11 Melodrama to Quagmire in Iraq: A Rhetorical History," *Rhetoric & Public Affairs* 10, no. 2 (Summer 2007): 184, http://www.jstor.org/stable/41940142.

39. Charles W. Eagles, "Toward New Histories of the Civil Rights Era," *Journal of Southern History* 56, no. 4 (November 2000): 834–35, https://doi.org/10.2307/2588012.

40. Theoharis, *A More Beautiful and Terrible History*, 99.

41. Edward H. Peeples, "Richmond Journal: Thirty Years in Black & White," in *Race Traitor*, ed. John Garvey and Noel Ignatiev (New York: Routledge, 1996), 82.

42. Michael Eric Dyson, *Tears We Cannot Stop: A Sermon to White America* (New York: St. Martin's Press, 2017), 132–33.

43. Davis W. Houck, "Textual Recovery, Textual Discovery: Returning to Our Past, Imagining Our Future," in *The Handbook of Rhetoric and Public Address*, ed. Shawn J. Parry-Giles and J. Michael Hogan (Malden, MA: Wiley-Blackwell, 2010), 114.

44. J. Waties Waring to Rev. Donald Harrington, November 16, 1950, and December 11, 1951, box 110-12, folder 292, J. Waties Waring Papers, Moorland-Spingarn Research Center, Howard University.

45. Waties's speeches to the National Lawyers Guild in 1949, Council of Civic Unity in 1950, and naturalization ceremony in 1950 were recorded and transcribed. Elizabeth spoke from a manuscript at the Coming Street YWCA in Charleston and Tindley Temple Methodist Church in Philadelphia. Her appearance on *Meet the Press* was transcribed.

46. Elizabeth Waring to Poppy Cannon and Walter White, January 15, 1950, box 7, folder 216, Walter Francis White and Poppy Cannon Papers, Yale Collection of American Literature, Beinecke Rare Book and Manuscript Library, Yale University.

47. Leah Ceccarelli, *On the Frontier of Science: An American Rhetoric of Exploration and Exploitation* (Lansing: Michigan State University Press, 2013), 11.

48. Pamela VanHaitsma, "Between Archival Absence and Information Abundance: Reconstructing Sallie Holley's Abolitionist Rhetoric through Digital Surrogates and Metadata," *Quarterly Journal of Speech* 106, no. 1 (February 2020): 28, https://doi.org/10.1080/00335630.2019.1706188.

49. VanHaitsma, "Between Archival Absence and Information Abundance," 34.

50. Lee Ann Bell, *Storytelling for Social Justice*, 2nd ed. (New York: Routledge, Taylor & Francis Group, 2020), 44, 55.

51. Bell, *Storytelling for Social Justice*, 28.

52. Bell, *Storytelling for Social Justice*, 47.

53. Theoharis, *A More Beautiful and Terrible History*, xxi, 210.

54. Jacquelyn Dowd Hall, "The Long Civil Rights Movement and the Political Uses of the Past," *Journal of American History* 91, no. 4 (March 2005): 1234–35, https://doi.org/10.2307/3660172.

55. Theoharis, *A More Beautiful and Terrible History*, 18.

56. Steven J. Crossland, "*Brown's* Companions: *Briggs*, *Belton*, and *Davis*," *Washburn Law Journal* 43, no. 2 (Winter 2003–2004): 382, https://contentdm.washburnlaw.edu/digital/collection/wlj/id/5394/.

57. Winfred B. Moore Jr. and Orville Vernon Burton, eds., *Toward the Meeting of the Waters: Currents in the Civil Rights Movement of South Carolina during the Twentieth Century*, (Columbia: University of South Carolina Press, 2008), 144.

58. Robert Asen, "Women, Work, Welfare: A Rhetorical History of Images of Poor Women in Welfare Policy Debates," *Rhetoric & Public Affairs* 6, no. 2 (Summer 2003): 288, https://www.jstor.org/stable/41940315.

CHAPTER 1: BAPTISM

1. "'Home Alive by 45': Operation Magic Carpet," October 2, 2020, National WWII Museum, https://www.nationalww2museum.org/war/articles/operation-magic-carpet-1945.

2. R. Alton Lee, "The Army 'Mutiny' of 1946," *Journal of American History* 53, no. 3 (December 1966): 556–57, https://doi.org/10.2307/1887571.

3. Isaac Woodard Jr., Enlisted Record and Report of Separation, Papers of the NAACP, Part 8, Discrimination in the Criminal Justice System, Series B: Legal Department and

Central Office Records 1940-1950 (Frederick, MD: University Publications of America), microfilm, reel 29, frame 178.

4. Steven F. Lawson, ed., *To Secure These Rights: The Report of President Harry S. Truman's Committee on Civil Rights* (Boston: Bedford/St. Martin's, 2004), 5.

5. John Dittmer, *Local People: The Struggle for Civil Rights in Mississippi* (Urbana and Chicago: University of Illinois Press, 1994), 94.

6. Kari Frederickson, "'The Slowest State' and 'Most Backward Community': Racial Violence in South Carolina and Federal Civil-Rights Legislation, 1946–1948," *South Carolina Historical Magazine* 98, no. 2 (April 1997): 179, https://www.jstor.org/stable/i27570226.

7. Gail Williams O'Brien, *The Color of the Law: Race, Violence, and Justice in the Post-World War II South* (Chapel Hill: University of North Carolina Press, 1999), 29–30.

8. Frederickson, "'The Slowest State' and 'Most Backward Community,'" 180.

9. "5 Crosses Burned on Stone Mountain in Klan Initiation," *News and Courier*, May 10, 1946, 2.

10. Lawson, *To Secure These Rights*, 7–8.

11. Isaac Woodard Deposition, April 23, 1946, Papers of the NAACP, Part 8, Discrimination in the Criminal Justice System, Series B: Legal Department and Central Office Records 1940-1950 (Frederick, MD: University Publications of America), microfilm, reel 28, frame 1012.

12. Robert Patterson to Walter White, June 17, 1946, Papers of the NAACP, Part 8, Discrimination in the Criminal Justice System, Series B: Legal Department and Central Office Records 1940-1950 (Frederick, MD: University Publications of America), microfilm, reel 28, frame 714.

13. Tom Clark to Walter White, July 25, 1946, Papers of the NAACP, Part 8, Discrimination in the Criminal Justice System, Series B: Legal Department and Central Office Records 1940-1950 (Frederick, MD: University Publications of America), microfilm, reel 28, frame 758.

14. Walter White to Orson Welles, July 24, 1946, Papers of the NAACP, Part 8, Discrimination in the Criminal Justice System, Series B: Legal Department and Central Office Records 1940-1950 (Frederick, MD: University Publications of America), microfilm, reel 28, frame 742.

15. "Aiken is Angered at Welles Charge," *New York Times*, August 9, 1946, 15.

16. Newspaper Clipping, n.d., Papers of the NAACP, Part 8, Discrimination in the Criminal Justice System, Series B: Legal Department and Central Office Records 1940-1950 (Frederick, MD: University Publications of America), microfilm, reel 28, frame 695.

17. Robert L. Carter to Harold Boulware, August 13, 1946, Papers of the NAACP, Part 8, Discrimination in the Criminal Justice System, Series B: Legal Department and Central Office Records 1940-1950 (Frederick, MD: University Publications of America), microfilm, reel 28, frame 823.

18. Affidavit of Lincoln Miller, August 8, 1946, Papers of the NAACP, Part 8, Discrimination in the Criminal Justice System, Series B: Legal Department and Central Office Records 1940-1950 (Frederick, MD: University Publications of America), microfilm, reel 28, frame 790.

19. Harold R. Boulware to Robert L. Carter, August 9, 1946, Papers of the NAACP, Part 8, Discrimination in the Criminal Justice System, Series B: Legal Department and Central Office Records 1940-1950 (Frederick, MD: University Publications of America), microfilm, reel 28, frame 814.

20. Memorandum from Robert L. Carter to A. V. Owens, August 19, 1946, Papers of the NAACP, Part 8, Discrimination in the Criminal Justice System, Series B: Legal Department and Central Office Records 1940-1950 (Frederick, MD: University Publications of America), microfilm, reel 28, frame 847.

21. Lawson, *To Secure These Rights*, 9.

22. United States of America v. Lynwood Lanier Shull, Case No. 16,603 Court File, Eastern District of South Carolina, National Archives, Morrow, GA.

23. "Police Chief Bonded in Beating of Negro," *New York Times*, September 29, 1946, 20.

24. Julius Waties Waring, *The Reminiscences of J. Waties Waring*, Columbia University Oral History Collection (Glen Rock, NJ: Microfilming Corporation of America, 1972), 215.

25. To avoid confusion, I depart from convention and refer to Judge J. Waties Waring as "Waties" and Elizabeth Avery Waring as "Elizabeth."

26. J. Waties Waring, interview by unidentified interviewer, 1948, box 110-179, J. Waties Waring Papers, Moorland-Spingarn Research Center, Howard University.

27. Tinsley E. Yarbrough, *A Passion for Justice: J. Waties Waring and Civil Rights* (New York: Oxford University Press, 1987), 10–11.

28. Yarbrough, *A Passion for Justice*, 4, 6.

29. *Reminiscences*, 128A.

30. Yarbrough, *A Passion for Justice*, 42.

31. Harry Simonhoff, "U. S. Judge J. Waties Waring: Reformer or Martyr," *Jewish Floridian*, 3, box 110-43, folder 1269, J. Waties Waring Papers, Moorland-Spingarn Research Center, Howard University.

32. Septima Poinsette Clark, *Ready from Within: Septima Clark and the Civil Rights Movement, A First Person Narrative*, ed. Cynthia Stokes Brown (Navarro, CA: Wild Trees Press, 1986), 24.

33. "Crack Federal Lawyer Put on Florida Case," *Atlanta Daily World*, August 21, 1946, 1.

34. H. H. Edens, "Memorial to Claud N. Sapp," *South Carolina Law Quarterly* 1, no. 2 (1948): 110, https://scholarcommons.sc.edu.

35. "Shull Trial Set for Wednesday, Sapp Tells Press," *News and Courier*, November 3, 1946, 7; United States of America v. Lynwood Lanier Shull, Case No. 16,603 Court File.

36. United States v. Shull, unfiled memorandum, n.d., box 110-31, folder 938, J. Waties Waring Papers, Moorland-Spingarn Research Center, Howard University.

37. Isaac Woodard deposition, April 23, 1946.

38. The account of the witnesses' testimony, opening, and closing statements was culled from a number of sources including Waties's oral history, Papers of the NAACP, FBI file, and newspaper reports. In South Carolina, *The State*, *Columbia Record*, *Lighthouse and Informer*, *News and Courier*, and *Evening Post* covered the trial.

39. Franklin H. Williams to Thurgood Marshall, memorandum, November 12, 1946, Papers of the NAACP, Part 8, Discrimination in the Criminal Justice System, Series B: Legal

Department and Central Office Records 1940-1950 (Frederick, MD: University Publications of America), microfilm, reel 28, frame 1001.

40. "Police Chief Freed in Negro Beating," *New York Times*, November 11, 1946, 36.

41. *Christian Science Monitor*, n.d., box 110-41, folder 1250, J. Waties Waring Papers, Moorland-Spingarn Research Center, Howard University.

42. Franklin H. Williams to Thurgood Marshall, memorandum, November 12, 1946.

43. Franklin H. Williams to Thurgood Marshall, memorandum, November 12, 1946.

44. "Chief of Police Acquitted of Blinding Man," *Washington Post*, November 6, 1946, 9. Federal Bureau of Investigation File 44-HQ-1411, stamped Nov 6, 1946.

45. "Southern Police Chief Freed in Blinding of Negro Veteran," *Christian Science Monitor*, November 6, 1946.

46. *Reminiscences*, 221–22.

47. "Federal Jury Acquits Shull in Negro Case," *Lighthouse and Informer*, November 6, 1946, 1.

48. *Reminiscences*, 222.

49. Margaret Green, Archivist, Westover School, email message to author, February 7, 2013.

50. "Mrs. J. W. Waring, Widow of Judge," *New York Times*, November 1, 1968, 49; Lillian Scott, "The Warings of South Carolina: South's Most Courageous Couple," n.d., box 110-43, folder 1269, J. Waties Waring Papers, Moorland-Spingarn Research Center, Howard University.

51. Scott, "The Warings of South Carolina: South's Most Courageous Couple."

52. "WCS Wafts Mother's Voice to Youngsters," *Detroit Free Press*, March 14, 1923, 13.

53. Yarbrough, *A Passion for Justice*, 32; The *Detroit Free Press* reported on January 16, 1933, that the Mills were headed to Ormond. Elizabeth's Reno divorce from Mills was granted on March 26, 1934. She married Hoffman on March 31, 1934.

54. Stephanie E. Yuhl, *A Golden Haze of Memory: The Making of Historic Charleston* (Chapel Hill: University of North Carolina Press, 2005), 163–64. Quoted from brochure for Fort Sumter Hotel that opened in 1924.

55. Poppy Cannon, "The Eleanor Roosevelt of the Caribbean," *Negro Digest*, October, 1950, 56, box 110-1, folder 2, J. Waties Waring Papers, Moorland-Spingarn Research Center, Howard University.

56. No definitive account exists of when or where Elizabeth Hoffman and Waties Waring met. Most speculate they met when the Hoffmans stopped over in Charleston on their way to winter in Florida. A few speculate that they may have met in New York when Waties presided in court.

57. "Marriage Announcement 1," *New York Times*, November 5, 1913, 11.

58. Yarbrough, *A Passion for Justice*, 30.

59. Caryl Phillips, *Atlantic Sound*, (New York: Alfred Knopf, 2000), 240.

60. Quoted in Yarbrough, *A Passion for Justice*, 29.

61. *Reminiscences*, 402.

62. *Reminiscences*, 403.

63. Septima Poinsette Clark, interview by Jacquelyn Hall, July 25, 1976, interview G-0016, Southern Oral History Program Collection (#4007), http://docsouth.unc.edu/sohp/G-0016/G-0016.html.

64. *Reminiscences*, 403.

65. *Reminiscences*, 219.

66. Phillips, *Atlantic Sound*, 245.

67. *Reminiscences*, 224.

68. United States of America v. Lynwood Lanier Shull, Case No. 16,603 Court File.

69. *Reminiscences*, 224.

70. Thurgood Marshall to Tom Clark, November 14, 1946, Papers of the NAACP, Part 8, Discrimination in the Criminal Justice System, Series B: Legal Department and Central Office Records 1940-1950 (Frederick, MD: University Publications of America), microfilm, reel 28, frame 1007.

71. *Reminiscences*, 219.

72. *Reminiscences*, 221.

73. Ralph McGill, "One Word More: 'The Mind of the South,'" *Atlanta Constitution*, July 5, 1941, 6.

74. W. J. Cash, *The Mind of the South* (New York: Alfred A. Knopf, 1941), 103.

75. David R. Goldfield, *Black, White, and Southern: Race Relations and Southern Culture, 1940 to the Present* (Baton Rouge: Louisiana State University Press, 1990), 15.

76. Howard Dorgan, "Rhetoric of the United Confederate Veterans: A Lost Cause Mythology in the Making," in *Oratory in the New South*, ed. Waldo W. Braden (Baton Rouge: Louisiana State University Press, 1979), 171.

77. Joan Marie Johnson, *Southern Ladies, New Women: Race, Region, and Clubwomen in South Carolina, 1890–1930* (Gainesville: University Press of Florida, 2004), 2–3.

78. Cash, *The Mind of the South*, 124.

79. James W. Vander Zanden, *Race Relations in Transition: The Segregation Crisis in the South* (New York: Random House, 1965), 21–22.

80. Cash, *The Mind of the South*, 107.

81. J. Waties Waring, unidentified interviewer, 1948.

82. Cash, *The Mind of the South*, 429.

83. J. Waties Waring, "The Struggle for Negro Rights," *Lawyers Guild Review* 9, no. 1 (Winter 1949): 10, HeinOnline.

84. P. L. Prattis, "The Horizon," *Pittsburgh Courier*, January 29, 1944, 7.

85. Frances Gaither, "Democracy—the Negro's Hope," *New York Times*, April 2, 1944, BR7.

86. Prattis, "The Horizon," 7.

87. Gunnar Myrdal, *An American Dilemma: The Negro Problem and Modern Democracy* (New York: Harper & Brothers Publishers, 1944), 1, 4, 574.

88. Prattis, "The Horizon," 7.

89. Myrdal, *An American Dilemma*, 441.

90. Waring, "The Struggle for Negro Rights," 10.

91. *Reminiscences*, 236.

92. *Reminiscences*, 404–5.

93. Elizabeth Waring's Account of *Briggs v. Elliott*, box 110-3, folder 14, J. Waties Waring Papers, Moorland-Spingarn Research Center, Howard University.

94. *Reminiscences*, 399.

95. Garth E. Pauley, "Harry Truman and the NAACP: A Case Study in Presidential Persuasion on Civil Rights," *Rhetoric & Public Affairs* 2, no. 2 (Summer 1999): 214, https://www.jstor.org/stable/41939509.

96. Harry S. Truman, "Annual Message to the Congress," Washington, DC, January 6, 1947, https://www.trumanlibrary.gov/library/public-papers/2/annual-message-congress-state-union-2.

97. Michael R. Gardner, *Harry Truman and Civil Rights: Moral Courage and Political Risks* (Carbondale: Southern Illinois University Press, 2002), 26.

98. William E. Juhnke, "President Truman's Committee on Civil Rights: The Interaction of Politics, Protest, and the Presidential Advisory Commission," *Presidential Studies Quarterly* 19, no. 3 (Summer 1989): 597, http://www.jstor.org/stable/40574372.

99. "Agency History," Records of the President's Committee on Civil Rights Record Group 220, Harry S. Truman Library & Museum, accessed May 12, 2020, https://www.trumanlibrary.gov/library/federal-record/records-presidents-committee-civil-rights-record-group-220.

100. Samuel Grafton, "Lonesomest Man in Town," *Collier's*, April 29, 1950, 49.

CHAPTER 2: IT ALL STARTED WITH A BUS

1. "SC Governor," Our Campaigns (website), accessed January 11, 2021, https://www.ourcampaigns.com/RaceDetail.html?RaceID=31141. Waties cited the number of voters in *Elmore v. Rice*, 72 F. Supp. 516 (E.D.S.C. 1947).

2. John H. McCray, "Enters Suit Against S.C. Primary Bill," *Pittsburgh Courier*, March 1, 1947, 1.

3. Julius Waties Waring, *The Reminiscences of J. Waties Waring*, Columbia University Oral History Collection (Glen Rock, NJ: Microfilming Corporation of America, 1972), 248.

4. Harold Boulware to Thurgood Marshall, March 11, 1947, Papers of the NAACP, Part 3, The Campaign for Educational Equality, Series B: Legal Department and Central Office Records 1940–1950 (Frederick, MD: University Publications of America), microfilm, reel 14, frame 301.

5. *Reminiscences*, 248, 256–58.

6. John H. Wrighten to Board of Trustees, August 17, 1946, Papers of the NAACP, Part 3, The Campaign for Educational Equality, Series B: Legal Department and Central Office Records 1940–1950 (Frederick, MD: University Publications of America), microfilm, reel 14, frame 272.

7. Patricia Sullivan, *Lift Every Voice: The NAACP and the Making of the Civil Rights Movement* (New York: The New Press, 2009), 339.

8. R. Scott Baker, *Paradoxes of Desegregation: African American Struggles for Educational Equity in Charleston, South Carolina, 1926–1972* (Columbia: University of South Carolina Press, 2006), 78.

9. Sullivan, *Lift Every Voice*, 339–40.

10. "Negro Disenfranchisement: A Challenge to the Constitution," *Columbia Law Review* 47, no. 1 (January 1947): 80, https://doi.org/10.2307/1118552.

11. Gunnar Myrdal, *An American Dilemma: The Negro Problem and Modern Democracy* (New York: Harper & Brothers Publishers, 1944), 452.

12. McCray, "Enters Suit Against S.C. Primary Bill."

13. Thurgood Marshall, "The Rise and Collapse of the 'White Democratic Primary,'" *Journal of Negro Education* 26, no. 3 (Summer 1957): 249, https://doi.org/10.2307/2293407.

14. "Johnston Asks White Control," *Atlanta Constitution*, April 15, 1944, 2.

15. "New 'Carpetbaggers' Assailed," *New York Times*, April 15, 1944, 13.

16. Peter F. Lau, *Democracy Rising: South Carolina and the Fight for Black Equality Since 1865* (Lexington: University Press of Kentucky, 2006), 135.

17. Marshall, "The Rise and Collapse of the 'White Democratic Primary,'" 249.

18. Tinsley E. Yarbrough, *A Passion for Justice: J. Waties Waring and Civil Rights* (New York: Oxford University Press, 1987), 61.

19. *Reminiscences*, 255.

20. Franklin Williams to Harold Boulware, January 23, 1947, and Harold Boulware to Franklin Williams, January 31, 1947, Papers of the NAACP, Part 4, Voting Rights Campaign 1916–1950, Group II, Series B: Legal file: Voting, 1940–1955, ProQuest History Vault.

21. Garth E. Pauley, "Harry Truman and the NAACP: A Case Study in Presidential Persuasion on Civil Rights," *Rhetoric & Public Affairs* 2, no. 2 (Summer 1999): 213, https://www.jstor.org/stable/41939509.

22. Harry S. Truman, "Address before the National Association for the Advanced of Colored People," Lincoln Memorial, June 29, 1947, https://www.trumanlibrary.gov/library/public-papers/130/address-national-association-advancement-colored-people.

23. Elmore v. Rice, 72 F. Supp. 516 (E.D.S.C. 1947).

24. Carl T. Rowan, *South of Freedom* (New York: Alfred A. Knopf, 1954), 89–90.

25. "Stoney Condemns Court's Opinion Against Party," *Evening Post*, July 12, 1947, 1.

26. "Maybank Believes Primary Ruling 'Clearly Wrong,'" *Evening Post*, July 14, 1947, 1.

27. "Negroes Ruled Eligible in SC Primaries," and "NAACP Wants Amendment of Party Rules," *The State*, July 13, 1947, 1.

28. "Judge Waring's Decision on Enrolling of Negroes in SC Democratic Party," *The State*, July 22 and 23, 1947, 4.

29. "South Carolina Negroes Win Vote in Democratic Primary Elections," *New York Times*, July 13, 1947, 1; "A Party, Not a Club," *New York Times*, July 14, 1947, 20.

30. "Negroes Win Court Decision on Rights in S.C. Primary," *Washington Post*, July 13, 1947, M1.

31. "Clear and Unmistakable," *Atlanta Daily World*, July 15, 1947, 6.

32. "Vote Bias Smashed in South Carolina," *Pittsburgh Courier*, July 19, 1947, 1.

33. Walter White, "Judge Waring's Decision," *Chicago Defender*, July 26, 1947, 15.

34. "Welfare Conference Hails Waring Decision," *Atlanta Daily World*, July 16, 1947, 1.

35. Irwin Klibaner, "The Travail of Southern Radicals: The Southern Conference Educational Fund, 1946–1976," *Journal of Southern History* 49, no. 2 (May 1983): 179, https://doi.org/10.2307/2207502.

36. "Welfare Conference Hails Waring Decision."

37. Morton Sosna, *In Search of the Silent South: Southern Liberals and the Race Issue* (New York: Columbia University Press, 1977), 184.

38. Yarbrough, *A Passion for Justice*, 124n45.

39. Linda Reed, *Simple Decency & Common Sense: The Southern Conference Movement, 1938–1963* (Bloomington: Indiana University Press, 1991), 153–54.

40. Yarbrough, *A Passion for Justice*, 65–66.

41. Katherine Woods, "Rebecca West's Brilliant Mosaic of Yugoslavian Travel," *New York Times*, October 26, 1941, BR4.

42. J. Waties Waring to Rebecca West, August 23, 1947, box 36, folder 1350, Rebecca West Papers, Beinecke Rare Book and Manuscript Library, Yale University.

43. For the definitive account of the lynching and trial, see William B. Gravely, *They Stole Him Out of Jail: Willie Earle, South Carolina's Last Lynching Victim* (Columbia: University of South Carolina Press, 2019).

44. Strom Thurmond, "Willie Earle Lynching Case," March 1, 1947. Strom Thurmond Collection, Clemson University Libraries, https://tigerprints.clemson.edu/strom/70.

45. Gravely, *They Stole Him*, xiii, 70.

46. Helene Huntington Smith, "Mrs. Tilly's Crusade," *Collier's*, December 30, 1950, 30. Special thanks to Brittany Slagle Pigford, the archivist at the Louise Pettus Archives and Special Collections at Winthrop University, for sending me documents via email.

47. John A. Salmond, "Flag-bearers for Integration and Justice: Local Civil Rights Groups in the South, 1940–1954," in *Before* Brown*: Civil Rights and White Backlash in the Modern South*, ed. Glenn Feldman (Tuscaloosa: University of Alabama Press, 2004), 227.

48. Smith, "Mrs. Tilly's Crusade," 29.

49. Rebecca West, "Opera in Greenville, *New Yorker*, June 14, 1947, 31–59, https://www.newyorker.com/magazine/1947/06/14/opera-in-greenville.

50. J. Waties Waring to Rebecca West, August 23, 1947.

51. N. Gordon Carper, "Slavery Revisited: Peonage in the South," *Phylon* 37, no. 1 (1st Quarter 1976): 85–99, https://doi.org/10.2307/274733.

52. "Federal Judge Sentences Man on Slave Count," *Asheville Citizen-Times*, December 4, 1947, 18.

53. "U. S. Uses Lindbergh Law to Prosecute S.C. Peonage Case," *Chicago Defender*, October 25, 1947, 1; "Hartsville Man Fined for Violation of Civil Liberties Act," *News and Courier*, December 3, 1947, 6; J. Waties Waring, unidentified interviewer, 1948, series N, box 110-179, J. Waties Waring Papers, Moorland-Spingarn Research Center, Howard University.

54. *Reminiscences*, 202.

55. J. Waties Waring, interview by unidentified interviewer, 1948, box 110-179, J. Waties Waring Papers, Moorland-Spingarn Research Center, Howard University.

56. $1,000 in 1948 equals $10,884.85 in 2020. "CPI Inflation Calculator," U.S. Bureau of Labor Statistics, accessed May 31, 2020, http://data.bls.gov/cgi-bin/cpicalc.pl. Wade Kolb III, "*Briggs v. Elliott* Revisited: A Study in Grassroots Activism and Trial Advocacy from the Early Civil Rights Era," *Journal of Southern Legal History* 19, no. 1 (2011): 124, 126, HeinOnline.

57. Ophelia De Laine Gona, *Dawn of Desegregation: J. A. De Laine and* Briggs v. Elliott (Columbia: University of South Carolina Press, 2011), 3.

58. *Reminiscences*, 241.

59. Yabrough, *A Passion for Justice*, 173.

60. *Reminiscences*, 341.

61. Gona, *Dawn of Desegregation*, 11.

62. James Felder, *Civil Rights in South Carolina: From Peaceful Protests to Groundbreaking Rulings* (Charleston: The History Press, 2012), 44.

63. Kolb, "*Briggs v. Elliott* Revisited," 124.

64. Gona, *Dawn of Desegregation*, 21–23.

65. Pearson, James v. Clarendon County Board of Education 1947–48, Papers of the NAACP, Part 3, Series B: Schools South Carolina, Clarendon County 1940–1950 (Frederick, MD: University Publications of America), microfilm, reel 4, frame 761.

66. Levi Pearson addressed To Whom It May Concern, December 16, 1947, Joseph A. De Laine Papers, Digital Collections, South Caroliniana Library, https://digital.tcl.sc.edu/digital/collection/jad/id/593.

67. James Pearson v. County Board of Education for Clarendon County et al., Case No. 1909, Eastern District of South Carolina, National Archives, Morrow, GA.

68. Kolb, "*Briggs v. Elliott* Revisited," 131.

69. J. A. De Laine Jr., email message to author, February 20, 2013.

70. *Reminiscences*, 343.

71. Kolb, "*Briggs v. Elliott* Revisited," 131.

72. Walter White, "People, Politics and Places," *Chicago Defender*, July 26, 1947, 15.

73. "South Carolina 'White Primary' Invalidated," *Atlanta Daily World*, July 13, 1947, 6.

74. "Negro Vote Stands in South Carolina," *New York Times*, April 20, 1948, 1.

75. "Negro Vote Stands in South Carolina."

76. Yarbrough, *A Passion for Justice*, 69.

77. "South Carolina Democratic Party Case Now in Hands of Federal Court," *Cleveland Call and Post*, December 4, 1948, 2B.

78. "U. S. Court Order Opens S. C. Party," *New Journal and Guide*, July 24, 1948, E26A.

79. Brown v. Baskin, 78 F. Supp. 933 (E.D.S.C. 1948).

80. Kari Frederickson, *The Dixiecrat Revolt and the End of the Solid South, 1932–1968* (Chapel Hill: University of North Carolina Press, 2001), 3–5.

81. Strom Thurmond, "Keynote Address at the States' Rights Democratic Conference," in *Milestone Documents of American Leaders* (Boston: Credo Reference, 2017).

82. Jack Bass and Walter DeVries, *The Transformation of Southern Politics: Social Change and Political Consequences Since 1945* (New York: BasicBooks,), 253.

83. 80 Cong. Record H4654 (1948) (statement Rep. Dorn). Dorn introduced H. Res. 704.

84. Rivers represented the 1st Congressional district consisting of Charleston and other coastal counties.

85. 80 Cong. Record H9752 (1948).

86. "Waring Declines Comment," *News and Courier*, August 6, 1948, 1.

87. Roy Wilkins to Water White, August 2, 1948, Papers of the NAACP, Part 4, The Voting Rights Campaign 1916–1950 (Frederick, MD: University Publications of America), microfilm, reel 11, frame 0049.

88. Leslie S. Perry to Thurgood Marshall, August 6, 1948, Papers the NAACP, Part 4, The Voting Rights Campaign 1916–1950 (Frederick, MD: University Publications of America), microfilm, reel 11, frame 0051.

89. The only report of violence that surfaced after the August 10 primary occurred in Abbeville County, near the Georgia border. White men beat and stabbed a Black preacher as he left the polls. Police watched without taking any action to intervene. "Voting Pastor Flees Mob," *Afro-American*, August 28, 1948, 1.

90. "35,000 Race Voters in South Carolina," *New Journal and Guide*, August 21, 1948, 3.

91. Quoted in Yarbrough, *A Passion for Justice*, 65, 75–76.

92. Curtis Karlson to J. Waties Waring, n.d., box 110-23 folder 698, J. Waties Waring Papers, Moorland-Spingarn Research Center, Howard University.

93. P. B. Young to J. Waties Waring, July 23, 1948, Papers of the NAACP, Part 4, The Voting Rights Campaign 1916–1950 (Frederick, MD: University Publications of America), microfilm, reel 11, frame 46.

94. I have not discovered a manuscript of the speech. More than likely, one does not exist. Excerpts from the address to the New York City Chapter of the National Lawyers Guild were published in the *New York Times* (October 12, 1948), *Columbia Record* (October 14, 1948), and *Chicago Defender* (October 23, 1948). *The State* reprinted the *New York Times* article on October 17, 1948.

95. "Judge Knox Joins Guild Directors to Honor Judge Waring at Luncheon," *New York Guild Lawyer* 6, no. 10 (November 1948): 1.

96. "Jurist from South Assails Prejudice," *New York Times*, October 12, 1948, 31.

97. "Jurist from South Assails Prejudice," *New York Times*, October 12, 1948, 31.

98. "South Needs Outside Help to Solve Race Issue," *New York Amsterdam News*, November 6, 1948, 17.

99. "Judge Waring Gets Columbia Ku Klux Letter," *The State*, October 23, 1948, 7.

100. "Klan Tried to Influence Him in Negro Vote Case, Judge Says," *Washington Post*, October 23, 1948, 11.

101. W. D. W., "Mid-State Parade of Klan Is Held," *News and Courier*, September 6, 1948, 1.

102. Will Maslow and Joseph B. Robison, "Civil Rights: A Program for the President's Committee," *Lawyers Guild Review* 3, no. 7 (May/June 1947): 115, 118, HeinOnline.

103. Newspaper Clipping, December 6, 1950, box 110-40, folder 1238, J. Waties Waring Papers, Moorland-Spingarn Research Center, Howard University.

104. "Advances Towards Democracy," *New York Times*, December 3, 1948, 24.

105. J. Waties Waring to Harry S. Truman, December 6, 1948, box 110-19, folder 567, J. Waties Waring Papers, Moorland-Spingarn Research Center, Howard University.

106. Waring to Truman, December 6, 1948.

107. Harry S. Truman to J. Waties Waring, December 10, 1948, box 110-19, folder 567, J. Waties Waring Papers, Moorland-Spingarn Research Center, Howard University.

108. J. Waties Waring to Thurgood Marshall, December 4, 1948, box 110-15, folder 385, J. Waties Waring Papers, Moorland-Spingarn Research Center, Howard University.

109. J. Waties Waring, unidentified interviewer, 1948.

110. "West Coast Press Interviews Waring on Racial Problems," *Evening Post*, August 27, 1948, 3.

111. John H. McCray, "The Harvest Is Ready," box 2, folder 20, John Henry McCray Papers, South Caroliniana Library, University of South Carolina.

112. Howard H. Quint, *Profile in Black and White: A Frank Portrait of South Carolina* (Washington, DC: Public Affairs Press, 1958; reis.,Westport, CT: Greenwood Press, 1973), 37.

113. David R. Goldfield, *Black, White, and Southern: Race Relations and Southern Culture 1940 to the Present* (Baton Rouge: Louisiana State University Press, 1990), 27.

114. *Reminiscences*, 303, 256.

115. Isabella Finnie to Elizabeth Waring, July, 1947, box 110-5, folder 93, J. Waties Waring Papers, Moorland-Spingarn Research Center, Howard University.

CHAPTER 3: I HOPE TO MAKE MORE FRIENDS

1. Peter F. Lau, "Hinton, James Miles," *South Carolina Encyclopedia*, updated May 17, 2016, https://www.scencyclopedia.org/sce/entries/hinton-james-miles/.

2. John H. McCray, "'Kidnap' NAACP Official," *Chicago Defender*, April 30, 1949, 1.

3. "Alleged Threat to be Probed," *Times and Democrat* (Orangeburg), January 27, 1949, 1.

4. "The Kidnapping of Hinton," *Atlanta Daily World*, April 26, 1949, 6.

5. "KKK Parade Reported in Lexington," *The State*, January 6, 1949, 21.

6. "K. K. K. Visits Ellenton. No Trouble Reported," *Aiken Standard*, January 12, 1949, 1.

7. "Klansmen Stage Peaceful Parade in Orangeburg," *Florence Morning News*, January 16, 1949, 1.

8. W. D. W., "Klansmen Fail to Frighten Denmark Folk," *News and Courier*, February 10, 1949, 1.

9. Box 110-42, folders 1257–1959 in Waties's papers at the Moorland-Spingarn Research Center are filled with articles about Klan activity, lynchings, beatings, and acquittals during 1949.

10. Julius Waties Waring, *The Reminiscences of J. Waties Waring*, Columbia University Oral History Collection (Glen Rock, NJ: Microfilming Corporation of America, 1972), 257.

11. Charles M. Payne, "'The Whole United States Is Southern!': *Brown v. Board* and the Mystification of Race," *Journal of American History* 91, no 1 (June 2004): 90, https://doi.org/10.2307/3659615.

12. "Books and Authors," *New York Times*, October 31, 1947, 20.

13. *To Secure These Rights*, Harry S. Truman Library & Museum, accessed June 9, 2020, https://www.trumanlibrary.gov/library/to-secure-these-rights#3.

14. Harry S Truman, "Special Message to the Congress on Civil Rights," February 2, 1948. Public Papers of the Presidents of the United States, January 1 to December 31, 1948. Washington: United States Government Printing Office, 1964, n. 20, https://glc.yale.edu/special-message-congress-civil-rights.

15. Democratic Party Platforms, 1948 Democratic Party Platform Online by Gerhard Peters and John T. Woolley, The American Presidency Project, accessed January 14, 2021, https://www.presidency.ucsb.edu/node/273225.

16. Address by Senator Hubert H. Humphrey to the Annual Convention of the National Association for the Advancement of Colored People, Oklahoma City, Oklahoma,

June 29, 1952, Papers of the NAACP, Group II, Series A: Supplement to Part 1, 1951–1955 (Frederick, MD: University Publications of America), microfilm, reel 6, frame 0777.

17. Alan Brinkley, "The New Deal and Southern Politics," in *The New Deal and the South: Essays*, ed. James C. Cobb and Michael V. Namorato (Jackson: University Press of Mississippi, 1984), 113.

18. William S. White, "South's Senators Warn Against 'Gag,'" *New York Times*, February 1, 1949, 28.

19. Cabell Phillips, "Filibuster Issue Clouds the Truman Program," *New York Times*, March 6, 1949, E6.

20. George Hatcher, "South Firmly Backs Filibuster in Senate," *New York Times*, March 13, 1949, E10.

21. "Trouble in Congress," *New York Times*, March 17, 1949, 24.

22. "Digest of Speeches on Civil Rights Made by Senator Hubert H. Humphrey on the Floor of the Senate, March 14 and 16, 1949," Minnesota Historical Society, http://www.mnhs.org/library/findaids/00442/pdfa/00442-00214.pdf.

23. "Filibustering Marches On," *Pittsburgh Courier*, March 26, 1949, 14.

24. J. Waties Waring to Donald Harrington, November 16, 1950, box 110-12, folder 292, J. Waties Waring Papers, Moorland-Spingarn Research Center, Howard University.

25. Ninth Annual Convention of the National Lawyers Guild, Detroit, Michigan, February 20, 1949, box 110-39, folder 1231, J. Waties Waring Papers, Moorland-Spingarn Research Center, Howard University.

26. Sarah Hart Brown, *Standing Against Dragons: Three Southern Lawyers in an Era of Fear* (Baton Rouge: Louisiana State University Press, 1998), 21–22.

27. Register of the Robert W. Kenny Papers, 1823–1975, Online Archive of California, accessed July 25, 2015, http://oac.cdlib.org/findaid/ark:/13030/tf3199n6b1/.

28. "Our History," nlg.org, National Lawyers Guild, accessed July 25, 2015.

29. "Truman Criticized before Law Guild," *New York Times*, February 20, 1949. National Lawyers Guild Records, TAM 191, box 21, folder 18, Tamiment Library & Robert F. Wagner Labor Archives, Bobst Library, New York University. I want to thank Timothy Johnson at the Tamiment Library for so kindly sending me materials.

30. National Lawyers Guild Records, TAM 191, box 21, folder 18.

31. Thurgood Marshall to Robert J. Silberstein, February 23, 1949, Papers of the NAACP Part 4, The Voting Rights Campaign 1916–1950 (Frederick, MD: University Publications of America), microfilm, reel 11, frame 129.

32. Ninth Annual Convention of the National Lawyers Guild, Detroit, Michigan, February 20, 1949.

33. Three transcripts exist of "The Struggle for Negro Rights": An edited version in the *Lawyers Guild Review* (volume 9, page 5); Papers of the NAACP, Part 4, reel 11, beginning at frame 107; and a transcript from a Detroit court reporter in J. Waties Waring's papers at Moorland-Spingarn Research Center (box 110-39, folder 1231).

34. Clifford J. Durr, "Tribute to Judge J. Waties Waring," *Lawyers Guild Review* 9, no. 1 (Winter 1949): 5. HeinOnline.

35. Marshall's tribute was not published in *Lawyers Guild Review*. Page numbers referenced in parentheses are the page numbers of the transcript in the NAACP Papers.

36. Donald Harrington to J. Waties and Elizabeth Waring, May 26, 1954, box 110-12, folder 292, J. Waties Waring Papers, Moorland-Spingarn Research Center, Howard University.

37. Donald Harrington, "What Negros Can Do about the White Problem," Community Pulpit Series, no. 2 (New York: Community Church of New York, 1947), 3.

38. Laurence Coupe, *Kenneth Burke on Myth: An Introduction* (New York & London: Routledge, 2005), 98.

39. Kenneth Burke, "Four Master Tropes," *Kenyon Review* 3, no. 4 (Autumn 1941): 424, https://www.jstor.org/stable/4332286.

40. Harrington, "What Negroes Can Do," 14–15.

41. Morton Sosna, *In Search of the Silent South: Southern Liberals and the Race Issue* (New York: Columbia University Press, 1977), 149.

42. Eleanor Roosevelt, "My Day," June 3, 1949, Eleanor Roosevelt Papers Project, George Washington University, http://www.gwu.edu/~erpapers/myday/displaydoc.cfm?_y=1949&_f=md001296.

43. James Dombrowski to J. Waties Waring, June 8, 1949, box 110-10, folder 52, J. Waties Waring Papers, Moorland-Spingarn Research Center, Howard University.

44. Elizabeth Waring to Thurgood Marshall, June 7, 1949, Papers of the NAACP, Part 4, The Voting Rights Campaign 1916–1950 (Frederick, MD: University Publications of America), microfilm, reel 11, frame 145.

45. J. Waties Waring to Aubrey Williams, July 21, 1949, box 110-19, folder 614, J. Waties Waring Papers, Moorland-Spingarn Research Center, Howard University.

46. J. Waties Waring to Rebecca West, August 23, 1947, box 36, folder 1350, Rebecca West Papers, General Collection, Beinecke Rare Book and Manuscript Library, Yale University.

47. Harold Boulware to Rev. Joseph A. De Laine, March 8, 1949, Joseph A. De Laine Papers, Digital Collections, South Caroliniana Library, https://digital.library.sc.edu/collections/joseph-a-de-laine-papers-ca-1918-2000/.

48. J. A. De Laine, "The Clarendon County School Segregation Case," *A.M.E. Review*, 37–53, Papers of the NAACP, Part 26, Selected branch files 1940–1955, Series A: The South (Frederick, MD: University Publications of America), microfilm, reel 18, frame 280.

49. Wade Kolb III, "*Briggs v. Elliott* Revisited: A Study in Grassroots Activism and Trial Advocacy from the Early Civil Rights Era," *Journal of Southern Legal History* 19, no. 1 (2011): 135, HeinOnline.

50. South Carolina State Conference, 1949, Papers of the NAACP, Part 26, Selected Branch Files 1940–1955, Series A: The South Group II, Series B, Branch Department Files, Geographic File, folder: 001493-019-001; pp. 67, 68, 78, 82, ProQuest History Vault.

51. Eugene A. R. Mongtomery to J. A. De Laine Sr., November 14, 1949, Joseph A. De Laine Papers, Digital Collections, South Caroliniana Library, https://digital.library.sc.edu/collections/joseph-a-de-laine-papers-ca-1918-2000/.

52. Ophelia De Laine Gona, *Dawn of Desegregation: J. A. De Laine and* Briggs v. Elliott (Columbia: University of South Carolina Press, 2011), 192.

53. John H. McCray, "The Water is Fine," April 27, 1952, John Henry McCray Papers, Digital Collections, South Caroliniana Library, https://digital.library.sc.edu/collections/john-henry-mccray-papers-1929-1989/.

54. John H. McCray, "Address: Columbia Chapters, Omega Psi Phi Fraternity," March 13, 1949, John Henry McCray Papers, Digital Collections, South Caroliniana Library, https://digital.library.sc.edu/collections/john-henry-mccray-papers-1929-1989/.

55. "Fight for Freedom, Judge Tells Sixth District Q's," *The Oracle* 39, no. 5 (September 1949): 34, https://oppf12d.org/index.cfm?e=inner4&itemcategory=92692.

56. Benjamin E. Mays, "Judge Waties Waring Characterized as a Free Man, Both Morally, Spiritually," *Pittsburgh Courier*, May 21, 1949, box 110-42, folder 1260, J. Waties Waring Papers, Moorland-Spingarn Research Center, Howard University.

57. My account of the fraternity's meeting and Waties's remarks comes from newspaper clippings in J. Waties Waring Papers at Moorland-Spingarn Research Center, box 110-42, folder 1260.

58. Program, box 110-39, folder 1231, J. Waties Waring Papers, Moorland-Spingarn Research Center, Howard University.

59. Elizabeth Waring to Poppy Cannon and Walter White, November 28, 1949, box 7, folder 216, Walter Francis White and Poppy Cannon Papers, Yale Collection of American Literature, Beinecke Rare Book and Manuscript Library, Yale University.

60. Tinsley E. Yarbrough, *A Passion for Justice: J. Waties Waring and Civil Rights* (New York: Oxford University Press, 1987), 127.

61. John H. McCray, "Charleston YWCA Is Target After Talk from Mrs. Waring," *Lighthouse and Informer*, January 28, 1950, 1, box 110-42, folder 1264, J. Waties Waring Papers, Moorland-Spingarn Research Center, Howard University.

62. J. Waties Waring to Mr. and Mrs. Aubrey Williams, January 25, 1950, box 110-19, folder 615, J. Waties Waring Papers, Moorland-Spingarn Research Center, Howard University.

CHAPTER 4: BRICKBATS AND BOUQUETS

1. J. Waties Waring to Anne and Stanley Warren, January 13, 1950, box 110-20, folder 584, J. Waties Waring Papers, Moorland-Spingarn Research Center, Howard University.

2. J. Waties Waring to Thurgood Marshall, April 22, 1949, box 110-15, folder 386, J. Waties Waring Papers, Moorland-Spingarn Research Center, Howard University.

3. Elizabeth Waring to John Hammond and Palmer Weber, January 4, 1950, box 110-31, folder 984, J. Waties Waring Papers, Moorland-Spingarn Research Center, Howard University.

4. "Judge Waring Tells AP Writer He Has 'Passion for Justice,'" *News and Courier*, April 20, 1950, box 110-43, folder 1268, J. Waties Waring Papers, Moorland-Spingarn Research Center, Howard University.

5. Sharon Crowley and Debra Hawhee, *Ancient Rhetorics for Contemporary Students*, 2nd ed. (Boston & London: Allyn and Bacon, 1999), 31.

6. In *Phaedrus*, Plato remarks on the concept of the propriety of time for the rhetor, "when to speak and when to hold his tongue, when to use and when not to use . . . each of the specific devices of discourse he may have studied." Plato, *Phaedrus*, trans. W. C. Helmbold and W. G. Rabinowitz (Upper Saddle River, NJ: Prentice Hall, 1956), 64.

7. John H. McCray, "Charleston YWCA Is Target After Talk from Mrs. Waring," *Lighthouse and Informer*, January 28, 1950, 1, box 110-42, folder 1264, J. Waties Waring Papers, Moorland-Spingarn Research Center, Howard University.

8. Septima Poinsette Clark, interview by Jacquelyn Hall, Septima P. Clark Papers, box 1, folder 8, Avery Research Center, College of Charleston.

9. Nancy Marie Robertson, *Christian Sisterhood, Race Relations, and the YWCA, 1906–46* (Urbana & Chicago: University of Illinois Press, 2007), 175.

10. McCray, "Charleston YWCA Is Target After Talk from Mrs. Waring," 1.

11. J. Waties Waring to Anne and Stanley Warren, January 13, 1950.

12. Septima Clark, account of invitation to Elizabeth Waring to speak at the annual meeting of the Coming Street YWCA, box 110-34, folder 1035, J. Waties Waring Papers, Moorland-Spingarn Research Center, Howard University.

13. Septima Clark, account of invitation to Elizabeth Waring to speak at the annual meeting of the Coming Street YWCA.

14. Robertson, *Christian Sisterhood, Race Relations, and the YWCA*, 175.

15. "Judge's Wife Abused for Praising Negroes," n.d., box 110-42, folder 1264, J. Waties Waring Papers, Moorland-Spingarn Research Center, Howard University.

16. Elmer W. Henderson, "The Elimination of Segregation Through Protest, Propaganda and Education," *Journal of Negro Education* 20, no. 3 (Summer 1951): 477, https://doi.org/10.2307/2966019.

17. Michael Leff and Ebony A. Utley, "Instrumental and Constitutive Rhetoric in Martin Luther King, Jr.'s 'Letter from Birmingham Jail,'" *Rhetoric & Public Affairs* 7, no. 1 (Spring 2004): 41, https://www.jstor.org/stable/41939889.

18. J. Waties Waring to Anne and Stanley Warren, January 13, 1950.

19. Tinsley E. Yarbrough, *A Passion for Justice: J. Waties Waring and Civil Rights* (New York: Oxford University Press, 1987), 129, 131–32.

20. Elizabeth Waring to Thurgood Marshall, January 17, 1950, Papers of the NAACP, Part 4, The Voting Rights Campaign 1916–1950 (Frederick, MD: University Publications of America), microfilm, reel 11, frame 149.

21. Steven F. Lawson and Charles M. Payne, *Debating the Civil Rights Movement* (Lanham, MD: Rowman & Littlefield, 2006), 4.

22. "Scorn White Blacklist to Aid Dixie Negroes," *New York World-Telegram*, February 22, 1950, box 110-40, folder 1239, J. Waties Waring Papers, Moorland-Spingarn Research Center, Howard University.

23. "Negro 'Push' Is Urged to Win Equality," *New York Times*, January 18, 1950, 23; "Jurist's Wife Angers South with Remarks about Whites," *Washington Post*, January 18, 1950, 7.

24. Septima Poinsette Clark with LeGette Blythe, *Echo in My Soul* (New York: E. P. Dutton, 1962), 99.

25. "Speech made at Charleston, S.C. on January 16, 1950 to the Colored YWCA's Annual Meeting by Mrs. J. Waties Waring, Wife of federal Judge Waring," Frank W. and Lillian Spencer Collection, 1921–1987, series 1, folder 74, Armstrong Atlantic State University, Lane Library, Special Collections, Savannah, GA. I have located four versions of this speech. The version in the Spencer Collection appears to be the press manuscript because of the typed

heading and lack of handwritten revisions. Another version is available in the NAACP Papers (Part 4, reel 11, frame 0146). Two versions are located in the Judge's papers at the Moorland-Spingarn Research Center at Howard University (box 110-3, folder 27). Of the two versions at Howard University, one appears to be a draft and the other has handwritten notation "original copy from which I spoke." Unless otherwise indicated, all references to the speech come from the delivery copy.

26. Charles W. Lomas, *The Agitator in American Society* (Englewood Cliffs, NJ: Prentice-Hall, 1968), 120.

27. Sarah Patton Boyle, *The Desegregated Heart: A Virginian's Stand in Time of Transition*, ed. Jennifer Ritterhouse (1962; reis., Charlottesville: University Press of Virginia, 2001), 216.

28. "Mrs. Waring Meets the Press," *American Mercury* 70 (May 1950): 562.

29. Clark, *Echo in My Soul*, 100.

30. Megan Foley, "Sound Bites: Rethinking the Circulation of Speech from Fragment to Fetish," *Rhetoric & Public Affairs* 15, no. 4 (Winter 2012): 618, https://www.jstor.org/stable/41940624.

31. "Priorities at Home," Speech at YWCA, Philadelphia, PA, April 30, 1950, box 110-3, folder 14, J. Waties Waring Papers, Moorland-Spingarn Research Center, Howard University.

32. Elizabeth Waring to Bicknell Eubanks, January 3, 1951, box 1, folder 6, Ruby Pendergrass Cornwell Papers, Avery Research Center, College of Charleston.

33. Elizabeth Waring to Bicknell Eubanks, January 3, 1951.

34. Letter from Betty Ross Parker, Summerville, n.d., box 110-7, folder 173, J. Waties Waring Papers, Moorland-Spingarn Research Center, Howard University.

35. J. Waties Waring to Mr. and Mrs. Aubrey Williams, January 25, 1950, box 110-19, folder 615, J. Waties Waring Papers, Moorland-Spingarn Research Center, Howard University.

36. Hodding Carter, "A Southern Liberal Looks at Civil Rights," *New York Times*, August 8, 1948, SM10.

37. Hodding Carter, "A Southerner Looks at the South," *New York Times*, July 7, 1946, 81.

38. Hodding Carter, "Just Leave Us Alone," *Saturday Evening Post*, 222, no. 29 (January 14, 1950), 30. EBSCOhost.

39. Jeanne Theoharis, *A More Beautiful and Terrible History: The Uses and Misuses of Civil Rights History* (Boston: Beacon Press, 2018), 88.

40. Letter to the Editor, Mrs. Raymond Moore of Walterboro, *News and Courier*, January 21, 1950, 4.

41. Letter from Mrs. P. J. Simms, January 18, 1950, Cornelia, GA, box 110-23, folder 720, J. Waties Waring Papers, Moorland-Spingarn Research Center, Howard University.

42. Letter from S. M. Ramsey, January 21, 1950, box 110-23, folder 722, J. Waties Waring Papers, Moorland-Spingarn Research Center, Howard University.

43. Letter from George H. Lackey, Manning, SC, January 20, 1950, box 110-23, folder 722, J. Waties Waring Papers, Moorland-Spingarn Research Center, Howard University.

44. Elizabeth Gillespie McRae, *Mothers of Massive Resistance: White Women and the Politics of White Supremacy* (New York: Oxford University Press, 2018), 88.

45. Charles M. Payne and Adam Green, eds., *Time Longer than a Rope: A Century of African American Activism, 1850–1950* (New York: New York University Press, 2003), 2.

46. Letter from Mrs. Elizabeth Munn, January 18, 1950, box 110-23, folder 724, J. Waties Waring Papers, Moorland-Spingarn Research Center, Howard University.

47. Letter from "Magnolia White," n.d., box 110-23, folder 725, J. Waties Waring Papers, Moorland-Spingarn Research Center, Howard University.

48. Letter to the Editor, G. L. Ivey, *News and Courier*, January 21, 1950, 4.

49. Letter from Mrs. Charles Clifton, January 21, 1950, box 110-23, folder 725, J. Waties Waring Papers, Moorland-Spingarn Research Center, Howard University.

50. Newspaper Clipping *The Statesman* [Hapeville, GA], January 26, 1950, box 110-42, folder 1264, J. Waties Waring Papers, Moorland-Spingarn Research Center, Howard University.

51. Letter from Mrs. J. Ashley Turner, January 19, 1950, box 110-23, folder 710, J. Waties Waring Papers, Moorland-Spingarn Research Center, Howard University.

52. Letter to the Editor, Mrs. John Duncan, *News and Courier*, January 20, 1950, 5A.

53. Letter to the Editor, Mrs. Raymond Moore.

54. Newspaper Clipping from *Atlanta Journal*, letter to the editor from Mrs. Joan Gates, n.d., box 110-43, folder 1268, J. Waties Waring Papers, Moorland-Spingarn Research Center, Howard University.

55. John H. McCray, "Need for Changing and Mrs. Waring Told Them . . . ," *Lighthouse and Informer*, January 21, 1950, 4, box 110-42, folder 1265, J. Waties Waring Papers, Moorland-Spingarn Research Center, Howard University.

56. "Reaction to Talk by Wife of Federal Judge Is Reported," *News and Courier*, January 18, 1950, 8.

57. "S. C. Congressmen Answer Charges of Judge's Wife," *News and Courier*, January 19, 1950, 12.

58. Carter, "Just Leave Us Alone."

59. Virginius Dabney, *Liberalism in the South* (Chapel Hill: University of North Carolina Press, 1932), 154, 242.

60. Newspaper Clipping from *Tallahassee Democrat*, n.d., box 110-42, folder 1264, J. Waties Waring Papers, Moorland-Spingarn Research Center, Howard University.

61. Mark Anthony Brown ("A Yankee"), "Letters Discuss Racial Talk," *News and Courier*, January 20, 1950, 5A.

62. Letter from Della Kitching Livingston Scudder, January 18, 1950, box 110-23, folder 719, J. Waties Waring Papers, Moorland-Spingarn Research Center, Howard University.

63. Letter to the Editor, Mrs. John Duncan, *News and Courier*, January 20, 1950, 5A.

64. Letter from George H. Lackey, Manning, SC, January 20, 1950.

65. Letter from Ned Holland, Greenville, SC, January 17, 1950, box 110-23, folder 721, J. Waties Waring Papers, Moorland-Spingarn Research Center, Howard University.

66. Postcard from Mrs. B. S. [last name illegible], Savannah, GA, January 19, 1950, box 110-23, folder 721, J. Waties Waring Papers, Moorland-Spingarn Research Center, Howard University.

67. Letter from William Hussey Jr., January 21, 1950, box 110-23, folder 722, J. Waties Waring Papers, Moorland-Spingarn Research Center, Howard University.

68. Letter from "A True Southerner," Palmetto, FL, January 19, 1950, box 110-23, folder 722, J. Waties Waring Papers, Moorland-Spingarn Research Center, Howard University.

69. Letter from Barbara Means, Fort Worth, TX, January 18, 1950, box 110-23, folder 722, J. Waties Waring Papers, Moorland-Spingarn Research Center, Howard University.

70. Letter from Barbara Means, January 18, 1950.

71. Letter to Editor, Mrs. Joan Gates, *Atlanta Journal*.

72. John Dollard, *Caste and Class in a Southern Town* (New Haven: Yale University Press, 1937), 136.

73. Unsigned letter Fort Worth, TX, January 25, 1950, box 110-23, folder 723, J. Waties Waring Papers, Moorland-Spingarn Research Center, Howard University.

74. Letter from "A True Southerner," Palmetto, FL; Letter from William Hussey Jr., January 21, 1950.

75. Unsigned letter, postmarked New York, NY, January 18, 1950, box 110-23, folder 710, J. Waties Waring Papers, Moorland-Spingarn Research Center, Howard University.

76. Letter from "A True Democrat," Charleston, January 20, 1950, box 110-23, folder 725, J. Waties Waring Papers, Moorland-Spingarn Research Center, Howard University.

77. Postcard from Charleston, January 17, 1950, box 110-23, folder 721, J. Waties Waring Papers, Moorland-Spingarn Research Center, Howard University.

78. Letter from "Magnolia White," n.d., box 110-23 folder 725, J. Waties Waring Papers, Moorland-Spingarn Research Center, Howard University.

79. Unsigned, Tampa, FL, January 20, 1950, box 110-23, folder 722, J. Waties Waring Papers, Moorland-Spingarn Research Center, Howard University.

80. Newspaper Clipping from *Tallahassee Democrat*.

81. Although Carter described Elizabeth as "youngish," she was fifty-four years old when she delivered "Freedom Is Everybody's Job." Hodding Carter, "Bilboism Deserves Denunciation, but so Does Libel on Southern Whites," *Atlanta Journal*, January 29, 1950, 19A.

82. Newspaper Clipping, n.d., box 110-42, folder 1264, J. Waties Waring Papers, Moorland-Spingarn Research Center, Howard University.

83. Letter from "A Southerner," n.d., box 110-7, folder 177, J. Waties Waring Papers, Moorland-Spingarn Research Center, Howard University.

84. Unsigned letter, Laurens, SC, January 18, 1950, box 110-23, folder 710, J. Waties Waring Papers, Moorland-Spingarn Research Center, Howard University.

85. "'Damyankee,' Charleston Retort as Judge's Wife Assails Whites," UP, January 17, 1950, Johnson Publishing Company Clipping Files Collection, Archives Research Center, Robert W. Woodruff Library, Atlanta University Center.

86. John H. McCray, "Champions of Democracy Bear Cross of Insults from White Supremacists," *Pittsburgh Courier*, January 28, 1950, 7.

87. Letter from Mr. and Mrs. E. W. Glenn, January 1950, box 110-7, folder 170; Letter from the Byrd family, n.d., box 110-23, folder 690, J. Waties Waring Papers, Moorland-Spingarn Research Center, Howard University.

88. Letter from Mary Miles, February 14, 1950, box 110-7, folder 172, J. Waties Waring Papers, Moorland-Spingarn Research Center, Howard University.

89. Letter from Mrs. Brice, January 24, 1950, box 110-7, folder 167; Letter from Mrs. Camil L. Johnson, January 20, 1950, folder 110–7, folder 171, J. Waties Waring Papers, Moorland-Spingarn Research Center, Howard University.

90. Letter from George Gramblin, February 3, 1950, box 110-23, folder 695, J. Waties Waring Papers, Moorland-Spingarn Research Center, Howard University.

91. Letter from Rev. and Mrs. J. H. McKissick, February 2, 1950, box 110-23, folder 701, J. Waties Waring Papers, Moorland-Spingarn Research Center, Howard University.

92. Letter from Mrs. E. L. Wheeler Sr., January 19, 1950, box 110-23, folder 710, J. Waties Waring Papers, Moorland-Spingarn Research Center, Howard University. Pendleton is in the far western section of South Carolina.

93. Timothy B. Tyson, "Dynamite and 'The Silent South': A Story from the Second Reconstruction in South Carolina," in *Jumpin' Jim Crow: Southern Politics from Civil War to Civil Rights*, ed. Jane Dailey, Glenda Elizabeth Gilmore, and Bryant Simon (Princeton: Princeton University Press, 2000), 276.

94. Letter from Mr. and Mrs. H. R. Scott, January 23, 1950, box 110-7, folder 174, J. Waties Waring Papers, Moorland-Spingarn Research Center, Howard University.

95. Letter from Mrs. and Mrs. F. Taylor, n.d., box 110-23, folder 707, J. Waties Waring Papers, Moorland-Spingarn Research Center, Howard University.

96. "Achievement Clubs Hail Mrs. Waring," *Pittsburgh Courier*, February 4, 1950, 4.

97. "Mrs. Waring's Speech," *Atlanta Daily World*, January 20, 1950, 4.

98. "The Courier Salutes," *Pittsburgh Courier*, February 4, 1950, 18.

99. "Crushing of Bias Urged by Waring," *New York Times*, March 1, 1954, 23.

100. I hesitate to label white people who opposed Jim Crow as a counterpublic since they benefited from segregation.

101. Tom Poston, "Judge's Wife Tells of Gain in Fight on Biased South," *New York Post*, March 5, 1950, Johnson Publishing Company Clipping Files Collection Archives Research Center, Robert W. Woodruff Library, Atlanta University Center.

102. See Benedict R. O'G. Anderson, *Imagined Communities: Reflections on the Origin and Spread of Nationalism* (London: Verso, 1983).

103. Michael Warner, "Publics and Counterpublics," *Public Culture* 14, no. 1 (Winter 2002): 58–59, https://muse.jhu.edu/article/26277.

104. Letter from Joseph A. Saracini, St. Louis, MO, January 20, 1950, box 110-7, folder 174, J. Waties Waring Papers, Moorland-Spingarn Research Center, Howard University.

105. Elizabeth Waring to Thurgood Marshall, January 17, 1950.

106. John H. McCray, "Threats Made on Mrs. Waring," *Lighthouse and Informer*, January 21, 1950, 1, box 110-42, folder 1265, J. Waties Waring Papers, Moorland-Spingarn Research Center, Howard University; "Reaction to Talk by Wife of Federal Judge Is Reported," *News and Courier*, January 18, 1950.

107. McCray, "Champions of Democracy Bear Cross of Insults from White Supremacists."

108. "Judge's Wife Who Blasted 'Savage' South Unmoved by Threats to Leave," *Chicago Defender*, January 28, 1950, 1.

109. "Marching Through Charleston," *Time* 55, no. 5 (1950): 18. EBSCOhost.

110. Walter White, "Threats Against Mrs. Waring Blight on Grand Old Charleston," *Chicago Defender*, February 5, 1950, box 110-43, folder 1268, J. Waties Waring Papers, Moorland-Spingarn Research Center, Howard University.

111. John H. McCray, "Need for Changing and Mrs. Waring Told Them . . . ," *Lighthouse and Informer*, January 21, 1950, 4, box 110-42, folder 1265, J. Waties Waring Papers, Moorland-Spingarn Research Center, Howard University.

112. McCray, "Champions of Democracy Bear Cross of Insults from White Supremacists."

113. "Our Opinions," *Chicago Defender*, February 4, 1950, 6.

114. McCray, "Need for Changing."

115. James C. Scott, *Domination and the Arts of Resistance: Hidden Transcripts* (New Haven: Yale University Press, 1990), 19.

116. Laurence K. Frank to Elizabeth Waring, Strom Thurmond, and *Time* Magazine, February 9, 1950, box 1, folder 3, Ruby Pendergrass Cornwell Papers, Avery Research Center, College of Charleston.

117. Elizabeth may have mailed Dr. Frank's letters to other people besides Cornwell.

118. "Judge Waring Denounces Foes, Tells of Campaign," *Washington Post*, February 8, 1950, B11.

119. "4 Aiken Men Started Impeachment Petition," *News and Courier*, February 9, 1950, 11.

120. "Judge Waring Denounces Foes, Tells of Campaign."

121. J. Waties Waring to Mrs. and Mrs. Aubrey Williams, January 25, 1950.

122. Elizabeth Waring to Ruby Cornwell, February 20, 1950, box 1, folder 2, Ruby Pendergrass Cornwell Papers, Avery Research Center, College of Charleston.

CHAPTER 5: ONLY FORCE WILL WORK

1. Lloyd F. Bitzer, "Functional Communication: A Situational Perspective," in *Rhetoric in Transition: Studies in the Nature and Uses of Rhetoric*, ed. Eugene E. White (University Park: Pennsylvania State University Press, 1980), 24.

2. George Kenney, "Scorn White Blacklist to Aid Dixie Negroes," *New York World-Telegram*, box 110-40, folder 1239, J. Waties Waring Papers, Moorland-Spingarn Research Center, Howard University. Also published in *Richmond Times-Dispatch*, February 23, 1950, 11, box 1, folder 2, Ruby Pendergrass Cornwell Papers, Avery Research Center, College of Charleston.

3. Elizabeth Waring to John Hammond and Palmer Weber, January 4, 1950, box 110-32, folder 984, J. Waties Waring Papers, Moorland-Spingarn Research Center, Howard University.

4. I have found mention of additional speeches: Waties before the Baptist Ministers Conference (*New York Amsterdam News*, March 11, 1950), and Harlem YMCA (*New York Times*, March 18, 1950; *New York Amsterdam News*, March 18, 1950). However, I could not locate any media coverage of these speeches.

5. J. Robert Cox, "Perspectives on Rhetorical Criticism of Movements: Antiwar Dissent, 1964–1970," *Western Speech* 38, no. 4 (Fall 1974): 262, https://doi.org/10.1080/10570317409 373836.

6. This is a representative list of newspapers that covered the speech. It does not include all of them.

7. Martin Weil, "Martha Rountree Dies," *Washington Post*, August 25, 1999, B5; Richard Severo, "Lawrence E. Spivak, 93, Is Dead," *New York Times*, March 10, 1994, D21.

8. Unless otherwise indicated, all references to Elizabeth Waring's appearance on *Meet the Press* come from "Mrs. Waring Meets the Press," *American Mercury* 70 (May 1950): 562–69.

9. "Meet the Press," February 11, 1950, Papers of the NAACP, Part 4, The Voting Rights Campaign 1916–1950 (Frederick, MD: University Publications of America, 1986), microfilm, reel 11, frame 157.

10. "Meet the Press," February 11, 1950, Papers of the NAACP.

11. Gunnar Myrdal, *An American Dilemma: The Negro Problem and Modern Democracy* (New York: Harper & Brothers Publishers, 1944), 591.

12. Letter from R. T. Ashurst, April 26, 1950, box 110-23, folder 686, J. Waties Waring Papers, Moorland-Spingarn Research Center, Howard University.

13. "New World A'Coming," November 25, 1952, box 110-1, folder 3, J. Waties Waring Papers, Moorland-Spingarn Research Center, Howard University.

14. Elizabeth Waring to Bicknell Eubanks, January 3, 1951, box 1, folder 6, Ruby Pendergrass Cornwell Papers, Avery Research Center, College of Charleston.

15. Myrdal, *An American Dilemma*, 591–92.

16. Milton Mayer, "The Issue is Miscegenation," in *White Racism: Its History, Pathology and Practice*, ed. Barry N. Schwartz and Robert Disch (New York: Dell Publishing, 1970), 207.

17. Kimberley Johnson, *Reforming Jim Crow: Southern Politics and State in the Age before* Brown (New York: Oxford University Press, 2010), 10.

18. "Judge's Wife Discusses Civil Rights on Television," *News and Courier*, February 12, 1950, 5D.

19. Marion Wright and Arnold Shankman, *Human Rights Odyssey* (Durham: Moore Publishing Company, 1978), 93.

20. James. W. Vander Zanden, "The Ideology of White Supremacy," *Journal of the History of Ideas* 20, no. 3 (June–September 1959): 401, https://doi.org/10.2307/2708116.

21. Letter from Mrs. Ernest C. Wood, March 22, 1950, box 110-23, folder 725, J. Waties Waring Papers, Moorland-Spingarn Research Center, Howard University.

22. Anonymous letter, n.d., box 110-23, folder 721, J. Waties Waring Papers, Moorland-Spingarn Research Center, Howard University.

23. Anonymous letter, n.d., box 110-7, folder 177, J. Waties Waring Papers, Moorland-Spingarn Research Center, Howard University.

24. Jacquelyn Dowd Hall, *Revolt Against Chivalry: Jessie Daniel Ames and the Women's Campaign Against Lynching* (New York: Columbia University Press, 1993), 145, 152.

25. I do not mean to imply that the letters that Elizabeth Waring received are equivalent to the sexual assaults and threats that Black women endured.

26. Letter from Mrs. Robert Martin, February 15, 1950, box 110-7, folder 178, J. Waties Waring Papers, Moorland-Spingarn Research Center, Howard University.

27. Letter from "A True Southerner," n.d., box 110-7, folder 177, J. Waties Waring Papers, Moorland-Spingarn Research Center, Howard University.

28. Anonymous letter, March 21, 1950, box 110-7, folder 177, J. Waties Waring Papers, Moorland-Spingarn Research Center, Howard University.

29. Anonymous letter, n.d., box 110-7, folder 177.

30. Anonymous letter, n.d., box 110-23, folder 721.

31. Letter from John T. Panks, March 19, 1950, Atlanta, box 110-23, folder 704, J. Waties Waring Papers, Moorland-Spingarn Research Center, Howard University.

32. Letter from Fred H. Colvin, February 21, 1950, Point Pleasant, NJ, box 110-7, folder 168, J. Waties Waring Papers, Moorland-Spingarn Research Center, Howard University.

33. Telegram, n.d., box 110-7, folder 179, J. Waties Waring Papers, Moorland-Spingarn Research Center, Howard University.

34. Letter from R. A. Thompson, February 14, 1950, box 1, folder 3, Ruby Pendergrass Cornwell Papers, Avery Research Center, College of Charleston.

35. Letter from John H. Faulk, February 11, 1950, box 1, folder 3, Ruby Pendergrass Cornwell Papers, Avery Research Center, College of Charleston.

36. "A Joint Resolution," February 14, 1950, South Carolina Department of Archives and History, Columbia, South Carolina, https://digital.scetv.org/teachingAmerhistory/lessons/GenAsmRemovalofWaring.htm.

37. Anonymous letter, March 21, 1950.

38. Julius Waties Waring, *The Reminiscences of J. Waties Waring*, Columbia University Oral History Collection (Glen Rock, NJ: Microfilming Corporation of America, 1972), 398.

39. "Meet the Press," February 11, 1950, Papers of the NAACP.

40. James Booker, "Sees Either Equality or New Slavery," *New York Amsterdam News*, February 25, 1950, 1.

41. "U. S. Judge Says South Has a 'White Problem,'" *Philadelphia Tribune*, February 28, 1950, 1.

42. Kenney, "Scorn White Blacklist to Aid Dixie Negroes."

43. Tom Poston, "Judge's Wife Tells of Gain in Fight on Biased South," *New York Post*, March 5, 1950, Johnson Publishing Company Clipping Files Collection, Archives Research Center, Robert W. Woodruff Library, Atlanta University Center.

44. James Booker, "Dixie Crusader Hits 'Die-Hards,'" *New York Amsterdam News*, March 11, 1950, box 110-43, folder 1273, J. Waties Waring Papers, Moorland-Spingarn Research Center, Howard University.

45. Lillian Scott, "The Warings of South Carolina: South's Most Courageous Couple," n.d., box 110-43, folder 1269, J. Waties Waring Papers, Moorland-Spingarn Research Center, Howard University. Lillian Scott was a journalist for the *Chicago Defender*. However, searches in multiple Black newspaper databases yielded no article with this title. It may have been published in *Jet* or *Ebony*.

46. "Between 1945 and 1960, three dozen new states in Asia and Africa achieved autonomy or outright independence from their European colonial rulers." See "Decolonization of Asia and Africa, 1945–1960," Department of State, Office of the Historian, accessed December 6, 2020, https://history.state.gov/milestones/1945-1952/asia-and-africa.

47. "South Carolina Couple Speaks for Negro Rights," *Kingsport News*, April 3, 1950; "Gradualism No Way to Get Rights, Mrs. Waring Says," *New Journal and Guide*, April 8, 1950, box 110-43, folder 1268, J. Waties Waring Papers, Moorland-Spingarn Research Center, Howard University.

48. "'White Supremacy' Termed a Cancer," *New York Times*, February 27, 1950, 17.

49. "Waring Rapped and Lauded on Race Campaign," *Christian Science Monitor*, April 20, 1950, box 110-43, folder 1268, J. Waties Waring Papers, Moorland-Spingarn Research Center, Howard University.

50. Faiza Patel and Raya Koreh, "New Method, Same Strategy: Russia Has Long Exploited U.S. Racial Divisions," Brennan Center for Justice, October 23, 2018, https://www.brennancenter.org/our-work/analysis-opinion/new-method-same-strategy-russia-has-long-exploited-us-racial-divisions.

51. "Waring Says Force Needed to Ease Bias," *Atlanta Daily World*, April 7, 1950, 1.

52. "Waring Rapped and Lauded on Race Campaign."

53. Booker, "Sees Either Equality or New Slavery."

54. Poston, "Judge's Wife Tells of Gain in Fight on Biased South."

55. Margaret Kernodle, "Judge Wants 'Master's Voice' to Rule Southerners on Race," *News and Courier*, March 19, 1950, 7D, box 110-43, folder 1273, J. Waties Waring Papers, Moorland-Spingarn Research Center, Howard University.

56. Poston, "Judge's Wife Tells of Gain in Fight on Biased South."

57. Lillian Scott, "Judge Waring, An 'Island' in a Sea of Southern Hate," *Chicago Defender*, November 20, 1948, 1.

58. Robert L. Ivie, "Fire, Flood, and Red Fever: Motivating Metaphors of Global Emergency in the Truman Doctrine Speech," *Presidential Studies Quarterly* 29, no. 3 (September 1999): 577, 584, https://doi.org/10.1111/j.0268-141.2003.00050.x.

59. "Human Rights Citation for Judge and Mrs. Waring," *New Journal and Guide*, March 4, 1950, C1.

60. Charles M. Payne, "'The Whole United States Is Southern!': Brown v. Board and the Mystification of Race," *Journal of American History* 19, no. 1 (June 2004): 87, https://doi.org/10.2307/3659615.

61. Kenney, "Scorn White Blacklist to Aid Dixie Negroes."

62. "Human Rights Citation for Judge and Mrs. Waring."

63. Kernodle, "Judge Wants 'Master's Voice' to Rule Southerners on Race."

64. Poston, "Judge's Wife Tells of Gain in Fight on Biased South."

65. "Race Hatred Is a Disease, Warings Say," *Minneapolis Star Tribune*, March 31, 1950, 20, box 110-43, folder 1273, J. Waties Waring Papers, Moorland-Spingarn Research Center, Howard University.

66. "Force Can Break Race Bars—Mrs. Waring," *New Jersey Afro-American*, April 6, 1950, 13, box 110-43, folder 1268, J. Waties Waring Papers, Moorland-Spingarn Research Center, Howard University.

67. Elizabeth Waring to George M. Houser, November 29, 1950, box 110-12, folder 315, J. Waties Waring Papers, Moorland-Spingarn Research Center, Howard University.

68. "Waring Rapped and Lauded on Race Campaign."

69. Kenney, "Scorn White Blacklist to Aid Dixie Negroes."

70. John T. Kneebone, *Southern Liberal Journalists and the Issue of Race, 1920–1944* (Chapel Hill: University of North Carolina Press, 1985), 219.

71. "Race Hatred Is a Disease, Warings Say."

72. Sid Kline, "Equality Must Be Forced in South, Says Judge Waring Here," *The Sunday Compass*, February 19, 1950, box 110-43, folder 1272, J. Waties Waring Papers, Moorland-Spingarn Research Center, Howard University.

73. Booker, "Sees Either Equality or New Slavery."

74. Kenney, "Scorn White Blacklist to Aid Dixie Negroes."

75. Kneebone, *Southern Liberal Journalists and the Issue of Race*, 199.

76. Martin Luther King Jr., "The Other America," April 14, 1967, Stanford University. Civil Rights Movement Veterans, https://crmvet.org/docs/otheram.htm. King delivered a version of this speech on March 14, 1968, at Grosse Pointe High School in Elizabeth's native Detroit.

77. "Jurist from South Assails Prejudice," *New York Times*, October 12, 1948, 31.

78. Kenney, "Scorn White Blacklist to Aid Dixie Negroes."

79. "Waring Believes Civil Rights Fight Being Neglected," box 110-43, folder 1273, J. Waties Waring Papers, Moorland-Spingarn Research Center, Howard University.

80. "Threat of Impeachment Scorned by U.S. Jurist," *Afro-American*, April 8, 1950, box 110-43, folder 1268, J. Waties Waring Papers, Moorland-Spingarn Research Center, Howard University.

81. Booker, "Dixie Crusader hits 'Die-Hards.'"

82. "Waring Says Force Needed to Ease Bias," *Atlanta Daily World*, April 7, 1950, 1.

83. "Negro-Rights Backer, Ostracized in South, Finds 'Soul Refreshment' in New York City," *Richmond Times-Dispatch*, February 23, 1950, 11.

84. Booker, "Sees Either Equality or New Slavery."

85. "Small Cross Burned in Front of Home of Judge Waring," *News and Courier*, March 12, 1950, 2.

86. "Waring Accepts Klan Challenge," *Afro-American*, March 18, 1950, 1.

87. "Small Cross Burned in Front of Home of Judge Waring."

88. "Waring Accepts Klan Challenge."

89. "Judge Waring Defies Kluxers," *Chicago Defender*, March 18, 1950, 1.

90. "Congressmen Hear Bid for Waring Ouster," *Evening Post*, March 8, 1950, 1.

91. "S. C. Warned of Ouster," *Newport Daily News* (RI), March 15, 1950, 5.

92. "Expect Suit If Waring Impeachment Is Voted," *Chicago Defender*, March 25, 1950, 1. The article informed readers that if the South Carolina Senate and Governor approved the appropriation, then any interested South Carolinian taxpayer could file suit against it. The NAACP and John McCray were consulting to determine how to assist Waties, if necessary.

93. "U. S. Jurist Continues Blasting Bias," *Philadelphia Tribune*, March 21, 1950, 1.

94. "Judge Waring Defies Kluxers," *Chicago Defender*, March 18, 1950, 1; "Waring Accepts Klan Challenge," *Afro-American*, March 18, 1950, 1; "Cross Burned at Carolina Judge's Home," *Chicago Daily Tribune*, March 12, 1950, 2; Clippings from *Daily Mirror* and *New York Herald Tribune*, box 110-40, folder 1238, J. Waties Waring Papers, Moorland-Spingarn Research Center, Howard University.

95. "Waring Believes Civil Rights Fight Being Neglected."

96. "U. S. Jurist Continues Blasting Bias."

97. "'White Supremacy' Termed a Cancer."
98. "South Carolina Couple Speaks for Negro Rights."
99. "Gradualism No Way to Get Rights, Mrs. Waring Says," *New Journal and Guide*, April 8, 1950. Newspaper Clipping, box 110-43, folder 1268, J. Waties Waring Papers, Moorland-Spingarn Research Center, Howard University.
100. "Waring Says Force Needed to Ease Bias," *Atlanta Daily World*, April 7, 1950, 1.
101. "When the Judge Overspeaks," *Citizen* [Asheville, NC], April 4, 1950, box 110-43, folder 1268, J. Waties Waring Papers, Moorland-Spingarn Research Center, Howard University.
102. "S. C. Congressmen Answer Charges of Judge's Wife," *News and Courier*, January 19, 1950, 12.
103. 81 Cong. Rec. H4930–31 (April 6, 1950) (statement of Rep. Rivers).
104. 81 Cong. Rec. H4930–31 (April 6, 1950) (statement of Rep. Rivers).
105. "Dixicrats Grab at Straw in War Against Waring," *Afro-American*, April 15, 1950, 5.
106. All references to this speech are from "Priorities at Home," Speech delivered at Tindley Temple, Philadelphia, PA, April 30, 1950, box 110-3, folder 14, J. Waties Waring Papers, Moorland-Spingarn Research Center, Howard University.
107. Letter from Shaemas O'Sheel, February 27, 1950, box 110-23, folder 703, J. Waties Waring Papers, Moorland-Spingarn Research Center, Howard University.
108. "Meet the Press," February 11, 1950, Papers of the NAACP.
109. Poston, "Judge's Wife Tells of Gain in Fight on Biased South."
110. "Annual League Banquet Great Success," box 110-43, folder 1268, J. Waties Waring Papers, Moorland-Spingarn Research Center, Howard University.
111. Newspaper Clipping, box 110-40, folder 1238, J. Waties Waring Papers, Moorland-Spingarn Research Center, Howard University.
112. "$1000 Pledged to Judge Waring," *Afro-American*, May 13, 1950, 7.
113. "Judge Waring Grateful for Funds Pledge," *Philadelphia Tribune*, May 16, 1950, 1; "Judge Waring Expresses Gratitude for $1000 Offer," *Afro-American*, May 27, 1950, 6.
114. "Negroes Ask Fight for Judge Waring," *New York Times*, March 19, 1950, 40; "Waring's Foes Told 'Lay Off' By NAACP," *Chicago Defender*, April 1, 1950, 11.
115. Letter from Lloyd B. Foster, May 10, 1950, Inman, SC, box 110-23 folder 725, J. Waties Waring Papers, Moorland-Spingarn Research Center, Howard University.
116. Letter from Dorothy Kaltenbach, April 22, 1950, San Francisco, box 110-7, folder 177, J. Waties Waring Papers, Moorland-Spingarn Research Center, Howard University.
117. Letter from Robert S. Cahoon, April 25, 1950, box 110-23, folder 690, J. Waties Waring Papers, Moorland-Spingarn Research Center, Howard University.
118. Letter from Chas and Ann Murphy, April 21, 1950, box 110-23, folder 702, J. Waties Waring Papers, Moorland-Spingarn Research Center, Howard University.
119. Letter from Mrs. J. W. Curry, May 8, 1950, box 110-7, folder 168, J. Waties Waring Papers, Moorland-Spingarn Research Center, Howard University.
120. Letter from Julia Collins, April 24, 1950, Maywood, IL, box 110-23, folder 700, J. Waties Waring Papers, Moorland-Spingarn Research Center, Howard University.
121. "Events Today," *Daily Compass*, May 1, 1950, box 110-43, folder 1269, J. Waties Waring Papers, Moorland-Spingarn Research Center, Howard University.

122. Myles Horton to J. Waties Waring, February 21, 1950, box 110-12, folder 301, J. Waties Waring Papers, Moorland-Spingarn Research Center, Howard University.

123. J. Waties Waring to Robert J. Silberstein, May 12, 1950, box 110-18, folder 514, J. Waties Waring Papers, Moorland-Spingarn Research Center, Howard University.

124. J. Waties Waring to James Dombrowski, December 11, 1948, box 110-20, folder 252, J. Waties Waring Papers, Moorland-Spingarn Research Center, Howard University.

CHAPTER 6: THE YEAR OF DECISION

1. James Booker, "Sees Either Equality or New Slavery," *New York Amsterdam News*, February 25, 1950, 1.

2. Oliver Hill, interview by George Gilliam, *The Ground Beneath Our Feet Project*, Virginia Center for Digital History, University of Virginia, accessed January 17, 2021, http://www2.vcdh.virginia.edu/saxon/servlet/SaxonServlet?source=/xml_docs/modernva/modernva_transcripts.xml&style=/xml_docs/modernva/interview_modernva.xsl&level=single&id=Oliver_Hill.

3. Henderson v. United States, 339 U.S. 816 (1950).

4. McLaurin v. Oklahoma State Regents for Higher Education, 339 U.S. 637 (1950).

5. Sweatt v. Painter, 339 U.S. 629 (1950).

6. J. Waties Waring to Thurgood Marshall, November 14, 1949, Papers of the NAACP, Part 15, Segregation and Discrimination, Complaints and Responses 1940–1955, Series A: Legal Department Files, ProQuest History Vault.

7. Correspondence between J. Waties Waring and James Dombrowski, December 13 and 15, 1949, box 110-10, folder 252, J. Waties Waring Papers, Moorland-Spingarn Research Center, Howard University.

8. James Dombrowski to J. Waties Waring, December 17, 1949, and January 9, 1950, box 110-10, folders 252 and 254, J. Waties Waring Papers, Moorland-Spingarn Research Center, Howard University.

9. James Dombrowski to J. Waties Waring, January 9, 1950.

10. Henderson v. United States, 339 U.S. 816 (1950).

11. Sweatt v. Painter, 339 U.S. 629 (195).

12. Charles M. Payne, "'The Whole United States Is Southern!': *Brown v. Board* and the Mystification of Race," *Journal of American History* 19, no. 1 (June 2004): 90, https://doi.org/10.2307/3659615.

13. Mark V. Tushnet, *The NAACP's Legal Strategy Against Segregated Education* (Chapel Hill: University of North Carolina Press, 1987), 147.

14. James M. Nabrit Jr., "Resort to the Courts as a Means of Eliminating 'Legalized' Segregation," *Journal of Negro Education* 20, no. 3 (Summer 1951): 468, https://doi.org/10.2307/2966018.

15. "The Clarendon County, SC School Case," May 21, 1951, Papers of the NAACP, Part 3, The Campaign for Education Equality, Series C: Legal Department and Central Office

Records 1951–1955 (Frederick, MD: University Publications of America), microfilm, reel 3, frame 212.

16. Oliver Hill, interview by George Gilliam, Virginia Center for Digital History, University of Virginia.

17. "Suit Prepared in Clarendon Seeking 'Equal' Treatment in Schools for Negroes," *The State*, May 16, 1950, 15; *Evening Post*, May 15, 1950, 2; *Greenville News*, May 16, 1950, 7.

18. "Equal Facilities Suit Filed by Negro Leaders," *Atlanta Daily World*, May 16, 1950, 1.

19. In 1950, South Carolina was divided into two federal court districts, Eastern and Western. Columbia and Charleston were both in the Eastern District. "U.S. District Courts for the District of South Carolina: Meeting Places," Federal Judicial Center, accessed January 30, 2021, https://www.fjc.gov/history/courts/u.s.-district-courts-districts-south-carolina-meeting-places.

20. Briggs et al. v. Board of Trustees et al., May 15, 1950, box 1, folder 4, Ruby Pendergrass Cornwell Papers, Avery Research Center, College of Charleston.

21. J. Waties Waring, "Does White Supremacy Menace America?," *The Recorder* [San Francisco], August 7–8, 1950, box 110-42, folder 1266, J. Waties Waring Papers, Moorland-Spingarn Research Center, Howard University.

22. Irving Paul Babow and Edward Howden, *A Civil Rights Inventory of San Francisco* (Council for Civic Unity of San Francisco, 1958), 46, accessed January 17, 2021, https://archive.org/details/civilrightsinveno2babo/mode/2up.

23. In 2019, Congressman Jared Huffman introduced a bill to rename the courthouse in McKinleyville the "Judge Louis E. Goodman Courthouse." H. R. 4781, introduced October 22, 2019, accessed January 17, 2021, https://www.congress.gov/bill/116th-congress/house-bill/4781/actions?r=3&s=1.

24. Unless otherwise indicated, all direct quotations from the San Francisco speech are from "Does White Supremacy Menace America?," *The Recorder* [San Francisco], August 7–8, 1950, box 110-42, folder 1266, J. Waties Waring Papers, Moorland-Spingarn Research Center, Howard University.

25. Box 1, folder 2, Ruby Pendergrass Cornwell Papers, Avery Research Center, College of Charleston.

26. Elizabeth Waring to John Hammond and Palmer Weber, January 4, 1950, box 110-32, folder 984, J. Waties Waring Papers, Moorland-Spingarn Research Center, Howard University.

27. John McCray, "Dixie Hate-Mongers Converted Mrs. Waring," *Afro-American*, February 23, 1952, 11.

28. "Mrs. Waring Says Dixie Can Change," *Philadelphia Tribune*, October 3, 1950, 16.

29. "Woman Furthers Cause of Negroes," *Providence Journal*, September 16, 1950, 4; Lydia Brown, "Mrs. Waring Tells Islanders of Social Snubs in Carolina," *Afro-American*, September 30, 1950, 11, box 110-42, folder 1267, J. Waties Waring Papers, Moorland-Spingarn Research Center, Howard University.

30. "Nab Klan Head on Riot Rap," *New York Amsterdam News*, September 9, 1950, 1.

31. Scrapbooks #8 & #9 (box 110-42, folders 1263–1267 in Waring Papers at Moorland-Spingarn Research Center) are filled with newspaper articles about the violence at Happy Hill.

32. Elizabeth Waring to Ruby Cornwell, September 9, 1950, box 1, folder 2, Ruby Pendergrass Cornwell Papers, Avery Research Center, College of Charleston.

33. "Summerville Officer Shoots Man to Death," *The State*, October 2, 1950, 1.

34. Newspaper Clippings, box 110-42, folder 1265, J. Waties Waring Papers, Moorland-Spingarn Research Center, Howard University.

35. J. A. De Laine to Elizabeth Waring, September 23, 1950, and November 1, 1950, box 110-5, folder 85, J. Waties Waring Papers, Moorland-Spingarn Research Center, Howard University.

36. "Home of Judge Waring Pelted with Missiles; FBI Called In," *Washington Post*, October 10, 1950, 1.

37. Anonymous letter, January 17, 1950, box 110-23, folder 721, J. Waties Waring Papers, Moorland-Spingarn Research Center, Howard University.

38. Letter from James C. Laring, October 3, 1950, box 110-23, folder 715, J. Waties Waring Papers, Moorland-Spingarn Research Center, Howard University.

39. Letter signed K.K.K., n.d., box 110-7, folder 177, J. Waties Waring Papers, Moorland-Spingarn Research Center, Howard University.

40. Julius Waties Waring, *The Reminiscences of J. Waties* Waring, Columbia University Oral History Collection (Glen Rock, NJ: Microfilming Corporation of America, 1972), 308.

41. "Home of S.C. Judge, Civil Rights Champion, Stoned by Hoodlums," *New York Post*, October 12, 1950.

42. Ted Poston, "FBI Probes Waring Attack Under Orders," *New York Post*, October 14, 1950.

43. "Home of Judge Waring Pelted with Missiles; FBI Called In."

44. Press Release to United Press, October 10, 1950, box 110-1, folder 5, J. Waties Waring Papers, Moorland-Spingarn Research Center, Howard University.

45. "U. S. Guards Judge in South," *New York Times*, October 12, 1950, 50.

46. "FBI Still Is Probing 'Stoning,'" n.d., box 110-42, folder 1264, J. Waties Waring Papers, Moorland-Spingarn Research Center, Howard University.

47. "Guard Restored at Waring Home," *New York Post*, November 1, 1950.

48. Letter from George Smith, October 14, 1950, box 110-23, folder 717, J. Waties Waring Papers, Moorland-Spingarn Research Center, Howard University.

49. "Citation Planned for Judge Waring," *Chattanooga Daily Times*, November 25, 1950, 9.

50. "125 Persons Make 'Pilgrimage' to Waring's House," *Evening Post*, November 27, 1950, 7.

51. J. Waties Waring to George Houser, December 5, 1950, Congress of Racial Equality (CORE), Series 3 Executive Secretary's File, 1941–1962, ProQuest History Vault.

52. J. Waties Waring to Hubert Delaney, October 12, 1950, box 110-10, folder 249, J. Waties Waring Papers, Moorland-Spingarn Research Center, Howard University.

53. *Reminiscences*, 343, 345.

54. Quoted in Richard Kluger, *Simple Justice: The History of* Brown v. Board of Education *and Black America's Struggle for Equality* (New York: Alfred A. Knopf, 2004), 1026.

55. Tushnet, *The NAACP's Legal Strategy Against Segregated Education*, 141.

56. Jack Greenberg, *Crusaders in the Courts: How a Dedicated Band of Lawyers Fought for the Civil Rights Revolution* (New York: BasicBooks, 1994), 121–22.

57. *Reminiscences*, 363.

58. Greenberg, *Crusaders in the Courts*, 121.

59. Kluger, *Simple Justice*, 382.

60. Greenberg, *Crusaders in the Courts*, 122.

61. Barbara Woods Aba-Mecha, "Black Woman Activist in Twentieth Century: Modjeska Monteith Simkins" (PhD diss., Emory University, 1978), 270n7.

62. *Reminiscences*, 345.

63. *Reminiscences*, 349; J. Waties Waring to John J. Parker, January 12, 1951, Series 3. Official Papers, 1925–1958, folder 957, John Johnston Parker Papers, Wilson Special Collections Library, University of North Carolina.

64. Order, Briggs v. Elliott, January 31, 1951, Series 6. Three-Judge Court Cases, 1926–1957, folder 1337b, John Johnston Parker Papers, Wilson Special Collections Library, University of North Carolina.

65. James F. Byrnes, Inaugural Address, January 16, 1951, box 110-25, folder 744, J. Waties Waring Papers, Moorland-Spingarn Research Center, Howard University.

66. James F. Byrnes, Address to the General Assembly, January 24, 1951, box 110-25 folder 742, J. Waties Waring Papers, Moorland-Spingarn Research Center, Howard University.

67. James F. Byrnes, Address to South Carolina Education Association, March 16, 1951, box 12, folder 8, James F. Byrnes Papers, Clemson University Libraries' Special Collection and Archives. I want to thank Brenda Burk, Head of Special Collections at Clemson University, for emailing me the speech manuscript.

68. L. Marion Gressette Papers, Finding Aid, South Carolina Political Collections, Thomas Cooper Library, University of South Carolina, accessed June 4, 2021, https://archives.library.sc.edu/repositories/6/resources/167.

69. Box 110-44, folder 1279, J. Waties Waring Papers, Moorland-Spingarn Research Center, Howard University.

70. "Judge Waring will preside in NY Court," *Charlotte Observer*, box 110-44, folder 1277, J. Waties Waring Papers, Moorland-Spingarn Research Center, Howard University.

71. Waties also delivered "Are We Making Progress in Race Relations?" at Community Church in New York on March 11, 1951. Elizabeth delivered "Pandora's Box" to the Harlem Interracial Platform on February 24, 1951 and spoke to the Little Red House School Association on February 29, 1951. In Charleston, her friend Ruby Cornwell asked Elizabeth to speak at an AKA luncheon on April 21, 1951. Despite diligent searches, I could not locate any news media coverage or manuscripts for any of these speeches.

72. *Philadelphia Inquirer*, February 8, 1951, box 110-44, folder 1277, J. Waties Waring Papers, Moorland-Spingarn Research Center, Howard University.

73. "South Carolina Darker than Darkest Africa, Says Mrs. Waring," *Plain Dealer*, February 16, 1951, box 110-44, folder 1277, J. Waties Waring Papers, Moorland-Spingarn Research Center, Howard University.

74. *Sun Reporter*, n.d., box 110-44, folder 1277, J. Waties Waring Papers, Moorland-Spingarn Research Center, Howard University.

75. Anonymous letter, February 26, 1950, box 110-7, folder 177; Anonymous letter, February 28, 1950, box 110-7, folder 177; Anonymous letter, June 28, 1951, box 110-23, folder 724, J. Waties Waring Papers, Moorland-Spingarn Research Center, Howard University.

76. "Mrs. Waring Hits Bias in S. Carolina," *Atlanta Daily World*, February 13, 1951, 1.

77. CORE-lator, March 1951, Papers of the Congress of Racial Equality (Sanford, NC: Microfilming Corporation of America), microfilm, reel 49, frames 46–47.

78. George Houser to Judge and Mrs. J. Waties Waring, October 20, 1950. Congress of Racial Equality (CORE), Series 3 Executive Secretary's File, 1941–1962, ProQuest History Vault.

79. George Houser to J. Waties Waring, February 28, 1951. Congress of Racial Equality (CORE), Series 3 Executive Secretary's File, 1941–1962, ProQuest History Vault.

80. CORE-lator, March 1951; "Brotherhood Month 1951," box 110-40, folder 1238, J. Waties Waring Papers, Moorland-Spingarn Research Center, Howard University.

CHAPTER 7: THE DAY DREAMED AND PRAYED WOULD ARRIVE HAS COME

1. Wade Kolb III, "*Briggs v. Elliott* Revisited: A Study in Grassroots Activism and Trial Advocacy from the Early Civil Rights Era," *Journal of Southern Legal History* 19, no. 1 (2011): 137, HeinOnline. George Timmerman Jr. served as lieutenant governor under Strom Thurmond and James Byrnes. He served as governor from 1955 to 59 and led the South's efforts to defy *Brown v. Board of Education*.

2. Ophelia De Laine Gona, *Dawn of Desegregation: J. A. De Laine and* Briggs v. Elliott (Columbia: University of South Carolina Press, 2011), 144.

3. Richard Kluger, *Simple Justice: The History of* Brown v. Board of Education *and Black America's Struggle for Equality* (New York: Alfred A. Knopf, 2004), 381; Kolb, "*Briggs v. Elliott* Revisited," 137.

4. Kluger, *Simple Justice*, 381.

5. Gona, *Dawn of Desegregation*, 136.

6. Julius Waties Waring, *The Reminiscences of J. Waties Waring*, Columbia University Oral History Collection (Glen Rock, NJ: Microfilming Corporation of America, 1972), 358.

7. Elizabeth Waring's Account of *Briggs v. Elliott*, box 110-3, folder 14, J. Waties Waring Papers, Moorland-Spingarn Research Center, Howard University.

8. Elizabeth Waring's Account of *Briggs v. Elliott*.

9. Newspaper Clipping, n.d., box 1, folder 15, Ruby Pendergrass Cornwell Papers, Avery Research Center, College of Charleston.

10. Kluger, *Simple Justice*, 331.

11. "Digest of Survey of Schools in Summerton, South Carolina," Papers of the NAACP, Part 3, The Campaign for Education Equality. In present-day dollars (2020), this amount is $423,124. "CPI Inflation Calculator," US Bureau of Labor Statistics, accessed December 27, 2020, http://data.bls.gov/cgi-bin/cpicalc.pl.

12. John N. Popham, "Pupil Segregation Held Drag on U.S.," *New York Times*, May 29, 1951, 25.

13. Elizabeth Waring's Account of *Briggs v. Elliott*.

14. Howard H. Quint, *Profile in Black and White: A Frank Portrait of South Carolina* (Washington, DC: Public Affairs Press, 1958; reis., Westport, CT: Greenwood Press, 1973), 14.

15. Mark V. Tushnet, *The NAACP's Legal Strategy Against Segregated Education* (Chapel Hill: University of North Carolina Press, 1987), 119.

16. Kluger, *Simple Justice*, 385, 395.

17. Popham, "Pupil Segregation Held Drag on U.S."

18. *Reminiscences*, 358–59.

19. Elizabeth Waring's Account of *Briggs v. Elliott*.

20. Tinsley E. Yarbrough, *A Passion for Justice: J. Waties Waring and Civil Rights* (New York: Oxford University Press, 1987), 187, 193; Briggs et al. v. Elliott et al., 98 F. Supp. 529 (E.D.S.C. 1951).

21. Gona, *Dawn of Desegregation*, 148–49.

22. Daniel M. Berman, *It Is So Ordered: The Supreme Court Rules on School Segregation* (New York: W. W. Norton & Company, 1966), 106–7.

23. Briggs v. Elliott, 98 F. Supp. 529.

24. J. Louis Campbell, "The Spirit of Dissent," *Judicature* 66, no. 6 (February 1983): 306–7, HeinOnline.

25. Briggs v. Elliott, 98 F. Supp. 529.

26. J. Waties Waring to Hubert Delaney, June 28, 1951, box 110-10, folder 249, J. Waties Waring Papers, Moorland-Spingarn Research Center, Howard University.

27. Warren Earl Wright, "The Rhetoric of Learned Hand in Selected Civil Liberties Cases: A Method for Analysis of Judicial Opinion" (PhD diss., University of Illinois, 1960), 65, 72–73.

28. John Popham, "South Acts to Keep Pupil Segregation," *New York Times*, May 28, 1951, 16.

29. Elizabeth Waring's Account of *Briggs v. Elliott*.

30. J. Waties Waring to Thurgood Marshall, June 15, 1951, box 110-15, folder 387, J. Waties Waring Papers, Moorland-Spingarn Research Center, Howard University.

31. J. Waties Waring to Thurgood Marshall, July 26, 1951, box 110-27, folder 839, J. Waties Waring Papers, Moorland-Spingarn Research Center, Howard University.

32. J. Waties Waring to Walter White, October 5, 1951, box 110-20, folder 605, J. Waties Waring Papers, Moorland-Spingarn Research Center, Howard University.

33. J. Waties Waring to Hubert Delaney, June 28, 1951.

34. Jack Greenberg, *Crusaders in the Courts: How a Dedicated Band of Lawyers Fought for the Civil Rights Revolution* (New York: BasicBooks, 1994), 122.

35. *Reminiscences*, 378.

36. Mark V. Tushnet, *Making Civil Rights Law: Thurgood Marshall and the Supreme Court, 1936–1961* (New York: Oxford University Press, 1994), 165–66.

37. Kluger, *Simple Justice*, 673.

38. Briggs v. Elliott, 342 U.S. 350 (1952).

39. Kluger, *Simple Justice*, 673.

40. Yarbrough, *A Passion for Justice*, 209. Judge Dobie presided at the trial for *Davis et al. v. County School Board of Prince Edward County et al.*, the Virginia case that was also decided in *Brown*.

41. Kluger, *Simple Justice*, 676.

42. Quint, *Profile in Black and White*, 17.

43. J. Waties Waring to Hubert Delaney, January 28, 1952, box 110-10, folder 249, J. Waties Waring Papers, Moorland-Spingarn Center, Howard University.

44. J. Waties Waring to John Hammond, February 15, 1952, box 110-12, folder 288, J. Waties Waring Papers, Moorland-Spingarn Center, Howard University.

45. Elizabeth Waring's Account of *Briggs v. Elliott*.

46. *Reminiscences*, 375.

47. Neil R. McMillen, *The Citizens' Council: Organized Resistance to the Second Reconstruction, 1954–64* (Urbana and Chicago: University of Illinois Press, 1971), 185.

48. *Reminiscences*, 378.

49. J. Waties Waring, interview by unidentified interviewer, 1948, box 110-179, J. Waties Waring Papers, Moorland-Spingarn Research Center, Howard University.

50. *Reminiscences*, 378.

51. Sadie T. M. Alexander to J. Waties Waring, January 22, 1952, box 110-8, folder 184, J. Waties Waring Papers, Moorland-Spingarn Research Center, Howard University.

52. Letter from Elizabeth Waring printed in Bulletin for Little Red House School and Elisabeth Irvin High School, box 110-3, folder 14, J. Waties Waring Papers, Moorland-Spingarn Research Center, Howard University.

53. J. Waties Waring to Honorable J. Skelly Wright, November 25, 1960, box 110-1, folder 2, J. Waties Waring Papers, Moorland-Spingarn Research Center, Howard University.

54. J. Waties Waring to Louis Wright, June 18, 1952, Papers of the NAACP, Supplement to Part 1, 1951–1955 (Frederick, MD: University Publications of America), microfilm, reel 2, frame 305.

55. Papers of NAACP, Supplement to Part 1, 1951–1955 (Frederick, MD: University Publications of America), microfilm, reel 6, frame 84.

56. J. Waties Waring to Louis Wright, June 18, 1952.

57. Modjeska Simkins, interview by Jacquelyn Hall, July 28, 1976, interview G-0056-2, Southern Oral History Program Collection (#4007), http://docsouth.unc.edu/sohp/playback.html?base_file=G-0056-2.

58. J. Waties Waring to John Hammond, February 15, 1952.

59. J. Waties Waring to Hubert Delaney, January 28, 1952.

60. J. Waties Waring to Hubert Delaney, June 28, 1951.

61. "Ten Given Russworm Awards for Democratic Action," *Afro-American*, March 15, 1952, 14.

62. "Judge Waring Raps Racial Gradualists," *Afro-American*, April 5, 1952, 9.

63. "Judge J. Waties Waring Gets 6th Abbott Award," *Chicago Defender*, April 26, 1952, 1.

64. Ralph Matthews, "Waring Blasts Bias at AME Convention," *Afro-American*, May 24, 1952, 18.

65. Henry Beckett, "Welcome to Our Town, Judge," *New York Post*, March 9, 1952, box 1, folder 9, Ruby Pendergrass Cornwell Papers, Avery Research Center, College of Charleston. I could not locate media coverage in the Black or white press of these speeches.

66. "Omegas' Conclave Dec. 27–30," *Pittsburgh Courier*, December 27, 1952, 3.

67. "Waring Calls Moores' Death 'Old Fashioned Lynching,'" *Philadelphia Tribune*, March 11, 1952, 1.

68. "Waring Calls Moores' Death 'Old Fashioned Lynching.'"
69. "Waring Calls Moores' Death 'Old Fashioned Lynching.'"
70. "Waring Challenges Politicians on Civil Rights," *Chicago Defender*, May 17, 1952, 1.
71. Elmore v. Rice, 72 F. Supp. 516 (E.D.S.C. 1947).
72. J. Waties Waring, "Does White Supremacy Menace America?," *The Recorder* [San Francisco], August 7–8, 1950, box 110-42, folder 1266, J. Waties Waring Papers, Moorland-Spingarn Research Center, Howard University.
73. "Ex-Judge Waring is Honored Here," *New York Times*, April 17, 1952, 42.
74. Arnold de Mille, "Cite Judge Waring for Legal Gains," *Chicago Defender*, April 5, 1952, 3.
75. "Waring Challenges Politicians on Civil Rights."
76. Ralph Matthews, "Waring Blasts Bias at AME Convention."
77. "Judge Waring Fires Guns at 'Gradual' Ending of Bias," *Pittsburgh Courier*, April 5, 1952, 32.
78. Thomas Jefferson Flanagan, "America Cannot Rest Upon White Supremacy," *Atlanta Daily World*, May 16, 1952, 3.
79. "Waring Challenges Politicians on Civil Rights."
80. Matthews, "Waring Blasts Bias at AME Convention."
81. "Judge Waring Raps Racial Gradualists."
82. Flanagan, "America Cannot Rest Upon White Supremacy."
83. "Waring Challenges Politicians on Civil Rights."
84. "Judge Waring Fires Guns at 'Gradual' Ending of Bias."
85. Flanagan, "America Cannot Rest Upon White Supremacy."
86. "Waring Challenges Politicians on Civil Rights."
87. Matthews, "Waring Blasts Bias at AME Convention."
88. "Judge Waring Receives Negro Fraternity Award," handwritten *News and Courier*, May 1, 1949, box 110-42, folder 1260, J. Waties Waring Papers, Moorland-Spingarn Research Center, Howard University.
89. "Judge Waring Raps Racial Gradualists."
90. "Judge Waring Fires Guns at 'Gradual' Ending of Bias."
91. "Waring Challenges Politicians on Civil Rights."
92. Tom Poston, "Judge's Wife Tells of Gain in Fight on Biased South," *New York Post*, March 5, 1950, Johnson Publishing Company Clipping Files Collection, Archives Research Center, Robert W. Woodruff Library, Atlanta University Center.
93. J. Waties Waring to Harry S. Truman, June 9, 1952, box 110-19, folder 567, J. Waties Waring Papers, Moorland-Spingarn Research Center, Howard University.
94. Anthony Leviero, "Truman Demands Civil Rights Based on Federal Power," *New York Times*, June 14, 1952, 1.
95. "South Building Schools to Buy Negroes—Waring," *New Journal and Guide*, June 21, 1952, 24A.
96. J. Waties Waring to Hubert Delaney, June 28, 1951.
97. Berman, *It Is So Ordered: The Supreme Court Rules on School Segregation*, 51–52.
98. Greenberg, *Crusaders in the Courts*, 120.

99. Davis et al. v. County School Board of Prince Edward County, Virginia, et al., 103 F. Supp. 337 (E.D. VA. 1952).

100. Greenberg, *Crusaders in the Courts*, 156.

101. Berman, *It Is So Ordered: The Supreme Court Rules on School Segregation*, 135.

102. Kluger, *Simple Justice*, 683.

103. Tushnet, *Making Civil Rights Law*, 164.

104. Kluger, *Simple Justice*, 683.

105. Quint, *Profile in Black and White*, 18.

106. Thurgood Marshall, Opening Argument, *Briggs et al. v. Elliott et al.*, December 9, 1952, Supreme Court, https://apps.lib.umich.edu/brown-versus-board-education/oral/Marshall&Davis.pdf.

107. James C. N. Paul, "The Decision and Some Alternatives—A Legal Analysis," in *The School Segregation Decision: A Report to the Governor of North Carolina on the Decision of the Supreme Court of the United States on the 17th of May 1954*, Institute of Government (Chapel Hill: University of North Carolina, 1954), 36.

108. Sydnor Thompson, "John W. Davis and His Role in the Public School Segregation Cases—A Personal Memoir," *Washington and Lee Law Review* 52, no. 5 (Winter 1995): 1692, https://scholarlycommons.law.wlu.edu/wlulr.

109. School Segregation Cases—Order of Argument, Record Group 267: Records of the Supreme Court, National Archives and Records Administration, accessed December 27, 2020, https://www.archives.gov/education/lessons/brown-case-order.

110. Brown v. Board of Education of Topeka, 374 U.S. 483 (1954).

CHAPTER 8: DEMOCRACY AND DECENCY PREVAIL

1. "To All on Equal Terms," *Time Magazine*, May 24, 1954, 23, EBSCOhost.

2. Poppy Cannon, *A Gentle Knight: My Husband, Walter White* (New York: Rinehart, 1956), 247.

3. Julius Waties Waring, *The Reminiscences of J. Waties Waring*, Columbia University Oral History Collection (Glen Rock, NJ: Microfilming Corporation of America, 1972), 365.

4. Press Release signed by J. Waties Waring, May 17, 1954, box 110-1, folder 5, J. Waties Waring Papers, Moorland-Spingarn Research Center, Howard University.

5. John McCray, "Judge and Mrs. Waring Given Rousing Testimonial in S.C.," *Afro-American*, November 20, 1954, 5.

6. *Reminiscences*, 401.

7. Modjeska Simkins to J. Waties Waring, November 4, 1954, box 110-18, folder 516, J. Waties Waring Papers, Moorland-Spingarn Research Center, Howard University.

8. McCray, "Judge and Mrs. Waring Given Rousing Testimonial in S.C."

9. Marion A. Wright Papers, South Caroliniana Library, University of South Carolina. When I researched Wright's papers in May 2018, the collection had not been processed.

10. McCray, "Judge and Mrs. Waring Given Rousing Testimonial in S.C."

11. Elizabeth Waring to Ruby and Aylwood "Connie" Cornwell, November 11, 1954, box 1, folder 14, Ruby Pendergrass Cornwell Papers, Avery Research Center, College of Charleston.

12. J. Waties Waring to Ruby and Aylwood "Connie" Cornwell, November 10, 1954, box 1, folder 14, Ruby Pendergrass Cornwell Papers, Avery Research Center, College of Charleston.

13. J. Waties Waring to Hubert Delaney, June 28, 1951, box 110-10, folder 249, J. Waties Waring Papers, Moorland-Spingarn Research Center, Howard University.

14. J. Waties Waring to John Hammond, February 15, 1952, box 110-12, folder 288, J. Waties Waring Papers, Moorland-Spingarn Research Center, Howard University.

15. Elizabeth Waring's Account of *Briggs v. Elliott*, box 110-3, folder 14, J. Waties Waring Papers, Moorland-Spingarn Research Center, Howard University.

16. John Hammond to J. Waties Waring, n.d., box 110-12, folder 288, J. Waties Waring Papers, Moorland-Spingarn Research Center, Howard University.

17. Tau Omega Alpha Kappa Alpha Sorority Tribute to J. Waties Waring, November 15, 1959, box 110-39, folder 1231, J. Waties Waring Papers, Moorland-Spingarn Research Center, Howard University.

18. "Snub Mrs. White, so Mrs. Waring Cuts NAACP Tea," *Chicago Defender*, March 11, 1950, 1.

19. "White Confirms Second Marriage," *Afro-American*, August 20, 1949, 1.

20. "Snub Mrs. White, so Mrs. Waring Cuts NAACP Tea."

21. Elizabeth Waring to Ruby Cornwell, July 13, 1951, box 1, folder 5, Ruby Pendergrass Cornwell Papers, Avery Research Center, College of Charleston.

22. Caryl Phillips, *Atlantic Sound* (New York: Alfred A. Knopf, 2000), 254.

23. McCray, "Judge and Mrs. Waring Given Rousing Testimonial in S.C."

24. John H. McCray, "Let's Rock Their Boat," Greenville, SC, March 16, 1952. John Henry McCray Papers, box 5, folders 17–23, Digital Collections, South Caroliniana Library. When I accessed the digital collection in April 2020, it had not been fully processed.

25. Albert J. Dunmore, "Judge Waring Fears Weak Negro Leaders," *Pittsburgh Courier*, July 7, 1951, 1.

26. Dunmore, "Judge Waring Fears Weak Negro Leaders."

27. Dunmore, "Judge Waring Fears Weak Negro Leaders."

28. J. Waties Waring to John Hammond, February 15, 1952.

29. "Let's Not be Unrealistic," *Pittsburgh Courier*, May 31, 1952, 8.

30. Miriam DeCosta to Elizabeth Waring, April 19, 1951, box 110-7, folder 146, J. Waties Waring Papers, Moorland-Spingarn Research Center, Howard University.

31. Miriam DeCosta to Elizabeth Waring, November 10, 1950, box 110-7, folder 150, J. Waties Waring Papers, Moorland-Spingarn Research Center, Howard University.

32. Elizabeth Waring to Ruby Cornwell, August 12, 1951, box 1, folder 5, Ruby Pendergrass Cornwell Papers, Avery Research Center, College of Charleston.

33. Isabella Finnie to Elizabeth Waring, May 27, 1954, box 110-5, folder 96, J. Waties Waring Papers, Moorland-Spingarn Research Center, Howard University.

34. "Negro-Right Judge Comes Here to Live," *New York Times*, February 24, 1952, 33.

35. Hodding Carter, "The Civil Rights Issue as Seen in the South," *New York Times*, March 21, 1948, SM15.

36. J. Waties Waring, interview by unidentified interviewer, 1948, box 110-179, J. Waties Waring Papers, Moorland-Spingarn Research Center, Howard University.

37. Letter from Mrs. Ernest C. Wood, March 22, 1950, box 110-23, folder 725, J. Waties Waring Papers, Moorland-Spingarn Research Center, Howard University.

38. James. W. Vander Zanden, "The Ideology of White Supremacy," *Journal of the History of Ideas* 20, no. 3 (June–September 1959): 399, https://doi.org/10.2307/2708116.

39. James C. N. Paul, "The Decision and Some Alternatives—A Legal Analysis," in *The School Segregation Decision: A Report to the Governor of North Carolina on the Decision of the Supreme Court of the United States on the 17th of May 1954*, Institute of Government (Chapel Hill: University of North Carolina, 1954), 37–38.

40. Michael J. Klarman, *From Jim Crow to Civil Rights: The Supreme Court and the Struggle for Racial Equality* (New York: Oxford University Press, 2004), 313.

41. Brown et al. v. Board of Education of Topeka et al., 349 U.S. 294 (1955).

42. "'White Supremacy' Termed a Cancer," *New York Times*, February 27, 1950, 17.

43. *Reminiscences*, 275, 203.

44. Charles M. Payne, "'The Whole United States Is Southern!': *Brown v. Board* and the Mystification of Race," *Journal of American History* 19, no. 1 (June 2004): 84, https://doi.org/10.2307/3659615.

45. Steven J. Crossland, "*Brown's* Companions: *Briggs, Belton*, and *Davis*," *Washburn Law Journal* 43, no. 2 (Winter 2003–2004): 382, https://contentdm.washburnlaw.edu/digital/collection/wlj/id/5394/.

46. Earl Caldwell, "Schools Remain Closed in Summerton, S.C.," *New York Times*, September 4, 1970, 11.

47. Jennifer Berry Hawes, Seanna Adcox, Paul Bowers, Thad Moore, and Glenn Smith, "Minimally Adequate," *Post and Courier*, November 14, 2018, https://www.postandcourier.com/news/minimally_adequate/.

48. Elizabeth Gillespie McRae, *Mothers of Massive Resistance: White Women and the Politics of White Supremacy* (New York: Oxford University Press, 2020), 112.

49. Septima Poinsette Clark, interview by Jacquelyn Hall, July 25, 1976, interview G-0016, Southern Oral History Program Collection (#4007), http://docsouth.unc.edu/sohp/G-0016/G-0016.html.

50. Ann Hyde, email message to author, July 31, 2013.

51. Septima Clark to Elizabeth Waring, July 30, 1950, box 4, folder 1, Ruby Pendergrass Cornwell Papers, Avery Research Center, College of Charleston.

52. Septima Clark, interview by Jacquelyn Hall, box 1, folder 8, Septima P. Clark Papers, Avery Research Center, College of Charleston.

53. J. Waties Waring to Ruby Cornwell, July 28, 1951, box 1, folder 5, Ruby Pendergrass Cornwell Papers, Avery Research Center, College of Charleston.

54. Margaret Green, Archivist, Westover School, email message to author, February 12, 2012.

55. Miriam DeCosta to Elizabeth Waring, September 19, 1950, box 110-7, folder 146, J. Waties Waring Papers, Moorland-Spingarn Research Center, Howard University.

56. J. A. De Laine Jr., email message to author, September 14, 2011.

57. J. Waties Waring to Walter White, December 18, 1951, box 110-20, folder 605, J. Waties Waring Papers, Moorland-Spingarn Research Center, Howard University.

58. J. A. De Laine Jr., interview with author, December 22, 2011, Charlotte, NC.

59. Correspondence between Sadie T. M. Alexander and J. Waties Waring, box 110-8, folder 184, J. Waties Waring Papers, Moorland-Spingarn Research Center, Howard University.

60. Trichita M. Chestnut, "Lynching: Ida B. Wells-Barnett and the Outrage over the Frazier Baker Murder," *Prologue* 40, no. 3 (Fall 2008): 23, https://www.archives.gov/files/publications/prologue/2008/fall/lynching.pdf. In 2018, Rep. James Clyburn (D-SC) sponsored H. R. 7230 to designate the Lake City post office as "Postmaster Frazier B. Baker Post Office." Press Release, Congressman James E. Clyburn, February 21, 2019, https://clyburn.house.gov/press-release/postmaster-frazier-b-baker-post-office-dedication-announced-new-lake-city-post-office.

61. J. A. De Laine Jr., interview.

62. Howard H. Quint, *Profile in Black and White: A Frank Portrait of South Carolina* (Washington, DC: Public Affairs Press, 1958; reis., Westport, CT: Greenwood Press, 1973), 36.

63. J. A. De Laine Jr., interview.

64. "Judge Waring Dies," *New York Times*, January 12, 1968, 27.

65. "Waring Honored by Schools Group," *New York Times*, November 21, 1954, 53.

66. J. Waties Waring to M. L. King and Ralph D. Abernathy, November 11, 1956, Martin Luther King Jr. Research and Education Institute, Stanford University, https://kinginstitute.stanford.edu/king-papers/documents/julius-waties-waring.

67. "Rights Leaders to Testify before Mrs. Roosevelt," *Chicago Daily Defender*, May 22, 1962, 7.

68. Thomasina Norford, "AKA's In Honor to Judge Waring," *New York Amsterdam News*, November 21, 1959, 1.

69. Elizabeth Waring to Ruby Cornwell, July 24, 1953, box 1, folder 11, Ruby Pendergrass Cornwell Papers, Avery Research Center, College of Charleston.

70. "Judge, Exiled by Dixie, Still Proud of His Rights Decisions," *Detroit Free Press*, August 30, 1963, 36.

71. Tinsley E. Yarbrough, *A Passion for Justice: J. Waties Waring and Civil Rights* (New York: Oxford University Press, 1987), 238–39.

72. "Few Whites Attend Judge Waring Rites," *New York Times*, January 18, 1968, 26.

73. Yarbrough, *A Passion for Justice*, 126.

74. Program, box 4, folder 23, Septima P. Clark Papers, Avery Research Center, College of Charleston.

CONCLUSION

1. "Editorial Excerpts from the Nation's Press on Segregation Ruling," *New York Times*, May 18, 1954, 19.

2. James D. Anderson, "The Jubilee Anniversary of *Brown v. Board of Education*: An Essay Review," *History of Education Quarterly* 44, no.1 (Spring 2004): 155, http://www.jstor.org/stable/3218122.

3. Anderson, "The Jubilee Anniversary of *Brown v. Board of Education*," 156.

4. Charles M. Payne, "The View from the Trenches," in *Debating the Civil Rights Movement, 1945–1968*, ed. Steven F. Lawson and Charles M. Payne (Lanham, MD: Rowman & Littlefield, 2006), 100.

5. Sean Patrick O'Rourke points out that often controversies over contested rights and responsibilities culminate in legal action and judicial review. See "Reading Bodies, Reading Books," in *Like Wildfire: The Rhetoric of the Civil Rights Sit-Ins* (Columbia: University of South Carolina Press, 2020), 135.

6. Charles M. Payne and Adam Green, eds., *Time Longer than a Rope: A Century of African American Activism, 1850–1950* (New York: New York University Press, 2003), 2.

7. Gunnar Myrdal, *An American Dilemma: The Negro Problem and Modern Democracy* (New York: Harper & Brothers Publishers, 1944), 558.

8. J. Waties Waring to James Dombrowski, November 6, 1952, box 110-10, folder 25, J. Waties Waring Papers, Moorland-Spingarn Research Center, Howard University.

9. Strom Thurmond, "Integration and How to Oppose," 1959, Citizens' Council Radio Forum, 597–910, Department of Special Collections, Mississippi State University.

10. Charles W. Lomas, *The Agitator in American Society* (Englewood Cliffs, NJ: Prentice-Hall, 1968), 2.

11. J. Waties Waring, "The Struggle for Negro Rights," National Lawyers Guild Annual Banquet, February 20, 1949, box 110-39, folder 1231, J. Waties Waring Papers, Moorland-Spingarn Research Center, Howard University.

12. Elizabeth Waring to Bicknell Eubanks, January 3, 1951, box 1, folder 6, Ruby Pendergrass Cornwell Papers, Avery Research Center, College of Charleston.

13. Julius Waties Waring, *The Reminiscences of J. Waties Waring*, Columbia University Oral History Collection (Glen Rock, NJ: Microfilming Corporation of America, 1972), 204.

14. Marguerite Cartwright, "J. Waties Waring: Latter Day Emancipation," *Negro History Bulletin*, December 1955, box 110-1, folder 2A, J. Waties Waring Papers, Moorland-Spingarn Research Center, Howard University.

15. Isabella Finnie to Elizabeth Waring, May 26, 1950, box 110-5, folder 94, J. Waties Waring Papers, Moorland-Spingarn Research Center, Howard University.

16. 81 Cong. Record C4930 (1950).

17. Interview of Gedney Howe, February 18, 1974, box 1, folder 5, Jack Bass/Walter DeVries Interview Papers, Avery Research Center, College of Charleston.

18. Samuel Grafton, "Lonesomest Man in Town," *Collier's*, April 29, 1950, 50.

19. Charles W. Eagles, "Toward New Histories of the Civil Rights Era," *Journal of Southern History* 66, no. 4 (November 2000): 838, https://doi.org/10.2307/2588012.

20. Joseph R. Biden Jr., Inaugural Address, January 20, 2021, The White House, https://www.whitehouse.gov/briefing-room/speeches-remarks/2021/01/20/inaugural-address-by-president-joseph-r-biden-jr/.

21. Jeanne Theoharis, *A More Beautiful and Terrible History: The Uses and Misuses of Civil Rights History* (Boston: Beacon Press, 2018), xvii.

22. Martin J. Medhurst, "Reconceptualizing Rhetorical History: Eisenhower's Farewell Address," *Quarterly Journal of Speech* 80, no. 2 (May 1994): 195–97, https://doi.org/10.1080/00335639409384067.

BIBLIOGRAPHY

PRIMARY SOURCES

Collections

Byrnes, James F. Papers. Special Collections and Archives, University Libraries, Clemson University.
Citizens' Council Radio Forum. Special Collections. Mississippi State University, Starkville, MS.
Clark, Septima P. Papers. Avery Research Center, College of Charleston, Charleston, SC.
Cornwell, Ruby Pendergrass. Papers. Avery Research Center, College of Charleston, Charleston, SC.
De Laine, Joseph A. Papers. South Caroliniana Library, University of South Carolina, Columbia, SC.
Gressette, L. Marion. Papers. South Carolina Political Collections, University of South Carolina, Columbia, SC.
Humphrey, Hubert H. Speech Text Files. Manuscript Collections, Minnesota Historical Society.
Johnson Publishing Company. Clipping Files Collection. Archives Research Center. Robert W. Woodruff Library, Atlanta University Center.
McCray, John Henry. Papers. South Caroliniana Library, University of South Carolina, Columbia, SC.
National Lawyers Guild. Records. Tamiment Library & Robert F. Wagner Labor Archives. Bobst Library, New York University.
Papers of the Congress of Racial Equality, 1941–1967 (Sanford, NC: Microfilming Corporation of America).
Papers of the NAACP. Parts 1, 3, 4, 8, 15, 26, and Supplement to Part 1, 1951–1955 (Frederick, MD: University Publications of America, 1986).
Parker, John Johnston. Papers. Southern Historical Collection. Louis Round Wilson Special Collections Library. University of North Carolina at Chapel Hill.
South Carolina Department of Archives and History, Columbia, South Carolina.

Southern Oral History Program Collection, Southern Historical Collection, Wilson Library, University of North Carolina at Chapel Hill.
Spencer, Frank W. and Lillian. Papers. Special Collections, Lane Library, Armstrong Atlantic State University, Savannah, GA.
Supreme Court of the United States. Records. National Archives and Records Administration.
Thurmond, Strom. Collection, Special Collections and Archives, University Libraries, Clemson University.
Tilly, Dorothy Rodgers. Papers. Louise Pettus Archives and Special Collections, Winthrop University, Rock Hill, SC.
Waring, J. Waties. Papers. Manuscript Division, Moorland-Spingarn Research Center, Howard University.
West, Rebecca. Papers. General Collection. Beinecke Rare Book and Manuscript Library, Yale University.
White, Walter Francis and Poppy Cannon. Papers. Yale Collection of American Literature, Beinecke Rare Book and Manuscript Library, Yale University.
Wright, Marion A. Papers. South Caroliniana Library, University of South Carolina, Columbia, SC.

Interviews and Oral Histories

Bass, Jack and Walter DeVries Interview Papers. Avery Research Center, College of Charleston, Charleston, SC.
De Laine, J. A., Jr., interview by author, December 22, 2011, Charlotte, NC.
Hill, Oliver. Virginia Center for Digital History, University of Virginia, Charlottesville, VA.
Waring, Julius Waties. *The Reminiscences of J. Waties Waring*, Columbia University Oral History Collection (Glen Rock, NJ: Microfilming Corporation of America, 1972).

Government Documents

Congressional Record (1948, 1950)
Federal Bureau of Investigation, File 44-HQ-1411
The School Segregation Decision: A Report to the Governor of North Carolina on the Decision of the Supreme Court of the United States on the 17th of May 1954

Court Cases

Belton v. Gebhart, 32 Del. Ch. 343 (Del. Ch. 1952)
Bolling v. Sharpe, 344 U.S. 873 (1952)
Briggs et al. v. Elliott et al., 98 F. Supp. 529 (E.D.S.C. 1951)
Briggs et al. v. Elliott et al., 342 U.S. 350 (1952)
Brown et al. v. Board of Education of Topeka et al., 347 U.S. 483 (1954)
Brown et al. v. Board of Education of Topeka et al., 349 U.S. 294 (1955)
Brown v. Baskin, 78 F. Supp. 933 (E.D.S.C. 1948)

Davis et al. v. County School Board of Prince Edward County, Virginia et al., 103 F. Supp. 337 (E.D. Va. 1952)
Elmore v. Rice, 72 F. Supp. 516 (E.D.S.C. 1947)
Henderson v. United States, 339 U.S. 816 (1950)
McLaurin v. Oklahoma State Regents for Higher Education, 339 U.S. 637 (1950)
James Pearson v. County Board of Education for Clarendon County et al., Case No. 1909, Eastern District of South Carolina
Plessy v. Ferguson, 163 U.S. 537 (1896)
Sweatt v. Painter, 339 U.S. 629 (1950)
United States of America v. Lynwood Lanier Shull, Case No. 16,603, Eastern District of South Carolina

Newspapers and Periodicals

Afro-American, 1948–1950, 1952, 1954
Aiken Standard, 1949
American Mercury, 1950
Asheville Citizen-Times, 1947
Atlanta Constitution, 1941, 1944
Atlanta Daily World, 1946, 1947, 1949–1952
Atlanta Journal, 1950
Chattanooga Daily Times, 1950
Chicago Daily Defender, 1962
Chicago Daily Tribune, 1950
Chicago Defender, 1947–1950, 1952
Christian Science Monitor, 1946, 1950
Cleveland Call and Post, 1948
Collier's Magazine, 1950
Columbia Record, 1948
Detroit Free Press, 1923, 1933, 1963
Evening Post, 1947, 1948, 1950
Florence Morning News, 1949
Greenville News, 1950
Kingsport News, 1950
Lawyers Guild Review, 1949
New Journal and Guide, 1948, 1950–1952
New Republic, 1944
New York Amsterdam News, 1948, 1950, 1959
New York Guild Lawyer, 1948
New York Post, 1950
New York Times, 1913, 1941, 1944, 1946–1952, 1954, 1968, 1970, 1994
New Yorker, 1947
Newport Daily News, 1950
News and Courier, 1946–1950

The Oracle, 1949
Philadelphia Tribune, 1950, 1952
Pittsburgh Courier, 1944, 1947, 1949–1952
Post and Courier, 2018
Richmond Times-Dispatch, 1950
Saturday Evening Post, 1950
The State, 1947–1950
Time, 1950, 1954
Times and Democrat, 1949
Washington Post, 1946–1948, 1950, 1999

SECONDARY SOURCES

Books and Journal Articles

Anderson, Benedict R. O'G. *Imagined Communities: Reflections on the Origin and Spread of Nationalism*. London: Verso, 1983.

Anderson, James D. "The Jubilee Anniversary of *Brown v. Board of Education*: An Essay Review." *History of Education Quarterly* 44, no.1 (Summer 2004): 149–57. http://www.jstor.org/stable/3218122.

Asen, Robert. "Women, Work, Welfare: A Rhetorical History of Images of Poor Women in Welfare Policy Debates." *Rhetoric & Public Affairs* 6, no. 2 (Summer 2003): 285–312. https://www.jstor.org/stable/41940315.

Baker, R. Scott. *Paradoxes of Desegregation: African American Struggles for Educational Equity in Charleston, South Carolina, 1926–1972*. Columbia: University of South Carolina Press, 2006.

Bass, Jack Bass, and Walter DeVries. *The Transformation of Southern Politics: Social Change and Political Consequences Since 1945*. New York: BasicBooks, 1976.

Bell, Lee Ann. *Storytelling for Social Justice*. 2nd edition. New York: Routledge, Taylor & Francis Group, 2020.

Benson, Thomas W., ed. *Rhetoric and Political Culture in Nineteenth-Century America*. East Lansing: Michigan State University Press, 1997.

Berman, Daniel M. *It Is So Ordered: The Supreme Court Rules on School Segregation*. New York: W. W. Norton & Company, 1966.

Bowser, Benjamin P. "Racism: Origin and Theory." *Journal of Black Studies* 48, no. 6 (September 2017): 572–90. https://doi.org/10.1177/0021934717702135.

Boyle, Sarah Patton. *The Desegregated Heart: A Virginian's Stand in Time of Transition*. Charlottesville: University Press of Virginia, 2001. First published 1962 by Morrow.

Braden, Waldo W., ed. *Oratory in the New South*. Baton Rouge: Louisiana State University Press, 1979.

Brown, Sarah Hart. *Standing Against Dragons: Three Southern Lawyers in an Era of Fear*. Baton Rouge: Louisiana State University Press, 1998.

Burke, Kenneth. "Four Master Tropes." *Kenyon Review* 3, no. 4 (Autumn 1941): 421–28. https://www.jstor.org/stable/4332286.

Campbell, J. Louis, III. "The Spirit of Dissent." *Judicature* 66, no. 6 (February 1983): 302–12. HeinOnline.

Cannon, Poppy. *A Gentle Knight: My Husband, Walter White*. New York: Rinehart, 1956.

Carper, N. Gordon. "Slavery Revisited: Peonage in the South." *Phylon* 37, no. 1 (1st Quarter 1976): 85–99. https://doi.org/10.2307/274733.

Cash, W. J. *The Mind of the South*. New York: A. A. Knopf, 1941.

Ceccarelli, Leah. *On the Frontier of Science: An American Rhetoric of Exploration and Exploitation*. East Lansing: Michigan State University Press, 2013.

Chestnut, Trichita M. "Lynching: Ida B. Wells-Barnett and the Outrage over the Frazier Baker Murder." *Prologue* 40, no. 3 (Fall 2008): 21–29. National Archives.

Clark, Septima Poinsette, with LeGette Blythe. *Echo in My Soul*. New York: E. P. Dutton, 1962.

Clark, Septima Poinsette. *Ready from Within: Septima Clark and the Civil Rights Movement, A First Person Narrative*. Edited by Cynthia Stokes Brown. Navarro, CA: Wild Trees Press, 1986.

Cobb, James C., and Michael V. Namorato, eds. *The New Deal and the South: Essays*. Jackson: University Press of Mississippi, 1984.

Condit, Celeste Michelle. "Democracy and Civil Rights: The Universalizing Influence of Public Argumentation." *Communication Monographs* 54, no. 1 (March 1987): 1–18. https://doi.org/10.1080/03637758709390213.

Condit, Celeste Michelle, and John Louis Lucaites. *Crafting Equality: America's Anglo-African Word*. Chicago: University of Chicago Press, 1993.

Coupe, Laurence. *Kenneth Burke on Myth: An Introduction*. New York & London: Routledge, 2005.

Cox, J. Robert. "Perspectives on Rhetorical Criticism of Movements: Antiwar Dissent, 1964–1970." *Western Speech* 38, no. 4 (Fall 1974): 254–68. https://doi.org/10.1080/10570317409373836.

Crossland, Steven J. "*Brown's* Companions: *Briggs, Belton*, and *Davis*." *Washburn Law Journal* 43, no. 2 (Winter 2003–2004): 381–428. https://contentdm.washburnlaw.edu/digital/collection/wlj/id/5394/.

Crowley, Sharon, and Debra Hawhee. *Ancient Rhetorics for Contemporary Students*. 2nd edition. Boston & London: Allyn and Bacon, 1999.

Dailey, Jane, Glenda Elizabeth Gilmore, and Bryant Simon, eds. *Jumpin' Jim Crow: Southern Politics from Civil War to Civil Rights*. Princeton: Princeton University Press, 2000.

Dabney, Virginius. *Liberalism in the South*. Chapel Hill: University of North Carolina Press, 1932.

Dittmer, John. *Local People: The Struggle for Civil Rights in Mississippi*. Urbana and Chicago: University of Illinois Press, 1994.

Dollard, John. *Caste and Class in a Southern Town*. New Haven: Yale University Press, 1937.

Dyson, Michael Eric. *Tears We Cannot Stop: A Sermon to White America*. New York: St. Martin's Press, 2017.

Eagles, Charles W. "Toward New Histories of the Civil Rights Era." *Journal of Southern History* 66, no. 4 (November 2000): 815–48. https://doi.org/10.2307/2588012.

Edens, H. H. "Memorial to Claud N. Sapp." *South Carolina Law Quarterly* 1, no. 2 (1948): 107–18. https://scholarcommons.sc.edu.

Felder, James L. *Civil Rights in South Carolina: From Peaceful Protests to Groundbreaking Rulings*. Charleston: The History Press, 2012.

Feldman, Glenn, ed. *Before* Brown: *Civil Rights and White Backlash in the Modern South*. Tuscaloosa: University of Alabama Press, 2004.

Foley, Megan. "Sound Bites: Rethinking the Circulation of Speech from Fragment to Fetish." *Rhetoric & Public Affairs* 15, no. 4 (Winter 2012): 613–22. https://www.jstor.org/stable/41940624.

Frederickson, Kari. *The Dixiecrat Revolt and the End of the Solid South, 1932–1968*. Chapel Hill: University of North Carolina Press, 2001.

Frederickson, Kari. "'The Slowest State' and 'Most Backward Community': Racial Violence in South Carolina and Federal Civil-Rights Legislation, 1946–1948." *South Carolina Historical Magazine* 98, no. 2 (April 1997): 177–202. https://www.jstor.org/stable/i27570226.

Gardner, Michael R. *Harry Truman and Civil Rights: Moral Courage and Political Risks*. Carbondale: Southern Illinois University Press, 2002.

Garvey, John, and Noel Ignatiev, eds. *Race Traitor*. New York: Routledge, 1996.

Gergel, Richard. *Unexampled Courage: The Blinding of Sgt. Isaac Woodard and the Awakening of President Harry S. Truman and Judge J. Waties Waring*. New York: Sarah Crichton Books/Farrar, Straus & Giroux, 2019.

Goldfield, David R. *Black, White, and Southern: Race Relations and Southern Culture, 1940 to the Present*. Baton Rouge: Louisiana State University Press, 1990.

Gona, Ophelia De Laine. *Dawn of Desegregation: J. A. De Laine and* Briggs v. Elliott. Columbia: University of South Carolina Press, 2011.

Gravely, William B. *They Stole Him Out of Jail: Willie Earle, South Carolina's Last Lynching Victim*. Columbia: University of South Carolina Press, 2019.

Greenberg, Jack. *Crusaders in the Courts: How a Dedicated Band of Lawyers Fought for the Civil Rights Revolution*. New York: BasicBooks, 1994.

Hall, Jacquelyn Dowd. "The Long Civil Rights Movement and the Political Uses of the Past." *Journal of American History* 91, no. 4 (March 2005): 1233–63. https://doi.org/10.2307/3660172.

Hall, Jacquelyn Dowd. *Revolt Against Chivalry: Jessie Daniel Ames and the Women's Campaign Against Lynching*. New York: Columbia University Press, 1993.

Harrington, Donald. "What Negros Can Do about the White Problem." Community Pulpit Series, no. 2. New York: Community Church of New York, 1947.

Hasian, Marouf, Jr., Celeste Michelle Condit, and John Louis Lucaites. "The Rhetorical Boundaries of 'The Law': A Consideration of the Rhetorical Culture of Legal Practice and the Case of the 'Separate But Equal' Doctrine." *Quarterly Journal of Speech* 82, no. 4 (November 1996): 323–42. https://doi.org/10.1080/00335639609384161.

Henderson, Elmer W. "The Elimination of Segregation Through Protest, Propaganda and Education." *Journal of Negro Education* 20, no. 3 (Summer 1951): 475–84. https://doi.org/10.2307/2966019.

Ivie, Robert L. "Fire, Flood, and Red Fever: Motivating Metaphors of Global Emergency in the Truman Doctrine Speech." *Presidential Studies Quarterly* 29, no. 3 (September 1999): 570–91. https://doi.org/10.1111/j.0268-141.2003.00050.x.

Johnson, Joan Marie. *Southern Ladies, New Women: Race, Region, and Clubwomen in South Carolina, 1890–1930*. Gainesville: University Press of Florida, 2004.

Johnson, Kimberley. *Reforming Jim Crow: Southern Politics and State in the Age before Brown*. New York: Oxford University Press, 2010.

Juhnke, William E. "President Truman's Committee on Civil Rights: The Interaction of Politics, Protest, and the Presidential Advisory Commission." *Presidential Studies Quarterly* 19, no. 3 (Summer 1989): 593–610. https://www.jstor.org/stable/40574372.

Kiewe, Amos, and Davis W. Houck, eds. *The Effects of Rhetoric and the Rhetoric of Effects: Past, Present, Future*. Columbia: University of South Carolina Press, 2015.

Klarman, Michael J. *From Jim Crow to Civil Rights: The Supreme Court and the Struggle for Racial Equality*. New York: Oxford University Press, 2004.

Klibaner, Irwin. "The Travail of Southern Radicals: The Southern Conference Educational Fund, 1946–1976." *Journal of Southern History* 49, no. 2 (May 1983): 179–202. https://doi.org/10.2307/2207502.

Kluger, Richard. *Simple Justice: The History of* Brown v. Board of Education *and Black America's Struggle for Equality*. New York: Alfred A. Knopf, 2004.

Kneebone, John T. *Southern Liberal Journalists and the Issue of Race, 1920–1944*. Chapel Hill: University of North Carolina Press, 1985.

Kolb, Wade, III. "*Briggs v. Elliott* Revisited: A Study in Grassroots Activism and Trial Advocacy from the Early Civil Rights Era." *Journal of Southern Legal History* 19, no. 1 (2011): 123–75. HeinOnline.

Konvitz, Milton R. "The Extent and Character of Legally-Enforced Segregation." *Journal of Negro Education* 20, no. 3 (1951): 425–35. https://doi.org/10.2307/2966015.

Lau, Peter F., ed. *From the Grassroots to the Supreme Court:* Brown v. Board of Education *and American Democracy*. Durham: Duke University Press, 2004.

Lawson, Steven F., and Charles M. Payne. *Debating the Civil Rights Movement, 1945–1968*. Lanham, MD: Rowman & Littlefield Publishers, 1998.

Lawson, Steven F., ed. *To Secure These Rights: The Report of President Harry S. Truman's Committee on Civil Rights*. Boston: Bedford/St. Martin's, 2004.

Lee, R. Alton. "The Army 'Mutiny' of 1946." *Journal of American History* 53, no. 3 (December 1966): 555–71. https://doi.org/10.2307/1887571.

Leff, Michael. "Textual Criticism: The Legacy of G. P. Mohrmann." *Quarterly Journal of Speech* (November 1986) 72, no. 4: 384. https://doi.org/10.1080/00335638609383783.

Leff, Michael, and Ebony A. Utley. "Instrumental and Constitutive Rhetoric in Martin Luther King, Jr.'s 'Letter from Birmingham Jail.'" *Rhetoric & Public Affairs* 7, no. 1 (Spring 2004): 37–51. https://www.jstor.org/stable/41939889.

Leff, Michael C., and Fred J. Kauffeld, eds. *Texts in Context: Critical Dialogues on Significant Episodes in American Political Rhetoric*. Davis, CA: Hermagoras Press, 1989.

Lomas, Charles W. *The Agitator in American Society*. Englewood Cliffs, NJ: Prentice-Hall, Inc., 1968.

Marshall, Thurgood. "The Rise and Collapse of the 'White Democratic Primary.'" *Journal of Negro Education* 26, no. 3 (Summer 1957): 249–54. https://doi.org/10.2307/2293407.

Marshall, Thurgood. "The Supreme Court as Protector of Civil Rights: Equal Protection of the Laws." *Annals of the American Academy of Political and Social Science* 275, no. 1 (May 1951): 101–10. https://doi.org/10.1177/000271625127500113.

Maslow, Will, and Joseph B. Robison. "Civil Rights: A Program for the President's Committee." *Lawyers Guild Review* 3, no. 7 (May/June, 1947): 112–21. HeinOnline.

McMillen, Neil R. *The Citizens' Council: Organized Resistance to the Second Reconstruction, 1954–64*. Urbana and Chicago: University of Illinois Press, 1971.

McRae, Elizabeth Gillespie. *Mothers of Massive Resistance: White Women and the Politics of White Supremacy*. New York: Oxford University Press, 2020.

Medhurst, Martin J. "Thirty Years Later: A Critic's Tale." *Rhetoric Review* 25, no. 4 (2006): 379–83. http://www.jstor.org/stable/20176743.

Medhurst, Martin J. "Reconceptualizing Rhetorical History: Eisenhower's Farewell Address." *Quarterly Journal of Speech* 80, no. 2 (May 1994): 195–218. https://doi.org/10.1080/00335639409384067.

Moore, Winfred B., Jr., and Orville Vernon Burton, eds. *Toward the Meeting of the Waters: Currents in the Civil Rights Movement of South Carolina during the Twentieth Century*. Columbia: University of South Carolina Press, 2008.

Motley, Constance Baker. "The Historical Setting of *Brown* and Its Impact on the Supreme Court's Decisions." *Fordham Law Review* 61, no. 1 (October 1992): 9–18. https://ir.lawnet.fordham.edu/flr/.

Myrdal, Gunnar. *An American Dilemma: The Negro Problem and Modern Democracy*. New York: Harper & Brothers, 1944.

Nabrit, James M., Jr. "Resort to the Court as a Means of Eliminating 'Legalized' Segregation." *Journal of Negro Education* 20, no. 3 (Summer 1951): 460–74. https://doi.org/10.2307/2966018.

"Negro Disenfranchisement: A Challenge to the Constitution." *Columbia Law Review* 47, no. 1 (1947): 76–98. https://doi.org/10.2307/1118552.

Newby, I. A., ed. *The Development of Segregationist Thought*. Homewood, IL: The Dorsey Press, 1968.

O'Brien, Gail Williams. *The Color of the Law: Race, Violence, and Justice in the Post-World War II South*. Chapel Hill: University of North Carolina Press, 1999.

O'Rourke, Sean Patrick, and Lesli K. Pace, eds. *Like Wildfire: The Rhetoric of the Civil Rights Sit-Ins*. Columbia: University of South Carolina Press, 2020.

Parry-Giles, Shawn, and J. Michael Hogan, eds. *The Handbook of Rhetoric and Public Address*. Malden, MA: Wiley-Blackwell, 2010.

Pauley, Garth E. "Harry Truman and the NAACP: A Case Study in Presidential Persuasion on Civil Rights." *Rhetoric & Public Affairs* 2, no. 2 (Summer 1999): 211–41. https://www.jstor.org/stable/41939509.

Payne, Charles M. "'The Whole United States Is Southern!': *Brown v. Board* and the Mystification of Race." *Journal of American History* 91, no. 1 (June 2004): 83–91. https://doi.org/10.2307/3659615.

Payne, Charles M., and Adam Green, eds. *Time Longer than a Rope: A Century of African American Activism, 1850–1950*. New York: New York University Press, 2003.

Phillips, Caryl. *Atlantic Sound*. New York: Alfred A. Knopf, 2000.
Plato. *Phaedrus*. Translated by W. C. Helmbold and W. G. Rabinowitz. Upper Saddle River, NJ: Prentice Hall, 1956.
Prentice, Robert A. "Supreme Court Rhetoric." *Arizona Law Review* 25, no. 1 (1983–84): 85–122. HeinOnline.
Quint, Howard H. *Profile in Black and White: A Frank Portrait of South Carolina*. Washington, DC: Public Affairs Press, 1958; reis., Westport, CT: Greenwood Press, 1973.
Reed, Linda. *Simple Decency & Common Sense: The Southern Conference Movement, 1938–1963*. Bloomington: Indiana University Press, 1991.
Robertson, Nancy Marie. *Christian Sisterhood, Race Relations, and the YWCA, 1906–46*. Urbana and Chicago: University of Illinois Press, 2007.
Rowan, Carl T. *South of Freedom*. New York: Knopf, 1952.
Schwartz, Barry N., and Robert Disch, eds. *White Racism: Its History, Pathology and Practice*. New York: Dell Publishing, 1970.
Scott, James C. *Domination and the Arts of Resistance: Hidden Transcripts*. New Haven: Yale University Press, 1990.
Simons, Herbert W. "From Post-9/11 Melodrama to Quagmire in Iraq: A Rhetorical History." *Rhetoric & Public Affairs* 10, no. 2 (Summer 2007): 183–93. http://www.jstor.org/stable/41940142.
Sosna, Morton. *In Search of the Silent South: Southern Liberals and the Race Issue*. New York: Columbia University Press, 1977.
Sullivan, Patricia. *Lift Every Voice: The NAACP and the Making of the Civil Rights Movement*. New York: The New Press, 2009.
Theoharis, Jeanne. *A More Beautiful and Terrible History: The Uses and Misuses of Civil Rights History*. Boston: Beacon Press, 2018.
Thomas, Brook, ed. Plessy v. Ferguson: *A Brief History with Documents*. Boston & New York: Bedford Books, 1979.
Thompson, Sydnor. "John W. Davis and His Role in the Public School Segregation Cases—A Personal Memoir." *Washington and Lee Law Review* 52, no. 5 (1995): 1679–1695. https://scholarlycommons.law.wlu.edu/wlulr.
Turner, Kathleen J., ed. *Doing Rhetorical History: Concepts and Cases*. Tuscaloosa: University of Alabama Press, 1998.
Tushnet, Mark V. *Making Civil Rights Law: Thurgood Marshall and the Supreme Court, 1936–1961*. New York: Oxford University Press, 1994.
Tushnet, Mark V. *The NAACP's Legal Strategy Against Segregated Education*. Chapel Hill: University of North Carolina Press, 1987.
Vander Zanden, James W. "The Ideology of White Supremacy." *Journal of the History of Ideas* 20, no. 3 (June–September 1959): 385–402. https://doi.org/10.2307/2708116.
Vander Zanden, James W. *Race Relations in Transition: The Segregation Crisis in the South*. New York: Random House, 1965.
VanHaitsma, Pamela. "Between Archival Absence and Information Abundance: Reconstructing Sallie Holley's Abolitionist Rhetoric through Digital Surrogates and Metadata." *Quarterly Journal of Speech* 106, no. 1 (February 2020): 25–47. https://doi.org/10.1080/00335630.2019.1706188.

Ward, Brian, and Tony Badger, eds. *The Making of Martin Luther King and the Civil Rights Movement*. New York: New York University Press, 1996.
Ware, Leland B. "Setting the Stage for *Brown*: The Development and Implementation of the NAACP's School Desegregation Campaign, 1930–1950." *Mercer Law Review* 52, no. 2 (2001): 631–73. https://digitalcommons.law.mercer.edu/jour_mlr.
Waring, J. Waties. "The Struggle for Negro Rights." *Lawyers Guild Review* 9, no. 1 (Winter 1949): 9–12. HeinOnline.
Warner, Michael. "Publics and Counterpublics." *Public Culture* 14, no. 1 (Winter 2002): 49–90. https://muse.jhu.edu/article/26277.
White, Eugene E., ed. *Rhetoric in Transition: Studies in the Nature and Uses of Rhetoric*. University Park: Pennsylvania State University Press, 1980.
Wright, Marion, and Arnold Shankman. *Human Rights Odyssey*. Durham: Moore Publishing Company, 1978.
Yarbrough, Tinsley E. *A Passion for Justice: J. Waties Waring and Civil Rights*. New York: Oxford University Press, 1987.
Yuhl, Stephanie E. *A Golden Haze of Memory: The Making of Historic Charleston*. Chapel Hill: University of North Carolina Press, 2005.
Yuval-Davis, Nira. *The Politics of Belonging: Intersectional Contestations*. Los Angeles & London: Sage, 2011.

Unpublished Theses, Dissertations, and Manuscripts

Aba-Mecha, Barbara Woods. "Black Woman Activist in Twentieth Century: Modjeska Monteith Simkins." PhD diss., Emory University, 1978.
Wright, Warren Earl. "The Rhetoric of Learned Hand in Selected Civil Liberties Cases: A Method for Analysis of Judicial Opinion." PhD diss., University of Illinois, 1960.

Websites

American Presidency Project, https://www.presidency.ucsb.edu/
Brennan Center for Justice, https://www.brennancenter.org
Civil Rights Movement Veterans, https://crmvet.org
James E. Clyburn, House of Representatives, https://clyburn.house.gov/
Department of State, Office of the Historian, https://history.state.gov
Federal Judicial Center, https://www.fjc.gov
Internet Archive, San Francisco Public Library, https://archive.org
Martin Luther King Jr. Research and Education Institute, https://kinginstitute.stanford.edu
Gilder Lehrman Center for the Study of Slavery, Resistance, and Abolition https://glc.yale.edu/
National Lawyers Guild, https://www.nlg.org/
National World War II Museum, https://www.nationalww2museum.org
Online Archive of California, https://oac.cdlib.org/
Our Campaigns, https://www.ourcampaigns.com

Eleanor Roosevelt Papers Project, https://erpapers.columbian.gwu.edu/
South Carolina Encyclopedia, https://www.scencyclopedia.org
Harry S. Truman Library & Museum, https://www.trumanlibrary.gov
US Bureau of Labor Statistics Inflation Calculator, https://data.bls.gov/cgi-bin/cpicalc.pl
The White House, https://www.whitehouse.gov

INDEX

Afro-American, 95, 101, 107, 109, 112, 123
Alexander, Raymond Pace, 112
Alexander, Sadie T. M., 110, 144, 169
allies, 14, 16, 89, 172–74, 176
American Creed, 30–31, 52–53, 121, 140, 149, 170, 180
American Dilemma, An (Myrdal), 28, 30, 73, 96–97
American Fund for Public Service (Garland Fund), 4
audience response, 8, 10, 16, 80–81, 85, 88, 90–93, 104, 111, 113, 132, 172–73, 175–77, 180

Belton v. Gebhart, 153–54, 156
Bilbo, Theodore G., 8, 48
Black Freedom Struggle, 11, 14–15, 78, 179, 181
Bolling v. Sharpe, 154, 156
Boulware, Harold, 19–20, 36, 43–44, 68, 119
Briggs v. Board of Trustees, 119, 127–29
Briggs v. Elliott, 5–6, 14, 16, 129, 133, 135, 139–41, 145, 151, 158, 168, 173, 176; appeal to Supreme Court, 142, 153–55, 179
Brown v. Baskin, 45–49, 175
Brown v. Board of Education (1954), 5–6, 9–11, 14, 15–16, 118, 156, 158–59, 164, 165, 169–70, 172–74, 179–81; in Topeka, Kansas, 118, 153–54, 156, 158
Brown v. Board of Education (1955), 165–66, 169–70
Byrnes, James F., 129–32, 137–38, 150, 162

Cannon, Poppy, 25, 74, 96, 156, 160
Carter, Hodding, 81–82, 84, 87–88, 96, 164
Carter, Robert L., 20, 118–19, 155, 157
Cash, W. J., 8, 28–30, 39, 73
Chicago Defender, 37, 91, 95, 102, 107, 146, 151
circulation, 7–8, 50, 58, 76–77, 80, 90–93, 97, 104, 111–12, 132, 173, 177, 180
civil rights, 4, 20, 22, 24, 31–32, 36, 51–52, 55, 57, 71, 76–77, 94–97, 123, 125, 148, 151–52, 167
civil rights movement, 5, 14–16, 179–80
Clarendon County, 5, 12, 16, 42–44, 53, 68–71, 73, 79–80, 92, 95, 119–20, 125, 127–31, 135, 142, 145–46, 153, 166, 168–69, 173, 175–76, 179–80
Clark, Septima, 22, 27, 72, 73–76, 92, 166, 167, 169
Collier's, 102, 113, 166, 178
communism, 38, 59, 67, 102, 124, 148–49
Congress of Racial Equality (CORE), 13, 114, 133, 146
Cornwell, Ruby P., 27, 74, 92–93, 99, 125, 157–58, 160, 163, 167
Council for Civic Unity, 120
courage, 7, 14–15, 38, 44, 59–62, 65–66, 73–75, 80, 89–91, 93, 99, 103, 111–13, 157, 162, 176–77

Davis v. County School Board, 153–54, 156
De Laine, Reverend Joseph A., 43–44, 68–70, 119, 125, 168–70
Delaney, Hubert, 49, 127, 129, 143

Democratic Party, National, 46, 56, 152
Democratic Party, South Carolina, 21, 22, 33, 35–37, 45–48, 92, 129, 157
digital surrogates, 13–14, 174
Dixiecrats (States' Rights Democratic Party), 46, 56–57, 74, 94, 96, 123, 143, 148, 152
Dombrowski, James, 38, 67, 113, 116–17, 127, 173–74
Dudley, Edward, 44, 64, 66

Earle, Willie, 39–40, 68, 124
Elmore v. Rice, 33, 35–39, 45–48, 93, 107, 148, 175

Fair Employment Practice Commission, 45, 56, 96, 115
fear, 7–9, 40, 49, 51, 56, 60, 62, 66–67, 69, 77, 90, 100, 103, 108, 110–12, 160, 164, 177, 179
federal antilynching law, 27, 56, 81, 94, 124
Fifteenth Amendment, 30, 35, 51, 62
Fifth Amendment, 154
Finnie, Isabella, 53, 178
Fourteenth Amendment, 22, 30, 31, 35, 43, 62, 117, 139, 154

gradualism, 49, 58, 62, 65, 67, 79, 82, 103–6, 108–10, 120, 132, 134, 148–49, 162–63, 174, 178

Hammond, John, 74, 129, 145, 158–59
Harrington, Donald, 58, 62–64
Henderson, Elmer W., 6, 76, 101, 115–16
Henderson v. United States, 115–17, 141, 151
Highlander Folk School, 113–14
Hill, Oliver, 4, 115, 119
Hinton, James, 37, 54, 69, 157, 162
Horton, Myles, 113, 173
House Un-American Activities Committee (HUAC), 38, 59, 114
Houston, Charles Hamilton, 4, 5, 115, 119, 155, 164
Howard University, 4, 5, 115, 118, 152, 153, 155, 169
Humphrey, Hubert, 56–57, 110, 112

impeachment, 5, 46–47, 52, 92–93, 101, 107–10, 112, 134, 177
interracial sex, 86, 96–98, 143–44, 166
interracial marriage, 96–98

Jim Crow, 3, 4, 6, 7, 8, 11, 18, 31, 46, 55, 58, 73, 77, 78, 80, 81, 82, 83, 84, 85, 86, 89, 90, 92, 100, 102, 103, 111, 118, 121, 122, 123, 127, 130, 132, 134, 135, 138, 164, 166, 167, 172, 173, 176, 177, 179, 180

King, Martin Luther, Jr., 15, 105, 170
Ku Klux Klan (KKK), 18, 23, 28, 34, 50, 54–55, 81, 92–93, 106–8, 124–27, 134, 161, 169, 175

Legal Defense and Educational Fund, 5, 44, 64, 68, 69, 118–19, 145
Lighthouse and Informer, 50, 52, 70, 83, 91, 188n38
Lost Cause, 29, 68, 80, 84, 108, 130, 174
lynching, 7, 11, 19, 39–40, 51, 55, 68, 102, 124, 147, 170, 177

Margold, Nathan, 4
Marshall, Thurgood, 4, 6, 28, 35, 44, 47–48, 49, 52, 59–61, 64, 66, 68–71, 73, 76, 90, 116, 118–19, 127–29, 134, 135–38, 140–42, 147, 154–55, 158, 161
master narrative, 14–15, 179
Mays, Benjamin, 71, 140
McCray, John H., 50, 52, 70, 83, 91, 129, 161, 162
McLaurin v. Oklahoma, 115–17, 138, 141, 151
Mind of the South, The (Cash), 8, 28–30, 73
Montgomery, Eugene A. R., 69–70
Moore, Harry and Harriette, 147–48
Motley, Constance Baker, 3
Myrdal, Gunnar, 28, 30, 39, 73, 96–97, 137, 174

NAACP (National Association for the Advancement of Colored People), 3–5,

16, 18–20, 23, 24, 27–28, 33, 35–37, 42, 44–45, 47, 52, 54, 60, 64, 68–69, 73–74, 79, 89, 94, 96, 112, 117–19, 124, 128–29, 131, 135–36, 139, 141–47, 156–60, 162, 164, 169, 171, 173, 180–81
Nabrit, James, Jr., 5, 118, 154, 155
National Lawyers Guild, 58–59, 65, 103, 104, 113, 117, 123; New York chapter, 48, 58; Washington, DC, chapter, 101
noblesse largesse, 81, 131

Omega Psi Phi, 70–71, 146, 151
ostracism, 7, 47, 52–53, 60, 74, 75, 87, 103, 106, 111, 134, 144, 167, 176

Parker, John J., 9, 129, 135, 137–42, 143, 154
Pearson, James v. County Board of Education for Clarendon County, 43–44, 69, 118, 156, 173, 179
peonage, 41, 147
Perry, Leslie, 47
Pittsburgh Courier, 37, 57, 71, 90, 91, 95, 161–62
Plessy, Homer, 3
Plessy v. Ferguson, 3, 4, 5, 6, 34, 42, 115, 117, 131, 135, 137, 138, 151, 156, 157, 159, 164, 165, 180
poll tax, 51, 56, 81, 94, 124
President's Committee on Civil Rights, 6, 31–32, 55–56, 169
Prince Edward County, 4, 153

Reconstruction, 29–30, 34–35, 48, 68, 84
rhetorical culture, 6–8, 89, 111, 172–73, 175, 177
rhetorical history, 9–11, 14, 16, 180
Rivers, L. Mendel, 47, 84, 101, 109–10, 112, 114, 122, 126, 178
Roosevelt, Eleanor, 67, 72, 170
Roosevelt, Franklin D., 21, 22, 38, 58–62, 65, 120
Rowan, Carl, 36

second-class citizen, 4, 11, 36, 55, 102, 122, 127, 147, 157, 174, 180

separate but equal, 3, 6, 34, 42, 65, 67, 98, 115, 117–18, 129–30, 135, 137, 139, 142–43, 150, 155, 156–57, 159, 180
Shull, Lynwood L., 17–24
Smith, Lillian, 7–8, 112
Smith v. Allwright, 35–38, 44, 60, 61, 122
Solid South, 35, 38, 123
Southern Conference Educational Fund (SCEF), 8, 38, 67, 116
Southern Conference for Human Welfare (SCHW), 38, 113–14
Southern Regional Council, 32, 98, 157
Soviet Union, 95, 102, 121, 132, 148–49
Sweatt v. Painter, 115–17, 138, 141, 151

textual recovery, 12–14
Thirteenth Amendment, 4, 30, 62
Thurmond, J. Strom, 33, 39, 46, 48, 84, 92, 124, 136, 174
Tilly, Dorothy, 32, 39–40, 98
Timmerman, George, Sr., 21–22, 33–34, 129, 135, 137–40, 154
To Secure These Rights, 55, 94
Truman, Harry S., 9, 20, 31, 36, 46, 51, 55–57, 74, 80, 94, 96, 100, 102–3, 123, 143, 152

United States Department of Justice, 18, 20, 22–23, 28, 41, 56, 116, 125, 155
United States of America v. Shull, 27–28, 31, 33, 34, 39–40, 49, 55, 58, 73, 111, 123, 125, 129, 174, 179
United States Supreme Court, 3–6, 10, 30, 35, 38, 44–45, 51–52, 60, 65, 115–17, 122, 128, 131–32, 138, 140–43, 146, 151, 153–56, 158–59, 164–66, 168, 172, 179–81

Waring, Elizabeth Avery: first marriage and life in Detroit, 25; *Meet the Press*, 95–97; second marriage, 25; speech to Coming Street YWCA (Charleston), 75–80
Waring, J. Waties: dissent in *Briggs v. Elliott*, 14, 138–40, 143, 146, 156–59, 161, 164, 176; first marriage and divorce, 26–27, 167; rulings in primary cases, 36–38, 45–46, 49–50

Weber, Palmer, 74, 144–45, 158
Welles, Orson, 19–20
West, Rebecca, 39–40, 68
White, Walter, 19, 37, 71, 74, 91, 96, 124, 129, 141, 145, 156, 158–60, 168
Williams, Aubrey, 67–68, 80, 112, 127, 173
Williams, Franklin, 24, 36, 128–29
Woodard, Isaac, Jr., 9, 17–24, 27–28, 118, 129, 147, 150
Wright, Marion, 98, 157

Wrighten, John H. v. Board of Trustees of the University of South Carolina, 33–34, 37, 116

Young Women's Christian Association (YWCA): Coming Street (Charleston), 8, 72–73, 74–75, 76, 77, 79, 81–82, 88–89, 95, 104, 109, 133, 146, 149, 175–76; national, 75–76, 101, 110; Society Street (Charleston), 75, 77

ABOUT THE AUTHOR

Wanda Little Fenimore's research focuses on the rhetorical dimensions of racial injustice in the US South. Dr. Fenimore recovers the historical antecedents to present-day social issues. Her scholarship has been recognized with awards at conferences and published in academic journals. She received her bachelor's degree from Randolph-Macon Woman's College, master's from Hollins University, and doctorate from Florida State University. Dr. Fenimore was awarded the Mellon/American Council of Learned Societies Community College Faculty Fellowship in 2020. A native of Virginia, she has resided in the Palmetto State since 2015.

www.ingramcontent.com/pod-product-compliance
Lightning Source LLC
Chambersburg PA
CBHW022005220426
43663CB00007B/962